Experiencing God in Late Medieval and Early Modern England

Experiencing God in Late Medieval and Early Modern England

DAVID J. DAVIS

OXFORD
UNIVERSITY PRESS

Great Clarendon Street, Oxford, OX2 6DP,
United Kingdom

Oxford University Press is a department of the University of Oxford.
It furthers the University's objective of excellence in research, scholarship,
and education by publishing worldwide. Oxford is a registered trade mark of
Oxford University Press in the UK and in certain other countries

© David J. Davis 2022

The moral rights of the author have been asserted

First Edition published in 2022

Impression: 1

All rights reserved. No part of this publication may be reproduced, stored in
a retrieval system, or transmitted, in any form or by any means, without the
prior permission in writing of Oxford University Press, or as expressly permitted
by law, by licence or under terms agreed with the appropriate reprographics
rights organization. Enquiries concerning reproduction outside the scope of the
above should be sent to the Rights Department, Oxford University Press, at the
address above

You must not circulate this work in any other form
and you must impose this same condition on any acquirer

Published in the United States of America by Oxford University Press
198 Madison Avenue, New York, NY 10016, United States of America

British Library Cataloguing in Publication Data

Data available

Library of Congress Control Number: 2022931635

ISBN 978–0–19–883413–7

DOI: 10.1093/oso/9780198834137.001.0001

Printed and bound by
CPI Group (UK) Ltd, Croydon, CR0 4YY

Links to third party websites are provided by Oxford in good faith and
for information only. Oxford disclaims any responsibility for the materials
contained in any third party website referenced in this work.

To Nan and Wes

Acknowledgments

The idea for this book began with a scattered collection of conversations held on both sides of the Atlantic. Beginning with a question about an odd, recurring phrase in Protestant commentaries, the book slowly mushroomed over the course of eight years into a reassessment of large swathes of English intellectual and religious culture.

This journey has indebted me to many individuals, two of whom I owed a great deal long before this project began. Alexandra Walsham and the late Margaret Aston commented on different aspects of my embryonic considerations and sent me off on especially productive trains of thought. Laela Zwollo, Garthine Walker, Randy Hatchett, Jennifer Evans, Liam Temple, and the anonymous readers at Oxford University Press offered important suggestions at significant moments in my research. Their direction proved invaluable. Over many coffees and other beverages, my colleagues at Houston Baptist University have been a source of intellectual refreshment, particularly the members of the Pantalogia workshop that suffered through draft chapters and working papers. Also, I owe a special thanks to my graduate students—Becca, Camryn, Julia, Kathryn, Noah, Paige, Richard, Rocio, and Tim—for trudging alongside me through four centuries of English religion in the early stages of my research. Finally, I am forever grateful to Lisa Carroll-Davis, David Grubbs, Tyler McNabb, Adam Morton, Cress Ann Posten, Emily Stelzer, Joel Swann, and Jerry Walls, who read portions of the manuscript before it was finalized. Their comments not only contributed key insights I would not have reached on my own, but also encouraged me in the overall narrative.

The research for this book was supported by generous fellowships from the Renaissance Society of America, the Huntington Library, and the Johannes a Lasco Bibliothek, as well as a semester-long sabbatical from my teaching responsibilities at HBU. Much of the book was written during the Covid-19 pandemic, which severely limited my ability to travel and access archives in person. As such, librarians and archivists played an even more significant role in getting the materials I needed. The staff at the Huntington Library, Houghton Library (Harvard), the Bodleian Library, Cambridge University Library, the University of Illinois Urbana-Champaign Library, the Rijksmuseum (Amsterdam), the Lanier Theological Library (Houston), and the Dunham Bible Museum (Houston) have been incredibly patient with my requests. Their efforts on behalf of scholarship in a time of global pandemic have been inspiring.

Between the genesis and completion of this project, two of my closest family members departed this life. They both were wellsprings of encouragement, kindness, and joy, and they are dearly missed. I dedicate this book to their memory.

Contents

List of Figures	xi
List of Abbreviations	xiii
Introduction: The Culture of Divine Revelation	1

PART I. THE DISCOURSE OF EXPERIENCING GOD

1. 'The entrance to my joys': *Raptus* in Contemplative Devotion	15
2. 'Wee should bee rapt vp into the third heauen': The Reformation of Revelation	37
3. 'Pictures are ... not for Worship': Images of God in Early Modern England	56

PART II. *RAPTUS* AS PRAYER AND POETRY

4. 'A love-token of Christ to the Soul': Prayer and Devotion after the Reformation	95
5. 'Language of the Angels': The Poetics of Divine Ravishment	118

PART III. CHALLENGES TO THE CULTURE OF DIVINE REVELATION

6. 'So unsatisfying ... is Rapture': The Word and the Spirit in the Seventeenth Century	143
7. 'The foundation of all Knowledge': The Rationale of Divine Revelation	165
Conclusion	189

Bibliography	195
Index	219

List of Figures

1. Giovanni di Paolo, *Saint Catherine of Siena Exchanging Her Heart with Christ* (1461–1482). The Metropolitan Museum of Art.   31

2. Albrecht Dürer, *Revelation of St. John: The Adoration of the Lamb* (1511). Gift of the Print Club of Cleveland, The Cleveland Museum of Art.   42

3. 'The Crucifixion' in *The book of common prayer* (London: John Bill and Christopher Barker, 1664). By permission of the Rare Book and Manuscript Library, University of Illinois at Urbana-Champaign.   61

4. Francis Quarles, *Emblems* (London: M. G. and W, 1696), 240. The Huntington Library, San Marino, California.   65

5. 'The Circumcision of Christ' in *The book of common prayer* (London: John Bill and Christopher Barker, 1664). By permission of the Rare Book and Manuscript Library, University of Illinois at Urbana-Champaign.   68

6. 'Trinity Sunday' in *The book of common prayer* (London: John Bill and Christopher Barker, 1664). By permission of the Rare Book and Manuscript Library, University of Illinois at Urbana-Champaign.   71

7. 'The Conversion of Paul' in *The book of common prayer* (London: John Bill and Christopher Barker, 1664). By permission of the Rare Book and Manuscript Library, University of Illinois at Urbana-Champaign.   73

8. William Malone, *A reply to Mr. Iames Vssher his ansvvere* (Douai?: Permissu superiorum, 1627), title page. By permission of the Huntington Library, San Marino, California.   75

9. George Hakewill, *An apologie or Declaration of the povver and providence of God in the gouernment of the world* (Oxford: William Turner, 1635), title page. By permission of the Rare Book and Manuscript Library, University of Illinois at Urbana-Champaign.   77

10. Aegidius Sadeler, *Steniging van de heilige Stefanus* (1580–1629). Rijksmuseum, Amsterdam.   80

11. Hans Holbein, *Drieëenheid* (1538). Rijksmuseum, Amsterdam.   81

12. 'The Household of God' in *The book of common prayer* (London: John Bill and Christopher Barker, 1664). By permission of the Rare Book and Manuscript Library, University of Illinois at Urbana-Champaign.   84

13. Jan Christoffel Jegher, *Heilinge Drie-eenheid* (1649). Rijksmuseum, Amsterdam.   86

14. Richard Vennard, *The right vvay to heauen* (London: Printed by Thomas Este, 1602). The Huntington Library, San Marino, California.   88

xii LIST OF FIGURES

15. Samuel Wesley, *The life of our blessed Lord & Saviour Jesus Christ* (1697), opposite title page. The Huntington Library, San Marino, California. 90

16. 'The House of Prayer' in *The Preaching Bible* (Cambridge: John Field, 1668). By permission of the Dunham Bible Museum, Houston Baptist University. 112

17. 'Peter and Mary Magdalene with Crucified Heart' in *The Preaching Bible* (Cambridge: John Field, 1668). By permission of the Dunham Bible Museum, Houston Baptist University. 132

18. Francis Quarles, *Emblems* (London: M. G. and W, 1696), 180. The Huntington Library, San Marino, California. 138

List of Abbreviations

BPI   British Printed Images to 1700 (https://bpi1700.org.uk/jsp/)

ODNB   Oxford Dictionary of National Biography (https://www.oxforddnb.com/)

PLRE   Private Libraries in Renaissance England (https://plre.folger.edu/)

RSTC   W. A. Jackson, J. F. Ferguson, and K. F. Pantzer (eds), *A Short-Title Catalogue of Books Printed in England, Scotland, & Ireland and of English books printed abroad 1475–1640* (2nd edn, London, 1986–91)

Wing   Donald G. Wing (ed.), *Short-title catalogue of books printed in England, Scotland, Ireland, Wales, and British America ... 1641–1700* (2nd edn, New York, 1994)

Introduction

The Culture of Divine Revelation

> The revelation goes on; it is their witness and yet their witness to an original source which forms the revelation.
>
> (Richard Swinburne, *Revelation*)

The ceiling of the Sheldonian Theatre in Oxford boasts an early baroque painting of Truth descending from heaven. Truth brings the light of understanding to the Arts and Sciences, which are personified as Muses. Completed in 1668 by London artist Robert Streater, the Sheldonian's ceiling celebrated both the completion of the new theatre and the Restoration of the monarchy under Charles II. The traditional notion of truth as a gift from God, as a form of divine revelation, aligned very nicely with the reaffirmation of the divine right of kings in Caroline England. The painting also highlights the epistemic importance placed upon such revelation, which most people considered to be the ultimate source for all human science and philosophy. Thus, a contemporary poetic *encomium* of the painting explained that Truth 'disperse(s) abroad' the enemies of understanding, 'Envy...Rapine and Brutality'. Like the sun, it is difficult (and dangerous) to look directly upon truth, but it provides light to everything else: 'So bright Truth seem's obscur'd to us below, / But every figure yield's the brighter shew'.[1]

Compared to much of the art of the eighteenth century, Streater's painting presents a very different way of thinking about Truth. The work of artists like Joseph Wright of Derby often depicted the light of Truth (or discovery) pouring out from a distinctly terrestrial source.[2] In these later renderings, Truth is not blinding but illuminating, it is not transcendent but rather entirely immanent, a product of human ingenuity and invention. Also, the movement of Truth in Streater's depiction between heaven and Earth reminded the viewer that Truth descended so that human beings might ascend: 'That the Beholder would become all Eye:...

---

[1] Robert Whitehall, *Urania* (1669), 4. Daughter of Zeus and Mnemosyne, Urania was the muse of astronomy and universal love, and was invoked by religious poets like Guillaume de Salluste Du Bartas and John Milton who associated her with the Holy Spirit.

[2] See e.g. Joseph Wright of Derby, *An Experiment on a Bird in the Air Pump* (1768) and *The Alchemist Discovering Phosphorous* (1771). Similar in this respect, though not with the same celebration of human ingenuity, is William Blake's *Newton* (1795).

Experiencing God in Late Medieval and Early Modern England. David J. Davis, Oxford University Press.
© David J. Davis 2022. DOI: 10.1093/oso/9780198834137.003.0001

A phan'sie makes essayes to Heauen to climb'.[3] Truth, via divine revelation, was a religious experience in that it involved the communion between God and human beings. It was also an epistemic experience that expanded human understanding, giving insight that could not have been obtained otherwise.

The idea for this book began with a curiosity. I found myself mentally glossing over a popular phrase that Protestant commentators used to describe the biblical prophets' experiences of divine revelation, which were often described in terms of being 'ravished', 'rapt', or 'rapt up' in the Spirit. I knew that similar language was present in the sensual poetry of the period as well as accounts of contemplative devotion. As I explored the popularity of such language, I began to wonder if this was more than a rhetorical turn-of-phrase, if there was a more robust discourse of divine revelation. Not only did the language appear in an unusual number of different (and different kinds of) texts, but it also possessed a commonly understood meaning about the physical and metaphysical experience that someone had when they were believed to have encountered God. Taken together, the examples present what the philosopher Owen Barfield once described as a 'collective representation' of late medieval and early modern English culture and thought. For Barfield, collective representations were commonly held ways of understanding and explaining human experiences, consisting of individual perceptions as well as preconceived ideas, biases, and beliefs that contribute to our making sense (and meaning) of our perceptions. Barfield explained, 'Like the words of a language...are common to the members' of a society, collective representations 'are transmitted from one generation to another, developing and changing only gradually in the process'.[4] Barfield believed that, at a fundamental level, collective representations provided the primary means through which human beings experience the world. While an individual's sense perception is theirs alone, the ways that we understand and make meaning out of our perceptions is most often done through shared representations about reality (even if the meaning we are making challenges those representations). Barfield's idea of collective representations is helpful in understanding how accounts of divine experiences corresponded, in many respects, with one another over a long period of English history. As we will see in the following chapters, the ways that late medieval and early modern English people understood the experience of divine revelation was built around certain textual and pictorial signs, which provided important discursive markers in identifying divine revelation. These signs not only supported certain presuppositions about how humans interacted with God, but also provided important means of legitimizing and delimiting what was and what was not considered to be an experience of God.

---

[3] Whitehall, *Urania*, 6–7.
[4] Owen Barfield, *Saving the Appearances* (1988), 33.

INTRODUCTION: THE CULTURE OF DIVINE REVELATION   3

While the collective representations of such experiences were not determinative, they contributed to ways of thinking and speaking of a profound experience with God, which, when taken together, constructed a broader culture of divine revelation in late medieval and early modern England.[5] In this book, we will trace the ways that people described and delimited divine revelation from late medieval contemplatives like Walter Hilton and Julian of Norwich through the religious changes of the Reformation and the intellectual cauldron of the seventeenth century, in the hopes of better understanding the workings of this culture and how it developed over time. Although this book admittedly covers a very long period of time, I hope to demonstrate that most people held at least one significant, common notion about divine revelation: that divine revelation was considered to be a divine act of direct intimacy, even absorption, of the human soul in the divine.[6] Looking at a variety of contexts—such as moral philosophy, devotional writings, religious polemic, sermons, poetry, biblical commentaries, and natural philosophy—this book focuses upon the way that divine revelation was understood to have been received, the experiential characteristics of what it was like to communicate with God. More specifically, I want to explore the different ways that emerged to describe and understand the means of experiencing God, the images and tropes that developed to help late medieval and early modern people conceptualize what was an unfamiliar, as well as religiously and epistemically profound, experience.

If we take Streater's painting too literally, then we would need to consider all knowledge as a product of some interaction with God, because divine truth was thought to enlighten even the most secular of university subjects. While I am sure there would be merit in such an investigation, I want to narrow the scope in this book to include only those experiences that were considered to be outside the norm of everyday life, only those experiences where the Christian God was thought to have immediately acted upon a person's soul (or mind), by which the person was enlightened, either emotionally or intellectually. This sort of experience, often referred to as divine revelation, has been described by the contemporary theologian Hans Urs van Balthasar as 'an inner, immediate spiritual experience of the divine', which 'is itself human', but nevertheless lays claim to an experience beyond human ability.[7] In general, these experiences consisted of God taking control of the person's soul, dissociating the person's internal self from their

---

[5] Divine revelation as a core feature of early modern thought and culture has not been attended to nearly enough in historical scholarship. Even most religious histories of the period do not address it to any great extent, often relegating it to the social and cultural fringes. See for example, in an otherwise excellent work, Kaspar von Greyerz, *Religion and Culture in Early Modern Europe* (Oxford, 2008). Von Greyerz uses the term 'inspiration' only in relation to groups like the Quakers and Pietists (pp. 171–83), and on the whole, makes very little study of such experiences.

[6] See e.g. Steven Katz, 'Language, Epistemology, and Mysticism', in *Mysticism and Philosophical Analysis* (Oxford, 1978), 4.

[7] Hans Urs von Balthasar, *Love Alone* (1992), 22.

physical senses, which oftentimes included the person losing any orientation of space and time.[8] Most late medieval and early modern experiences are reported to have been similar to those moments of divine revelation recorded in scripture by prophets and apostles, although the content of what was experienced varied considerably. Whereas biblical revelation was often filled with prophecy, late medieval and early modern accounts included a wide range of experiences, from visions of heaven and aural voices to an overwhelming sense of emotion, in which the person does not feel in control of their body.

Of course, exploring divine revelation as a historian presents many challenges. The most obvious challenge is the attempt to assert historical rigor upon an experience which happened to a particular individual outside the normal boundaries of the physical senses and was generally considered, at the time, to be beyond human comprehension. This challenge is compounded when studying divine revelation from the vantage point of a largely secularized society which has few, if any, analogous experiences. Even among practicing Christians, like myself, it is difficult to identify a commonly held way of thinking about divine revelation in the life of the believer that would reflect the notions and understanding that were predominant in late medieval and early modern England. While I do not think this challenge is entirely prohibitive, it does highlight the need, from the perspective of modern scholarship, to take careful account of this unique way of thinking about the world (because it is so unusual from our vantage point), in the hopes that we can better understand English society before the Enlightenment.

One important source that sheds light on the understanding of divine revelation in this period is Augustine's categories of *visio intellectualis* and *visio spiritualis*. The former is an experience of images and figures communicated through the imagination to what Augustine described as the human *ratio*; the latter is an unmediated communication to an individual's understanding from God.[9] In his *Confessions*, Augustine recalled his own version of *visio intellectualis*, which was described in the first English translation as a 'rauishing contemplation', when Augustine and his mother Monica were 'so wrappe[d] vp' with joy in a moment of 'vnderstanding' that they lost all sense of time and place. Such experiences of God were thought to surpass the physical senses as God communicated directly to the human soul in such a way that the experience carried epistemic currency

---

[8] It is worth noting that I have excluded several topics that some may consider examples of divine experience, like those of the ancient Greek sybils, the prophecies of Merlin, etc. Although many people of the period took such prophecies quite seriously, they were taken seriously more often in a different way than those which I explore in this book. See e.g. Tim Thornton, *Prophecy, Politics and the People* (Woodbridge, 2006).

[9] Laela Zwollo, *Augustine and Plotinus* (Leiden, 2019), 315–20. See also Laela Zwollo, 'St. Augustine on the Soul's Divine Experiences', *Studia Patristica* (2013), 85–92; John Peter Kenney, *The Mysticism of Saint Augustine* (Abingdon, 2005), 61–7, 129–35. The importance of Augustine's categories in the early modern world, to my knowledge, was first studied by Stuart Clark, *Vanities of the Eye* (Oxford, 2007), 2, 204.

INTRODUCTION: THE CULTURE OF DIVINE REVELATION 5

(i.e., understanding). In this regard, revelation and reason were very closely related, both operating in the same, superior regions of the human soul. Furthermore, the translation of Augustine's experience echoed a popular discourse of how God was experienced, which we will explore in the first few chapters. Augustine used the term *rapiat* to describe his experience, which was, for late medieval and early modern readers, an important linguistic marker indicating divine revelation.[10] Although describing an experience of divine revelation as a rapture (or ravishment) was not absolutely necessary, it was one of the more standardized methods of distinguishing the experience, which denoted an external agent violently acting upon someone or something and removing that person or thing from its current location.[11] God acted upon the soul to such a degree that the soul was dissociated from its bodily confines, which was believed to allow a more direct and clear communication between human and divine.[12]

Also important in understanding the culture of divine revelation is recognizing the relationship that such encounters with God had with human reason and rationality. Soul ravishings were neither simply a delightful, emotional experience nor an ordinary movement of intellectual ascent to some higher understanding. As John Peter Kenney explains, for Augustine, contemplative ravishment was an 'exceptional aperture into the transcendent', which relied entirely upon divine grace to transport the soul into heaven where it may access this transcendent reality. While divine ravishment throughout this period was closely aligned with the rational faculties, it also transcended natural, human reason.[13] From humanists like Desiderius Erasmus to reformers like John Calvin, the experience was understood to be counterintuitive to mere human reason because it was experienced outside the body and was an understanding that could not be accomplished by the human individual on their own.[14] In fact, both Erasmus and Calvin considered such encounters with God to be a necessity for our complete understanding of the world, both physical and metaphysical, because there were certain truths that were only accessible to human reason through the aid of divine revelation. In his study on Erasmus and Calvin, Kirk Essary explains, 'Not only is the human intellect in itself incapable of contemplating God on its own, but even

---

[10] Augustine, *Saint Augustines confessions* (1631), 542–3. The Latin text reads: '*et haec una rapiat et absorbeat et recondat in interiora gaudia spectatorem suum, ut talis sit sempiterna vita, quale fuit hoc momentum intellegentiae*': *The Confessions of Augustine* (Oxford, 1992), x.

[11] Thus, an early-seventeenth century English dictionary defined 'rauish' as 'to take away by force': Robert Cawdrey, *The First English Dictionary* (Oxford, 2007), 131.

[12] Importantly, the simple use of these terms did not denote divine revelation. Like most English words, rapture and ravishment carried several different possible meanings and many of these meanings had very little to do with God.

[13] Kenney, *The Mysticism of Saint Augustine*, 118.

[14] Erasmus celebrated those who pursued such pious experiences of divine ravishment: Erasmus, *The Praise of Folly* (New Haven, 1979), 132–8. For Augustine, the dissociation of the body and the soul constituted a kind of death: Kenney, *The Mysticism of Saint Augustine*, 134.

6   EXPERIENCING GOD IN LATE MEDIEVAL & EARLY MODERN ENGLAND

when illuminated by the Spirit, there is something more going on than intellectual comprehension. The self is divided, or is taken beyond itself'.[15]

Bringing this theoretical description down to Earth, it may be helpful to consider how a popular theological work from the seventeenth century deployed this discourse. Richard Baxter's *The saints everlasting rest* (1650) was an exhaustive study of the *telos* of the 'blessed saints': the 'beatifical vision' of God after this life.[16] Despite Baxter's work reaching to over eight hundred pages and fifteen hundred footnotes with extensive margin commentary, it was a very popular book, going through fifteen editions in fifty years. Popular with conforming and nonconforming Protestants, Baxter taught that the beatific vision was an experience to be had both now and in the afterlife. In this life, Baxter prayed that his book might help people to enjoy the 'transcendent Glory' of God, which 'will eternally pierce us, and warm our very Souls', so that the 'unworthy...soul' may be 'rapt up into heaven and closed in the armes of Christ'. Like most Calvinists, Baxter believed such glimpses of God were important to overcome the recalcitrant depravity of human nature. In other words, experiences of the beatific vision in this life were expressions of divine grace.

Importantly, Baxter deployed the language of 'ravish' and 'rapture' numerous times to describe the experiences of the biblical prophets, and nor was Baxter unusual in this regard.[17] One of his contemporaries, the minister Edward Reynolds, described this divine action upon the soul as 'extraordinarie', wherein 'the Soule is carried beyond the Spheres of Sense, and transported unto more raysed operations'. Both Baxter and Reynolds believed that the soul was the seat of the understanding and that the will, the imagination, and the soul possessed sensory faculties distinct from the physical senses. In ravishing the soul, divine revelation did not simply stir a person with religious sentiment; it stripped the soul of its bodily shackles, allowing a person's mind to experience truth, untainted by physical limitations. Citing the apostle Paul's account of his own revelation of the third heaven (2 Cor. 12.2–4), Reynolds wrote that all godly believers should be 'inspired with such heavenly Revelations', providing one example of many Protestant texts that set up Paul's revelation as a template for contemporary experiences. While the degree of dissociation of the body and soul varied in intensity, duration, etc., it was one of the most consistent elements of this discourse before 1700.[18] Importantly, many seventeenth-century divines, as we will

---

[15] Kirk Essary, *Erasmus and Calvin* (Toronto, 2017), 66, see also pp. 124–7. An earlier study of Erasmus in this regard is M. A. Screech, *Erasmus* (1980), 56–61, Ch. 5.

[16] Richard Baxter, *The saints everlasting rest* (1650), 774. Similar views on the beatific vision can be found among conformists and nonconformists (like Baxter), as we will see in later chapters.

[17] Baxter, *The saints*, 76, 78, see also pp. 329, 631, 760, 774.

[18] Edward Reynolds *A treatise of the passions and faculties of the soule of man* (1640), 8, 36. This kind of exhortation toward experiencing divine revelation can be found throughout the period: John Woolton, *A treatise of the immortalitie of the soule wherein is declared the origine, nature, and powers of the same* (1576), sigs. B1r–D8r; Thomas Traherne, *Christian Ethicks* (Ithaca, NY, 1968), 36–7;

INTRODUCTION: THE CULTURE OF DIVINE REVELATION   7

see in Chapter 6, rejected claims of contemporary, extra-biblical prophecy, believing that 'the Spirit onely Reveales what is Revealed already in the word; by illuminating us to understand it'. The divine experience that an early modern person might have, often referred to as *inspiration*, was a kind of 'divine Revelation, which we are certain that God doth any way Reveal' directly to human souls.[19] The content of what was experienced may have differed from similar experiences described in scripture, but the process was thought to track quite closely.[20]

While it is easy for us to dismiss this language as merely figures of speech or flowery rhetoric, the larger culture's emphasis upon divine revelation in such terms suggests that late medieval and early modern English culture took divine revelation very seriously and many people expectantly pursued it in their religious devotion. As we will see, divine ravishment was considered to be both desirable and possible across a wide stretch of English religious culture. Terms like ravish and rapture were not simply common signs to represent divine revelation; they carried a particular understanding of the epistemology and phenomenology of the experience, and its impact upon an individual. Using this language in contemplative works, biblical commentaries, deathbed visions, prophetic pamphlets, and devotional literature, people sought not only to legitimate certain experiences (and delegitimate others), through linguistic association (or disassociation), but also to recontextualize the traditional understanding of divine revelation into new settings.[21] In the middle ages, some sources likened the experience to an intellectual ascent, where others stressed the emotive qualities of the experience. During the Reformation, many Protestants condemned the seclusion of medieval hermits and contemplatives while still deploying the same discourse to describe the ideal Sabbath rest as well as the ritual of communion. Also, seventeenth century sectarian prophets incorporated the discourse into their own accounts of divine experiences, while at the same time many of the religious authorities (puritan, Anglican, and Catholic) attempted to demonstrate, within the same discourse, that the prophets were unbalanced or demonically possessed. Although there was not a consensus about who experienced divine revelation, there was a commonly held understanding of how legitimate divine encounters could be experienced.

Since this book focuses on collective representations of experiencing God that were shared by most pre-modern Englishwomen and men, there is an inevitable

---

John Scott, *The Christian Life* (1683), 75, 90. Among Catholic works, a similar understanding of the soul, its *telos*, and its senses can be seen in Robert Bellarmine, *Jacob's Ladder* (Doway, 1638), 198–9.

[19] Baxter. *The saints*, 118, 207.

[20] Baxter even chastized ministers who continued to preach without experiencing such 'heavenly delights' for themselves: *The saints*, 482.

[21] A helpful study on the ways that discourse can be recontextualized is Peter van Leeuwen, *Discourse and Practice* (Oxford, 2008), esp. pp. 3–22. Van Leeuwen identifies ten different elements in recontextualizing a discourse, including: eligibility criteria of participants, performance modes, presentation styles, times, and locations.

bias toward continuity, drawing connections across traditional divides, whether they be categorized as confessional, political, philosophical, societal, or gender-based. This bias is highlighted by the fact that my analysis overlaps the Reformation period, which is so often framed as a period of revolution and upheaval, rather than continuity.[22] In recent years, a few scholars have taken to task others who suggest that categories of religious identity and confession can conceal a certain amount of agreement and similarity across differing theological divides. I find this debate a helpful one in teasing out the layers of cultural, theological, and social continuity and discontinuity that emerged during the Reformation, as new religious identities were being fashioned from both innovative ideas and lasting traditions.[23] Chapters 3 and 5, for example, engage substantively with the scholarship that draws clear boundaries around how particular confessions and religious groups treated religious images and divine poetry, respectively. Certainly, context in such matters determines how great the gulf was between different groups. If the context is the nature of the sacrament or the civil authority's role in religion, the field will certainly look much different (and discontinuous) than, say, a question about the nature of God or, as Alec Ryrie has demonstrated, private devotion.[24] So, when it comes to understanding how people thought about and described experiences with God, I think there is a great deal of overlap and continuity across the expanse of English Christianity before 1700. That is to say, at least on this question, I do not think that an Anglican was essentially a Catholic beneath a reformed pelt; however, I do think that many Protestants, even puritans, had more in common with Roman Catholics than they would have liked to admit.

Because this bias runs the risk of overly homogenizing the religious culture by collapsing differences and conflating ideas and individuals that are better left distinct, I have tried to distinguish the different characters by their appropriate positions, time frames, and identities. Thus, when we look at late medieval contemplative literature, it is important to note the different traditions, whether it is the Dionysian apophatic literature, Augustinian works on intellectual ascent, or Bonaventure's notion of a journey inward toward God which permeated a great deal of late medieval writings. Thus, a hermit like Richard Rolle or a visionary like Catherine of Siena share a great deal in common with Augustinians like Thomas Kempis and Walter Hilton in their contemplative theology, but there were some key differences, which can prove just as revealing as the points of commonality.

---

[22] See e.g. Eamon Duffy, *Stripping of the Altars* (1992); James Simpson, *Permanent Revolution* (Cambridge, MA, 2019).

[23] Unfortunately, the tendentious pot-shots taken at Alec Ryrie throughout Peter Lake's and Isaac Stephens's *Scandal and Religious Identity in Early Stuart England* (Woodbridge, 2015) undermine what is otherwise an excellent work of scholarship. A much less polemical work by Tom Betteridge offers a particularly insightful study of confessionalization in Tudor England: *Literature and Politics in the English Reformation* (Manchester, 2004).

[24] Alec Ryrie, *Being Protestant in Reformation Britain* (Oxford, 2013).

INTRODUCTION: THE CULTURE OF DIVINE REVELATION 9

Likewise, when we turn to the early modern religious landscape, I try not to lose either the variety of confessional identities or the important organizational changes to English politics and religion which shaped many people's lives as well as large swathes of English history.

Throughout this book, I have relied upon the expertise of a wide array of scholars, whose knowledge of specific individuals, topics, and ideas far outstrips my own. At key moments in the following chapters, I have wrestled with certain scholarly debates when I found it helpful in understanding the landscape, and hopefully I have done so without following anyone's lead too slavishly. Also, while my narrative intentionally casts a very wide net, I will certainly have overlooked a favourite philosopher, poet, contemplative, and/or theologian, or will not have given them their due attention.[25] For this, I can only apologize in advance.

The following chapters are organized largely by different kinds of texts, and many of these texts were selected in part because of their broad cultural impact. For this reason, much of my analysis relies upon the popular texts of the fifteenth, sixteenth, and seventeenth centuries.[26] This includes several non-English voices (e.g. Catherine of Siena, Thomas Kempis, Heinrich Bullinger, Gaspar Loarte, Guillaume de Salluste Du Bartas) whose works were popular, or had a significant impact, in England. While it is certainly true that the number of editions does not demonstrate popularity in any definitive way, it does provide an indicator of influence and longevity. At the end of the day, if we cannot always get at what people thought, particularly the people who left no written record, we must be satisfied with what they were told to think, by reading what was available to them. At the same time, however, I attempted to pay heed to some sources who, while not serving as examples of what was in the popular mind, present examples of how different individuals responded to this larger literary culture. Thus, published works by people like James Harrington, Edward Benlowes, and Simon Patrick have been studied, even though they were not the most popular at the time and have received very little scholarly attention. Nevertheless, such sources provide us important touchpoints in our understanding of how individuals, whether they be soldiers, poets, or bishops, engaged with the discourse of experiencing God. Also, since a culture is more than its printed books, I included a variety of materials in my sources, where they were available and relevant. Commonplace manuscripts and readers' notes in book margins provide valuable evidence of individual engagement and examples of material culture (e.g. domestic décor, art)

---

[25] Even worse, I have ignored almost entire areas of scholarship that deserve further research (e.g. perhaps most significantly, the intersection of divine revelation and symbolic alchemy). A good starting point for this topic is Bruce Janacek, *Alchemical Belief* (University Park, PA, 2011).

[26] I have chosen, for better or worse, not to dive too deeply into the works of William Shakespeare and John Milton. Not only is there a large body of scholarship for both of these literary giants, but there is also a lush terrain of literary and devotional writings in their shadows, much of which too often goes unattended. However, references to both men's works have been made in a few places where they seemed most helpful.

illustrate the ways that experiences of God were privatized and personalized. Images provide scholars an important trajectory in studying cultural expression, as so much of the late medieval and early modern religious culture relied upon some form of visualization. Moreover, visual evidence allows us to consider what was on display in the late medieval and early modern eye of the mind, suggesting insight into the social and culture imaginaries of the period.

In Part I (chapters 1–3), I identify the essential contours of 'The Discourse of Experiencing God' in medieval contemplative literature, Protestant theology, and the religious visual culture of early English printing. These chapters explore how the language of *raptus* offered a way to describe the pinnacle of contemplative ascent. This discourse was incorporated largely wholesale into the later religious culture of the sixteenth and seventeenth centuries, and it is reflected in the continued popularity of religious images of God during and after the Reformation. Not only does the perpetuation of this discourse suggest a significant continuity between late medieval and early modern English religion, but also the differences in how the discourse was deployed, which can suggest important gaps emerging even within this relative continuity. The proliferation of religious images of God demonstrates that visualizations of the divine continued to play a role in English Protestantism as a significant expression of the culture of revelation.

Part II, chapters 4 and 5, surveys '*Raptus* as Prayer and Poetry', demonstrating how this discourse was an important aspect of both Protestant and Catholic devotional practice. The chapters present different ways that the discourse reached beyond the confines of contemplative writings and biblical commentaries to become a way of thinking and speaking about divine revelation that was dispersed into many more common and secular contexts. These different recontextualizations of the discourse often proved popular in printed literature, and at the same time, they impacted the evolution of how the collective representation of divine revelation was understood. Popular prayer books, sermons, pastoral theologies, and divine poetry encouraged everyday people to experience divine ravishment in different contexts, even encouraging people to make such a pursuit part of their regular routines. These works deployed different contexts such as the Sabbath and communion and domesticated imagery such as gardens and weddings to encourage people with familiar experiences that corresponded to parts of scripture.

Part III presents the 'Challenges to the Culture of Divine Revelation' that became most pressing in the seventeenth century, even though many of them were present in more subtle ways throughout the period. In chapters 6 and 7, we will examine how the emergence of radical sects, many claiming certain religious, even epistemic, authority based upon prophetic utterances. In addition, new philosophical and scientific systems challenged the traditional understanding of divine revelation. In this, I do not intend a decline-and-fall narrative of divine revelation. Although many late-seventeenth century writers took issue with different details and examples of contemporary prophecy as well as more general claims to divine revelation, the late medieval discourse continued to be recontextualized into a variety of contexts. The expansion of the discourse of experiencing God into a much more common and pervasive literary culture (in Part II) provides orthodox and heterodox readers a way of representing divine revelation. Enthusiasts like Francis Bampfield, Anglicans like Simon Patrick, puritans like John Owen, mechanical scientists like Robert Boyle, and empiricist philosophers like John Locke shared a high view of divine revelation as something that was epistemically valid. Both the enthusiasm of radical sects as well as the new philosophies of science and rationality presented problems that were as much internal as well as external to the religious culture.

Fifty years ago, studying how people experienced God in late medieval and early modern culture likely would have been considered an obscure topic, which was best left for religious studies or theological scholarship. If it was a historical topic at all, divine revelation as a cultural phenomenon was considered to be significant only in the ways that it influenced political and social movements.[27] Even today, while histories of religious emotion and belief are becoming standard fare, a historical study of people's experiences of direct divine encounter, particularly approached as a central feature of the religious culture, is not. Nevertheless, studies on the impact of religious belief as well as histories of devotional practice and private belief demonstrate the importance of understanding not only what people believed but how sincerely they believed it and how those beliefs were manifested.[28] Exploring the culture of how God was experienced raises a variety of questions and issues about other social and cultural norms. Notions of the individual self and personhood will become apparent, whether the human self was considered to be a soul within a body or a necessary combination of the two. If, as some scholars argue, the human self was considered to be 'fundamentally embodied', then how are we to understand such experiences in which the body was thought to be set aside, where the soul experiences things without the body?[29] Similarly, divine revelation highlights understood hierarchical, relational dynamics, not only between a transcendent deity and human beings, but also between humans who were said to be like God (or Christ) in their particular roles (e.g. kings, popes, husbands) and the people under their authority.

In recent years, other disciplines have developed their own robust literature on divine revelation, particularly in the realms of epistemology and the philosophy

---

[27] For e.g. Christopher Hill, *The World Turned Upside Down* (1972).

[28] For e.g. Ethan Shagan, *The Birth of Modern Belief* (Princeton, NJ, 2019); Peter Marshall, *Heretics and Believers* (New Haven, CT, 2017); Ryrie, *Being Protestant*; Alexandra Walsham, *Providence in Early Modern England* (Oxford, 1999).

[29] Elizabeth L. Swann, 'Nosce Teipsum', in *Literature, Belief and Knowledge in Early Modern England*, eds, Subha Mukherji and Tim Stuart-Battle (2018), 195–214.

of religion.[30] Scholars are beginning to engage with the impact that religious ways of thinking, often governed and directed by divine revelation, have had upon individual and social relations, even in our modern, secular society.[31] The erosion of Enlightenment rationalism as the unquestioned framework for intellectual discovery is allowing a reconfiguration of the questions that scholars ask concerning divine revelation as well as our assumptions about where beliefs, specifically about the ways that people experience the divine, have in academic research. What I hope this book offers to this larger literature is not only a historical account of how such experiences were understood in pre-eighteenth century England but also the beginnings of a historical narrative within which to place our own society's questions about human encounters with the divine.

Notes on the Text

The spelling, grammar, and italicization of quotations from pre-1700 sources has been kept in the original, however all archaic or unusual abbreviations have been spelled out.

The city of publication for book citations is London unless otherwise noted. All citations include a short title for books (see the BIBLIOGRAPHY for complete titles).

All biblical references are quoted from the 1599 Geneva Bible, unless otherwise noted.

---

[30] See e.g. Rolfe King, *Obstacles to Divine Revelation* (2011); William J. Abraham, *Crossing the Threshold of Divine Revelation* (Grand Rapids, MI, 2006); Richard Swinburne, *Revelation* (Oxford, 1992); Nicholas Wolterstorff, *Divine Discourse* (Cambridge, 1995); William P. Alston, *Perceiving God* (Ithaca, NY, 1991). See also the recent publication of *The Oxford Handbook of Divine Revelation* eds Balázs M. Mezei, Francesca Aran Murphy, and Kenneth Oakes (Oxford, 2021), which promises to offer a systemic approach to divine revelation across several disciplines.

[31] See e.g. John Milbank, *Beyond the Secular Order* (Hoboken, NY: Wiley, 2013); Mark Taylor, *After God* (Chicago, 2007); Charles Taylor, *A Secular Age* (Cambridge, MA, 2007).

PART I

THE DISCOURSE
OF EXPERIENCING GOD

1

'The entrance to my joys'

Raptus in Contemplative Devotion

To name is to know and remember.

Dana Gioia, 'Words'

I want to count him blessed and holy to whom such rapture has been vouchsafed in this mortal life...as if you were emptied and lost and swallowed up in God.

Bernard of Clairvaux, *On Loving God*

During Easter week 1196, Edmund, a monk at the Benedictine abbey in Eynsham, experienced a series of divine visions that began on Easter Friday and ended on Easter morning, in which he was guided by St. Nicholas through Hell, Purgatory, and Heaven. Edmund's visions were subsequently recorded by Adam of Eynsham, whose *Visio monachi de Eynsham* was one of the more popular medieval vision tales.[1] In fact, other than Dante Alighieri's *La divina commedia*, the *Visio* was the only such narrative of the afterlife to be printed before the sixteenth century, and, as Robert Easting explains, 'Adam's account' was particularly concerned with detailing 'Edmund's physical, mental, and spiritual states prior to the vision.'[2] According to Adam of Eynsham, Edmund's experience included a dissociation of his physical body, which left him without any feeling in his extremities, evidenced by the fact that he felt nothing when his brother monks prodded his feet with pins.[3] Furthermore, Adam insisted that Edmund was not sleeping nor hallucinating during the vision, suggesting that whatever was happening to Edmund could not be explained away easily. While Edmund had been ill earlier in the week, Adam is clear that he was awake, alert, and enquiring about the other monks on Maundy Thursday, the day before he 'was rapte in spirit by the wille of god'.

---

[1] The *Visio* survives in thirty-three manuscripts and was translated and printed in English in 1483, as one of William Caxton's first printed books.

[2] Adam of Eynsham, *The Revelation of the Monk of Eynsham*, ed. Robert Easting (Oxford, 2002), lxxx. Of course, this was not the first of such visions in Britain. The vision of Dryhthelm recorded by Bede is likely the earliest, followed by the Irish twelfth-century *Visio Tnugdali*.

[3] Formative in my own thinking on both the language of divine revelation and the phenomenological aspects of the experience is Dyan Elliott, 'The Physiology of Rapture and Female Spirituality', in *Medieval Theology and the Natural Body* (York, 1997), 141–74. Testing the contemplative's physical body seems to have been a standard practice (Elliott, 163).

Experiencing God in Late Medieval and Early Modern England. David J. Davis, Oxford University Press.
© David J. Davis 2022. DOI: 10.1093/oso/9780198834137.003.0002

16   EXPERIENCING GOD IN LATE MEDIEVAL & EARLY MODERN ENGLAND

Furthermore, Adam explained that Edmund had been lucid and free of any infirmity that may have clouded his reason. Then, after Edmund was found prostrate in the church 'betwixt the auter and the walle', the other monks could not wake him, even after they 'prickyd with neldys and scrapyd the solys of hys fete'.[4] After the experience had passed, Edmund relayed what he witnessed, evidencing a certain level of intellectual awareness, or remembrance of the experience, even though he was unaware of any physical sensation.

Medieval contemplative texts span several centuries. They include experiences of clergy and laity, workers and hermits, women and men, which were written as handbooks on prayer, guides to contemplative ascent, and accounts of other-worldly visions. In this chapter, I sketch a general understanding of how divine revelation, particularly by means of what was termed *raptus*, was described and delimited in late medieval England. For as much as divine revelation suggests the numinous and incommunicable, Steven Katz is correct that:

> Whatever else the world's mystics do with language, they do not, as a rule, merely negate it...they utilize language to convey meaning(s) and content(s) in a variety of amazingly imaginative ways. It is, indeed, their success at just this sort of substantive communication that allows us to speak of, to learn of, and to participate in mystical traditions at all.[5]

Among the accounts of divine revelation examined here, there are shifts in the meaning of common terms, images, and figurative descriptions.[6] Nevertheless, there are key discursive points of continuity that seem to hold true across much of the literature. These points, when taken together, illustrate a collective representation of how people experienced God that was consistently deployed in first-hand accounts, hagiographies, prayer books, and devotionals. This discursive representation helped people to communicate what happened when they encountered God, providing a certain degree of surety to the reader as well as a common frame of reference from which people could understand what was happening to the individual.

Raptus in the Medieval Tradition

Essential to the discourse that described divine revelation was the notion that spiritual rapture was a sudden, and seemingly violent, movement of a person's

---

[4] Eynsham, *The Revelation of the Monk of Eynsham*, 19, 25.
[5] Steven T. Katz, 'Mystical Speech and Mystical Meaning', in *Mysticism and Language* (Oxford, 1992), 33.
[6] The works of both Wolfgang Riehle and Steven Katz stand out for their attention to the discursive structures surrounding divine revelation. Along with Katz's works already cited, see Wolfgang Riehle, *The Middle English Mystics* (1981).

soul (or mind), dissociating it from the body. Robert McMahon explains that for medieval contemplatives, 'It is understood that God can abbreviate the ascent whenever he wills... by seizing the soul into his presence with a sudden influx of grace'.[7] Importantly, medieval authorities like Thomas Aquinas and St. Bonaventure tended to draw distinctions between *raptus* and other forms of mystical *extasis*, which were equally part of the contemplative tradition. While *extasis*, according to Aquinas, was ultimately rooted in human agency, *raptus* contained a certain sense of *violentiam* that included an external force acting upon the soul. This distinction tracked quite well with the legal use of *raptus* in English courts, which was used to describe instances of kidnapping and assault, as well as rape, but was not limited to sexual violence.[8] In describing individuals' experiences of God, rapture was an interaction in which God compelled the individual, whereas other ecstatic experiences are simply, 'a man... moving himself' toward God.[9] That is not to say that *extasis* was somehow unspiritual or lacking in devotion. Rather, *raptus* was an experience set apart, because it was completely contingent upon divine intervention, and contemplative writers described their experiences accordingly, often delineating these unique experiences with particular discursive markers.[10] According to Wolfgang Riehle, English contemplative texts used the term *raptus* 'almost exclusively', when describing such encounters with God, recontextualizing this broader term to connote a particular experience in contemplative devotion that was treated differently than almost any other kind of experience. While other contemplative traditions on the continent deployed these terms in various ways, by the mid-fifteenth century, if not earlier, English writers deployed *raptus* to identify only those experiences of God in which the individual was completely overwhelmed by the divine.[11]

A useful theological benchmark for the discourse of the *Visio* is the thought of Richard of St. Victor, writing in the generation before Edmund of Eynsham. By 1150, the Abbey of St. Victor, near Paris, was a hub for medieval humanism. Among the abbey's most important figures was the British prior Richard, with his writings on contemplative devotion. Richard's *The Twelve Patriarchs* (or *Benjamin Minor*) and *The Mystical Ark* (or *Benjamin Major*) explained that contemplative devotion began from a position of rational understanding, because the 'rational

---

[7] Robert McMahon, *Understanding the Medieval Mystical Ascent* (Washington, DC, 2006), 1.

[8] Corinnne J. Saunders, *Rape and Ravishment in the Literature of Medieval England* (Woodbridge, 2001), 20. See also Kathryn Gravdal, *Ravishing Maidens* (Philadelphia, 1991).

[9] Thomas Aquinas, *The Summa Theologica* (New York, 1947), 2a2ae.175.1.2.

[10] Riehle, *The Middle English Mystic*, 95. Marianne Schlosser, 'Bonaventure: Life and Works', in *The Companion to Bonaventure* (Leiden, 2014), 53n.114.

[11] Riehle, *The Middle English Mystic*, 94. One example of this linguistic recontextualization appears in the Huntington Library manuscript copy of the *Prickyng of Conscience* (HM 128). The scribe maintains the typical word 'rauashed' to describe the resurrection of the dead at the Judgment Day. However, the scribe avoided the word 'ravyste' about the Antichrist's pretended resurrection, even though the word appears in earlier copies of the text. Instead, he wrote, 'he shal him feyne to aryse from ded' (f. 46v.). For an example of different continental uses of these words, see Jean Gerson, *Early Works* (New York, 1998), 282–5.

18 EXPERIENCING GOD IN LATE MEDIEVAL & EARLY MODERN ENGLAND

soul…is the foremost and principal mirror for seeing God', and the committed devotee must attend to cleansing the mirror of the rational soul in order to see God.[12] The soul must endure a period of moral purification until, 'The mirror has been wiped and gazed into for a long time', so that 'a kind of splendour of divine light begins to shine in it and a great beam of unexpected vision appears to his eyes'.[13] Deploying the Old Testament patriarch Benjamin as a metaphor for religious contemplation, Richard outlined a method of prayer, study, and meditation—expressions of human reason (Rachel, Benjamin's mother)—which led a person to the edge of contemplation. Thus, as Rachel gave birth to Benjamin, so reason gives birth to contemplation.[14]

Contemplative literature generally focused on the period of purification more than other stages of the process, detailing regimens of either penitent suffering, self-castigation, spiritual discipline, or a combination of such things. Equally important was the role that sickness and other external trials played in spiritual purification, as the devotee moved themselves closer to a state of contemplative love. As Edmund of Eynsham was ill for several days leading up to his revelations, so too the late fourteenth-century anchorite Julian of Norwich was sent a sickness by God as part of her purification, which was so severe that after three days and three nights of suffering she was given Last Rites. Two days later, however, she received a miraculous healing immediately after looking at the cross, and her visions began shortly thereafter.[15] The fact that both Edmund and Julian experienced physical weakness is not insignificant. In both Neoplatonic and contemplative literature, there seems to have been an understanding that the soul was more easily rapt up in the spirit when the body's hold upon the soul was loosened. Other contemplative writers described hardships they imposed upon themselves, which included fasting, vows of chastity and silence, repentance of sins, and other acts of physical (and mental) self-negation to discipline and silence the demands of the self.

These purifying acts, however, were not prescribed universally in the contemplative literature. Late medieval texts like *The Cloud of Unknowing* emphasized mental and spiritual cleansing but warned against 'soche rude streynynges' of physical purification, which were more likely to make a person 'feestre in fantasie feinid of feende', than to prepare them for contemplation.[16] While many contemplatives stressed an austere and solitary life, *The Cloud* warned against such strivings that weakened the body and made it susceptible to demonic ('feende')

---

[12] Richard of St. Victor, *Richard of St. Victor: The Twelve Patriarchs, The Mystical Ark, and Book Three of The Trinity* (New York, 1979), 129.

[13] St. Victor, *The Twelve Patriarchs*, 129–30.

[14] On the continent, the influence of St. Victor, particularly concerning reason's relationship to revelation, is evident in Gerson, *Early Works*, 44, 106, 114.

[15] Julian of Norwich, *The Shewings of Julian of Norwich* (Kalamazoo, MI, 1994), part 1, lines 72–80.

[16] Anon., *The Cloud of Unknowing* (Kalamazoo, MI, 1997), lines 1627–9.

deception. Physical self-negation was not inherently dangerous, nor was it necessarily virtuous or a guaranteed path to spiritual ascent.

Either way, Richard said that the devotee should anticipate experiences of divine love during the purification, specifically in the form of an 'unexpected vision', which Richard considered to be the beginning of a person's longing for God. The time that most writers spent on describing this longing illustrates how pivotal the purification process was seen to be, and it is out of this longing that, as Richard wrote, 'Benjamin is born'. Following the biblical account of Rachel (Jacob's wife) giving birth to Benjamin (Gen. 35.16–18), Richard explained that, like Rachel, the mother of contemplation (human reason) must pass away, or perish, 'for if it were possible to approach that divine light by some argument or other then it would not be inaccessible'.[17] Whatever the methods employed to reach contemplation, reason, also described as human understanding, brought the devotee to the edge of contemplation. The contemplative mind must then move past the limits of reason into three, otherwise inaccessible, 'heavens' of contemplation.[18]

Richard and other writers do not seem to consider this experience to constitute a psychological collapse into subjectivity; nor was Richard championing a kind of spiritual irrationality. If anything, the movement beyond reason was a movement into greater objectivity, a supra-rational state that casts off the subjective self with both its passions and its analytical abilities. This is evidenced in his explanation, 'Benjamin kills his mother when he goes above all reason. However…he goes beyond even himself when he transcends the mode of human understanding in that which he comes to know from divine showing'. In The Mystical Ark, this contemplative movement above the self is compared to the rising of smoke, 'the soul ascends like smoke into supernal regions when, being impelled to this very thing by a burning love, her longing carries her away above herself'.[19] The love for God initiates the movement, but the soul could only go so far on its own without God ravishing it heavenward. In other words, the movement of the soul by its own means was ultimately 'vain' without divine agency: 'who has seen or might be able to see cherubim? But how shall I represent that form which I am not capable of seeing?…And so it is necessary to ascend to a high heart and by ecstasy of mind learn further from a showing from the Lord'.[20]

Certainly, other authorities, both before and after Richard of St. Victor, will be relevant as we go forward. I do not want to suggest that Richard was the fount from which all later English contemplative thought sprang, but his thinking

[17] St. Victor, The Twelve Patriarchs, 131. See also the middle English version of Benjamin Minor in MS Richardson 22, fols. 67v–68r.

[18] The three-fold model was based in Bonaventure's De triplici vita, and it became a commonplace in both late medieval and Tridentine Catholic texts, like Ignatius Loyola's Spiritual Exercises: Thomas H. Bestul, 'Meditatio/Meditation', in The Cambridge Companion to Christian Mysticism (Cambridge, 2012), 164–6. See also Zwollo, Augustine and Plotinus, 320.

[19] St. Victor, The Twelve Patriarchs, 145; St. Victor, The Mystical Ark, 318.

[20] St. Victor, The Mystical Ark, 267–8, see also pp. 319–20.

20   EXPERIENCING GOD IN LATE MEDIEVAL & EARLY MODERN ENGLAND

around the process and experience of divine revelation provides an influential exemplar of how *raptus* was understood and described in late medieval England. The basic framework that Richard describes of preparation, the soul's ascent, and the reliance upon divine agency shaped much of what later centuries of English contemplatives and divines believed about being ravished by God.

Understanding *Raptus*

The fourteenth century was an important hundred years for Middle English writing in general and works of contemplation in particular, as several influential texts appeared that would shape much of the contemplative thought of late medieval and early modern England. Alongside the literary achievements of Geoffrey Chaucer, John Gower, and the *Pearl* Poet, classics of medieval spirituality in Middle English began to appear. In this section, we examine three of the more significant of these works and the different ways they approached contemplative devotion and the notion of divine *raptus*.

One of the earliest Middle English contemplatives that drew directly from Richard's theology was the hermit of Hampole, Richard Rolle (d.1349). Born to Yorkshire farmers, Rolle seems to have rejected the opportunities of social-climbing offered to him, as he never held a clerical office nor participated in civil society. Early in life, he was blessed by Thomas de Neville, archdeacon of Durham Cathedral, with an education at Oxford.[21] Rolle, however, rejected a future in the ecclesiastical hierarchy, retreating to a hermitage near a Cistercian house outside Hampole. We can only speculate as to what drove Rolle into such seclusion. Even in a period when the Franciscan call to poverty and purity reached across Europe, Rolle's decades-long isolation was unusual. Despite what little we know of Rolle's life, the large hoard of his surviving manuscripts—from meditations on the Passion and accounts of his own contemplative experiences to theological treatises and biblical commentaries—speak volumes about his prodigious mind.[22] His most popular book, the *Incendium Amoris* (Fire of Love) survives in over forty medieval manuscripts, and it was among the very few contemplative texts 'utilized in the Counter-Reformation'.[23]

Part of the *Incendium*'s success is due to Rolle's intimate prose and the powerful metaphors he fashioned to explore the contours of his experience with God.

---

[21] Elaine Glanz, 'Richard Rolle's Imagery in *Meditations on the Passion B*', *Mystics Quarterly* 22 (1996), 58–68; Claire McIlroy, *The English Prose Treatises of Richard Rolle* (Woodbridge, 2004), 84.

[22] Bernard McGinn, *The Varieties of Vernacular Mysticism, 1350–1550* (New York, 2012), 344. See also the monumental work done by Hope Emily Allen, *Writings Ascribed to Richard Rolle* (Oxford, 1927). Rolle was so prolific and popular that many anonymous Middle English manuscripts have been attributed to him for no more significant reason than his popularity.

[23] Allen, *Writings Ascribed*, 4.

Comparing divine love to both a melody and a fire (two things capable of surrounding and immersing a person's perceptions), Rolle described *raptus* as:

> The very fervor of their sweet love ravishes them with the sight of their Beloved. Flowering through this loving flame into all virtue they rejoice in their Maker. Their mind is changed and passes into lasting melody. From now on their meditations become song. Melancholy has been driven out of the mansion of their spirit, and it now resounds with wondrous melody.[24]

For Rolle, the human soul is completely overwhelmed and 'changed' by the experience, taking into itself some of the substance ('lasting melody') of what it experienced in its encounter with God. The soul becomes a heavenly echo on Earth, which 'resounds' with the wonders of divine revelation. Importantly, Rolle put no stock in what is often referred to as the active life (a life of secular work and responsibilities). Complete dedication to the contemplative life was, for him, essential to the pursuit of *raptus*: 'A human soul cannot know the fire of eternal love unless he has first completely cut adrift from worldly vanity of every kind. There must be a serious intention to study heavenly things'.[25] Similarly, the very popular fourteenth-century devotional the Poor Caitiff seems to put rapturous experiences with God out of reach for the lay reader who would have been engaged in the active life. Without entirely denigrating the active life, the author of the Poor Caitiff encourages readers to focus upon more practical activities like following the Ten Commandments, meditating upon the love of God, and caring for their neighbors, while looking forward to enjoying the heavenly sights after death, which contemplatives can catch glimpses of.[26]

Both Rolle and the Poor Caitiff stress the necessity, within the contemplative life, of eschewing anything and everything that does not contribute to the life of the soul through a systematic purge of the flesh. Rolle's own purgation is carefully detailed in the *Incendium*. Among the many struggles Rolle accounts for (and almost revels in the details), he includes an explicit, and apparently long-standing, battle with sexual temptation. Apparently, on at least three separate occasions, Rolle was verbally rebuked by women because he inappropriately admired their bodies. The most outspoken of these women made him, Rolle admits, 'deservedly...feel uncomfortable', when she loudly chastised him for his lechery.[27] However, once his physical and spiritual purgation freed Rolle of such lusts, he

---

[24] Richard Rolle, *The Fire of Love* (New York, 1972), 60.

[25] Rolle, *The Fire of Love*, 55. Here, and elsewhere, there are distinct echoes of Bonaventure's *Itinerarium* in Rolle's work: *The Journey of the Mind to God* (Indianapolis, 1993), VII.6, 39.

[26] The Poor Caitiff survives in over fifty medieval manuscripts, containing instructions for daily devotional living and often appended with other practical works on saying the Mass and prayers for the souls in Purgatory (English MS 87) as well as short treatises on chastity and virginity (English MS 701).

[27] Rolle, *The Fire of Love*, 81.

22 EXPERIENCING GOD IN LATE MEDIEVAL & EARLY MODERN ENGLAND

then seems to have been ready to receive the love of God more completely. Stripped of his fleshly desires, Rolle began to see God as, 'the end of my grief...the goal of my toil...the entrance to my joys'. These passionate desires burned so powerfully, they even took on amorous overtones: 'Yes, I burn, I pant for you. If you come I will be safe' as if Rolle's physical lechery had been transformed into a desire for God. At the same time, Rolle expressed a certain level of dissatisfaction with the glimpses of God he received in ravishment, 'Ravished though I be with love, yet I still cannot enjoy fully what I so desperately want; not until I taste that joy you are going to give me'. The tension between experiencing God and the mounting need for that future joy finally culminates in Rolle asking 'Death, why do you delay?'[28]

Rolle's understanding of *raptus* included several important distinctives. First, for Rolle, the person (man or woman) who was rapt in the fire of love was a 'perfect man', because they had chastised the flesh and silenced any desires other than loving Christ. He or she 'enjoys the sort of sweetness that angels have in heaven' and 'does not need to be purged by fire after this life'.[29] This experience fundamentally changed a person into something more perfect than their former selves, so much so that they were excused from Purgatory. Rolle concluded that the raptured soul did not need to 'say his prayers the same way as other men however righteous they may be, because his mind is raised to great exaltation and is rapt with love for Christ. He is taken out of himself into indescribable delight, and the divinest music floods into him'.[30] While righteousness can be found in the active life, only the contemplative life leads to the level of understanding and spiritual pleasure Rolle detailed. Finally, toward the end of the *Incendium*, Rolle argued that the experience of being 'enraptured can be understood in two ways'. The first way follows the tradition set out by Richard of St. Victor, Aquinas, and others, wherein 'a man is rapt out of all physical sensation, so that at the time of his rapture his body quite clearly feels nothing and does nothing. He is not dead, of course, but alive'. Rolle pointed to examples of biblical saints who had been so enraptured 'for their own good, and for others' enlightenment'. Of course, among the best of these examples was the fact that 'Paul was rapt to the third heaven', in a manner that dissociated his soul from his physical senses.[31] The second way of rapture, which Rolle considered, was different in at least one important way. This rapture 'comes through the lifting up of the mind to God in contemplation'. In this way, the human mind was the agent of rapture, even though it remains just as supernatural as the first way. Interestingly, there does not seem to be an overt dissociation of body and soul, and Rolle insisted that 'This second way is most desirable and lovely. For Christ was always contemplating God, yet it never detracted

[28] Rolle, *The Fire of Love*, 96.
[29] Rolle, *The Fire of Love*, 113–14.
[30] Rolle, *The Fire of Love*, 114.
[31] Rolle, *The Fire of Love*, 166.

from his self-possession'.[32] Christ was the ultimate model for Rolle's understanding of contemplation; the perfected contemplative mind could enjoy God in the same manner as Christ. While the contemplative approach seems always to be characterized by a surrendering of a person's will to God, here the retention of 'self-possession' is the quality that sets the second way of rapture above the first. That is to say, Rolle seems to value the retention of his individual agency above that of being overwhelmed completely by God, which for someone like Richard of St. Victor would seem to undermine the movement of the soul beyond reason.

Another writer who drew directly from Richard was the Augustinian canon Walter Hilton (d.1396), whose popularity rivalled that of Thomas Kempis in late medieval England.[33] Unlike most middle English works, Hilton's *The Scale of Perfection* was translated into Latin early in the fifteenth century, allowing it to be read by a broader audience on the continent. Also, along with dozens of surviving manuscripts from the fifteenth century, Hilton's *Scale* was printed in English five times before 1534, and then twice more in the 1650s.[34] Hilton's popularity, in part, had to do with his style, which was both accessible and edifying. Marion Glasscoe writes that Hilton found 'a means of using the language of both physical experience and Scripture in an anagogical sense whereby contemplative experience may be both recognized and shared'.[35] In *The Scale*, Hilton guides the contemplative rather than inspiring them with stories of rapture, providing practical direction on prayer and meditation.[36] Even though Hilton presents a much less sensuous description of divine rapture than someone like Rolle, he too was committed to the language of *raptus* as a movement of the soul away from the body. Sketching out three stages of contemplative ascent, Hilton instructed readers to engage their reason, their affections, and their cognition (or understanding) in a spiritual union of knowledge and love with God. The final stage of this ascent was divine *raptus*, and it was the only stage in which the soul was not an active agent:

> The thridde partie of contemplactioun whiche is perfite as it may be here, lieth bothe in cognicion and in affeccion: that is for to seie, in knowyng and in perfight lovynge of God. And that is whanne a mannys soule first is cleensid from alle synnes and reformyd bi fulheed of vertues to the ymage of Jhesu: and after

---

[32] Rolle, *The Fire of Love*, 166.

[33] For Hilton's criticisms of Rolle see Michael Sargent, 'Contemporary Criticism of Richard Rolle', *Analecta Cartusiana* 55 (1981), 160–205.

[34] McGinn, *The Varieties*, 372. The Carthusian houses in the south of England were familiar with his *Scale of Perfection*, as were the Bridgettine sisters at Syon Abbey.

[35] Marion Glasscoe, *English Medieval Mystics* (Harlow, 1993), 144.

[36] Denise Nowakowski Baker, *Julian of Norwich's Showings* (Princeton, NJ, 1994); John P. H. Clark and Rosemary Dorwood, 'Introduction', in Walter Hilton, *The Scale of Perfection* (Mahwah, NJ, 1991), 13–57. While many scholars understand Hilton as a critical voice of writers like Rolle, Riehle does not see the harsh criticism that many have identified in Hilton's writings toward more sensual contemplatives: Wolfgang Riehle, *The Secret Within* (Ithaca, NY, 2014), 182.

24   EXPERIENCING GOD IN LATE MEDIEVAL & EARLY MODERN ENGLAND

whanne he is visitid and is taken up from alle eartheli and fleisschli affecciones, from veyn thoughtis and veyn ymaginacions of alle bodili thynges, and as it were mykil ravysschid out of the bodili wittes and thane bi the grace of the Holi Gost is illumined for to see bi undirstoondynge soothfastnesse, whiche is God, and also goostli thynges, with a soft swete brennande love in hym, so perfightli that bi ravyschynge of this love the soule is ooned for the tyme and conformyd to the ymage of the Trinité. The bigynnyng of this contemplacioun may be felid in this lif, but the fulheed of it is kepid in the blisse of hevene. Of this onynge and conformynge speketh Seynt Poul thus: *Qui adheret deo unus spiritus est cum illo* (1 Corinthians 6:17). That is to seie, whoso bi raveschynge of love is fastned to God, thane God and a soule aren not two but bothe oon. Not in fleisch, but in oo spirit. And sotheli in this onynge is the marriage maad bitwixe God and the soule, which schal nevere be brokyn.[37]

For Hilton, *raptus* was a movement of the soul that united an individual's understanding with the love of God, echoing earlier voices of divine *raptus*. In his way of thinking about contemplation, Hilton emphasized several key features of *raptus*, which were typical elements of this contemplative discourse. The contemplative reader must first be 'cleensid' and the whole human soul (both the 'affeccion' and 'cognicion') participated in the purification. One of Hilton's favourite methods of purification was simple meditation upon the name, life, and passion of Christ, whom Hilton considered to be both the beginning and ending of contemplation. In the third stage, one must be removed from their physical body. In the dissociation of mind and body, God's revelation bypassed the sinful flesh, presenting to the soul a clear 'ymage of the Trinité'.[38] Also, importantly, Hilton did not expect that everyone would reach the perfection necessary to receive this kind of rapturous experience. In fact, he stressed it was solely 'by the grace' of God that a person 'is taken up', suggesting that rather than unlocking the door of divine *raptus*, purgation only prepares a person to be welcomed in. Throughout *The Scale*, Hilton reiterated the point that *raptus* was at the discretion of God and empowered by 'the grace of the Holi Gost', and it could not be achieved through any human device.[39] Hilton conscientiously warned his readers against pride and self-deception, which were apparently typical vices to be found in those that desired to have divine visions. Where writers like Rolle described divine revelation as a consummative and enveloping experience, for Hilton, the third level of contemplation was, first and foremost, an 'onynge', a spiritual union, between God and the human soul. Anything that was seen or experienced during divine

---

[37] Walter Hilton, *The Scale of Perfection* (Kalamazoo, MI, 2000), I.8.

[38] Hilton, *The Scale*, I.8; Riehle, *The Secret Within*, 192.

[39] Hilton, *The Scale*, I.8. This point was also affirmed by the tradition of contemplative ascent rooted in the work of Pseudo-Dionysius. See his *The Celestial Hierarchy*, in *The Complete Works* (New York, 1987), Ch. IV.

raptus should be considered 'symple and secundarie' compared to the union of the human soul with God.[40] Ravishment in contemplation was the highest form of human understanding, or what Hilton calls 'illuminacion of undirstondynge', and the purpose of this understanding was the individual's communion with the divine.[41] The languages of seeing, understanding, and knowing occupy much more of the *Scale* than do bodily or spiritual visions, and this emphasis climaxes in the 'openynge of the goostli iye', with which one may experience the full understanding of contemplative practice. Like the rapturous experience, the spiritual eye 'mai not be geten thorugh studie ne bi mannys traveile oonli, but principali thorugh grace of the Hooli Goost'.[42]

Another text that tended to curtail, rather than encourage, rapturous experiences was the *Cloud of Unknowing*. Possibly written for the English Carthusian houses in the early fifteenth century, *The Cloud* echoed Hilton's theology very closely. With a general cautionary tone and a stress on divine agency, the *Cloud*-author insisted that no one was capable of experiencing an unobstructed vision of God the Father.[43] All divine visions, at least in some sense, the *Cloud*-author argued, are apophatic and at 'the tyme of ravisching...alle [is] at the ordynaunce and the disposicion of God, after theire abilines in soule that this grace of contemplacion and of goostly worching is goven to'.[44] Even though there is a 'cloude of unknowing...betwixt thee and Hym', God can with 'a beme of goostly light' at his own choosing 'schewe thee sum of His privete'.[45] Like Richard of St. Victor, the *Cloud*-author prescribed a regimen of study, meditation, reading, and prayer, which cleans the mirror of the soul sufficiently for the divine beam of light to be reflected. Interestingly, the *Cloud*-author contrasts the experience of *raptus* with Christ's Ascension into heaven (Acts 1.6–11), and he discourages anyone who believes they can ascend under their own power. While the contemplative's soul may be drawn into heaven, the body will not be separated until the 'Day of Doome', when it is, like Christ's body after the Resurrection 'clad with undeedines'.[46] Although Christ's Ascension may offer an attractive model for how divine revelation occurred, the *Cloud*-author warned against any efforts 'to streyne thin ymaginacion in the tyme of thi preier', thinking that such a thing is possible before the Apocalypse. In this regard, the *Cloud*-author contended with Rolle's teaching of Christ as the best model for contemplation: 'For tyme, stede, and

---

[40] Hilton, *The Scale*, I.10, 9. Like Richard Baxter (discussed in the Introduction), Hilton believed that people who experience the third stage of contemplation received only a glimpse of heaven, which would be realized fully in the final beatific vision after death.

[41] Hilton, *The Scale*, I.9; Tarje Park, 'Reflecting Christ', in *The Medieval Mystical Tradition in England*, ed. Marion Glasscoe (Cambridge, 1992), 18.

[42] Hilton, *The Scale*, II.40.

[43] It is possible that Hilton and the *Cloud*-author worked together to some extent: Clark and Dorwood, 'Introduction', 24–5.

[44] Anon., *The Cloud of Unknowing*, lines 2383–5, 2387.   [45] Anon., *The Cloud*, lines 1138–40.

[46] Anon., *The Cloud*, line 2072.

body, thees thre schuld be forgeten in alle goostly worching. And therefore bewar in this werk that thou take none ensaumple at the bodily assencion of Christe'.[47] Finally, the *Cloud*-author exhorted readers to pursue the substance of contemplation, 'undirstoondynge soothfastnesse'.[48] Reason and study were the preliminary stages of contemplation, or the 'schadewe of verry contemplacioun', where the human mind moved itself. The final stage of contemplation moved the soul (separate from the body) beyond these shadows into a supra-rational understanding of God's love by the grace of the Holy Spirit.

It is not insignificant that beginning in the twelfth and thirteenth centuries, the Holy Spirit's unique function within the Trinity began to be more fully developed in western theology. In the New Testament, the Holy Spirit was God's commissioning and consoling presence among the believers (Luke 11.13). It was the Holy Spirit that descended upon Christ at his baptism (Matthew 3.14), and on the day of Pentecost, the Holy Spirit descended upon the disciples in Jerusalem (Acts 2). Moreover, as the *Cloud* passage above states, the Spirit was believed to be both the principal means by which God communicated to human beings and the personality that drew both the Father and Son, as well as humans, toward one another. The third person of the Trinity served as the mutual exchange of love between the other two persons of the godhead, and subsequently between God and the created world.[49] In a certain respect, the Holy Spirit became the personification of divine love, uniting all things together in God. For Richard of St. Victor, the Holy Spirit was the 'impulse' that carried us 'away into higher things', as well as the 'ardor of celestial longing...when it brings the human soul to a vigorous boiling by means of divine love'.[50] Hilton extended this essential desire for God even to understanding the Word of God, which he says, 'is closed undir keie seelid with a signet of Jhesuis fyngir, that is the Holi Goost...withouten His love and His leve mai no man come in'.[51] For later contemplatives, the Spirit offered particular gifts, which aided in the journey of spiritual ascent, as well as serving as the primary conduit of ascent.

Experiencing *Raptus*

The discourse of experiencing God in *raptus* was not limited to the work of a few well-educated theologians and contemplatives. In many contexts, it was an

---

[47] Anon., *The Cloud*, lines 2088–93

[48] Dyan Elliott referred to these as 'things themselves': Elliott, 'The Physiology of Rapture and Female Spirituality', 142.

[49] Matthew Knell, *The Immanent Person of the Holy Spirit from Anselm to Lombard* (Eugene, OR, 2009), 91–3.

[50] St. Victor, *The Mystical Ark*, 319.   [51] Hilton, *The Scale*, II, 43.

ingredient in non-clerical, grassroots religious *praxis*.[52] One example of this is the Middle English poem 'Trentale Sancti Gregorii', which describes a vision that St. Gregory had of the Virgin Mary: 'He sawe a full swete syght:.../ That all the worlde was not so bryght, / Comely crowned as a qwene, .../ He was so Raueshed of that syght/ That nygh for Ioye he swoned Ryght'.[53] Similarly, the earliest English translations of Jacobus Voragine's hagiography deployed *raptus* to describe visions received by saints like the apostle Paul and Elizabeth of Hungary.[54] Also, the Benedictine poet Henry Bradshaw described St. Radegund as having had 'Her soule...rapt / her mynde in an extasy'.[55] Elsewhere, *raptus* found its way into localized accounts like the thirteenth-century Scottish tradesman and saint William of Perth, who was murdered while on pilgrimage. After the saint's death, a sick man living in Perth was 'ledde in a uysyon' into heaven to witness William's apotheosis. Afterward, 'when his spyryte was come agayne to the Bodye', he reported to the townspeople what he saw.[56] Edmund of Leversedge from Somerset in 1465 was said to have been 'raveschyd and departed fro...body' and taken by God into the afterlife so that he might better 'vndirstand' the dangers of damnation for a sinful life.[57]

Among the more well-known examples was Julian of Norwich's *Shewings*. Born in 1342, Julian was fortunate to survive the waves of bubonic plague that ravaged the East Anglian countryside when she was a young girl. Sometime after reaching adulthood, Julian became an anchoress to a small church in the market city of Norwich, where in May 1373 she fell gravely ill. Although the details of her illness are unclear, the experience served as a catalyst for Julian's divine shewings, which she detailed in two works. The Short Text which is a brief description of her raptures that was likely set down soon after the events, and the Long Text, almost six times longer and written twenty years later, contained a complex interpretation of what was revealed to her. Perhaps most important for our purposes is the stress that Julian placed upon the process by which she received her divine shewings as well as the close connection she made between the intellectual enlightenment she received and her love for God.[58] In one of Julian's first revelations, Christ showed her 'a littil thing', no larger than a hazelnut: 'I lokid there upon with eye of my understondyng and thowte...What may this be? And it was generally answered thus: *It is all that is made*'.[59] Whether Julian had in mind the exact same thing as

---

[52] Gwenfair Walters Adams, *Visions in Late Medieval England* (Leiden, 2007), 55–7.

[53] 'Trentale Sancti Gregorii' in *Political, Religious, and Love Poems*, ed. Frederick J. Furnivall (1903), 120.

[54] Jacobus Voragine, *Legenda aurea* (1483), sigs. 2C6r, 2C4r.

[55] Henry Bradshaw, *Here begynneth the lyfe of saynt Radegunde* (1525), f. 6v.

[56] Anon., *Newe Legende of Englande* (1516), sig. S2v.

[57] Adam of Eynsham, *The prologe of this reuelation* (1483), sig. A1r. See also the modern edition *The Vision of Edmund Leversedge* (Nijmegen, 1991).

[58] Julian of Norwich, *The Shewings of Julian of Norwich* (Kalamazoo, MI, 1994), Part I, lines 536–7, 781; Adams, *Visions in Late Medieval England*, 135.

[59] Norwich, *The Shewings*, I.148–51.

28   EXPERIENCING GOD IN LATE MEDIEVAL & EARLY MODERN ENGLAND

Hilton's ghostly eye is unclear; however, Hilton and Julian both emphasized the epistemic qualities of divine revelation to this internal eye. For Julian, the most significant intellectual discipline was expanding her 'knowledge of the bodily peynes of our Saviour', and over the next few days, Julian received both corporeal and 'ghostly' revelations.[60] Interestingly, Julian did not employ the language of *raptus* to the extent that someone like Rolle did; she seems to have been much more particular in where and when she deployed the discourse. Also, unlike other contemplatives, she usually oriented her experiences around the mental rather than the physical. For example, she writes, 'And this vision was a lernyng to myn understondyng that the continual sekyng of the soule plesith God ful mekyl'.[61] Elsewhere, Julian noted that at the beginning of her sixth revelation, 'myn understondyng was lifted up into Hevyn, where I saw our Lord as a lord in his owne house', and a similar phrase begins her ninth revelation. The reasons for why she used *raptus* when she did are not entirely clear. It may be that *raptus* and visions went hand in hand for Julian, although there is no definitive indication that this was the case. The ravishment of her understanding certainly preceded her visions, and she clearly treats them as two distinct events, both of which were part of the larger experience.

We have an equally intriguing example in another contemplative from southeast England. Margery Kempe was born into a well-to-do, middle class family in King's Lynn (Norfolk), and her life, married to a town official named John Kempe and having fourteen children, was much different than Julian's.[62] In *The Book of Margery Kempe*, written in the early 1430s, Margery portrays herself as a devout, merchant-class wife. She was active in the local guild of the Holy Trinity and also struggled with sexual temptations, social expectations, and financial pressures, which were not unusual for a person of her social status. That she was uneducated and married are not the only aspects of her autobiography that set Margery apart. Although her writings echo the passion of Rolle and others as well as a commitment to physical purgation and self-denial, she did not think it necessary to abandon her active (secular) life completely, even if she did restrict certain activities.

Margery's account also provides an important example of the distinction between divine visions and *raptus*, which the average person could make.[63] Thus,

---

[60] Norwich, *The Shewings*, I.48–9. Throughout her work, Julian distinguishes between these two kinds of experiences, where 'ghostly' were those that had 'no bodily liknes'.

[61] Norwich, *The Shewings*, I.401–2.

[62] Margery's popularity in this period is difficult to measure. Few manuscripts survive, and there was only one printing of her book, a much-abbreviated collection of excerpts: Margery Kempe, *Here begynneth a shorte treatyse of contemplacyon* (1501).

[63] Margery's knowledge of contemplative literature depended upon a cleric who read her works of devotion, which she embraced 'so excellently that sche herd nevyr / boke, neythyr Hyltons boke, ne Bridis boke, ne Stimulus Amorys, ne Incendium Amoris, / ne non other that evyr sche herd redyn that spak so hyly of lofe of God but that sche / felt as hyly in werkyng in hir sowle yf sche cowd or ellys mygth a schewyd as sche / felt': Margery Kempe, *The Book of Margery Kempe* (Kalamazoo, MI, 1996), I.I.898–902.

early in the text, Margery received a vision of Christ, which convinced her that she must swear off sexual relations with her husband at least for a period of time.[64] Then, two years passed in which she struggled with temptations and a lack of spiritual discipline. This period of purgation and abstinence was followed by a rapturous experience on the Friday before Christmas, while Margery was 'knelyng in a chapel of Seynt John wythinne a cherch of Seynt Margrete'. Margery explained that she was weeping in the chapel because of her moral failings, when 'owyr mercyful Lord Cryst Jhesu, blessed mot he be, ravysched hir spyryt and seyd onto hir: "Dowtyr, why wepyst thow so sor?"'.[65] Only here does the text introduce the language of *raptus*, highlighting the profundity of the moment. The stress that Margery places upon the term is heightened by Christ's opening question, which echoed his first words to Mary Magdalene after his Resurrection (John 20.13). Also, this experience is framed by the markings of rapturous contemplation outlined by Hilton. Margery underwent a spiritual purification, which was followed by divine *raptus* in a particularly important place and time. The period from Friday to Sunday became a recurring temporal site for Margery's visions. In one of these, Christ gave particular instructions to Margery, to fast from ordinary food as a preparation for her to 'etyn my flesch and my blod, that is the very body of Crist in the sacrament of the awter'.[66] Among other promises that Christ makes to Margery in this ravishment, he assured her that he will come to her and 'gefe to the hey medytacyon and very contemplacyon'.[67] It is interesting that this experience is one of the only moments in her book that Margery deployed the language of *raptus* to describe what happened to her. Rather than this absence suggesting some lack of significance, the importance of this moment highlights the greater likelihood that the use of *raptus* was intended to set this experience apart from Margery's other divine encounters. For Margery, this was a moment of commissioning, from which followed many more spectacular experiences.

In a final example of this sort, Catherine of Siena, a fourteenth-century Dominican tertiary, was almost as popular in England as she was in Italy.[68] Wynkyn de Worde's English edition of her life was based upon her confessor Raymond of Capua's *Legenda Maior*, and from the very beginning of the book, there is an overt effort to reassure readers of the veracity of Catherine's experiences.[69] De Worde's edition, titled *The Orchard of Syon*, informed readers that Pope Pius II

---

[64] Adams, *Visions in Late Medieval England*, 188.

[65] Kempe, *The Book of Margery Kempe*, I.366–9.

[66] Kempe, *The Book of Margery Kempe*, I.379–81. For more on Margery's description of divine revelation, see Marion Glasscoe, *English Medieval Mystics* (1993), 268–313; Adams, *Visions in Late Medieval England*, 137–9.

[67] Kempe, *The Book of Margery Kempe*, I.392.

[68] She was depicted in several English icons and church: Duffy, *Stripping of the Altars*, 167.

[69] C. Annette Grisé, 'Holy Women in Print' in *Medieval Mystical Tradition in England* (Woodbridge, 2004), 83–96, esp. pp. 84–5.

30 EXPERIENCING GOD IN LATE MEDIEVAL & EARLY MODERN ENGLAND

testified to Catherine's holiness, and a prefatory letter from Capua explained Catherine was 'very often (and in maner whan she wolde)...was rauyshed in spyryte vnto god and so she was acustomed in extasy to haue reuelacyons and dyologes bytwene cryste and her and after to endyte them'.[70] It would seem that Catherine was one of those contemplatives whom the *Cloud* described as 'so sotyl in grace and in spirit, and so homely with God in this grace of contemplacion, that thei mowe have it when thei wolen in the comoun state of mans soule'.[71] Unlike Julian, who weathered a near-mortal illness, or Margery, who battled against her own human frailty before being ravished by God, divine *raptus* seems to have come more naturally to Catherine.

Beginning at the age of 21 (1368), Catherine's divine encounters exemplify the most intense experiences one could have with God. First, she had visions of St. Dominic and the Virgin Mary before being given to Christ in a wedding ceremony (administered by the Virgin).[72] After this heavenly wedding, Catherine experienced regular visions of Christ as well as divine raptures, where she witnessed a variety of things. Almost whenever Catherine went to pray, Capua explained: 'she was so much elevated in the height of her spirite, and so rauished from her bodilie senses'. At times, she struggled to complete a single Pater Noster before she was ravished and apparently was never able to partake in the Eucharist without being overcome by the Holy Spirit. On one Shrove Tuesday, during the Mass, she was incapacitated for three days.[73]

Another of Catherine's more unique experiences happened during her daily prayers, when Christ responded to 'create in me a cleane hart'. Christ 'appeared to her after a verie comfortable maner...and opened her lefte side sensibly with his hand, and tooke out her hart, and so going his waie lefte her in deed without a hart'. The experience became an iconic moment in Catherine's life, serving as one of the more popular depictions of her divine revelations. Giovanni di Paolo's tempera painting of the event became a visual template for many printed images and other visual displays to commemorate this most unusual experience (Figure 1).[74]

Fortunately, several days later while she was praying in a chapel, 'she was rauished in spirite', and once that was 'done', she began walking home when Christ returned to her with his own heart and inserted it into her body.[75] The word 'sensibly' is not insignificant, as Catherine used it on several occasions to distinguish

---

[70] Raymond of Capua, *Here begynneth the orchard of Suon* (1519), sig. iiv.

[71] Anon., *The Cloud*, lines 2389–91.

[72] Interestingly, Catherine may have been inspired by another Catherine (of Alexandria) who was said to have had a similar marriage experience with Christ in the fourth century. In Capua's biography, it seems clear that Catherine is at the very least aware of this earlier saint's life. Moreover, the early Renaissance painter Berna (or Barna) di Siena created a panel representation of this earlier account at least a decade before Catherine of Siena was born (Museum of Fine Arts, Boston access #15.1145).

[73] Raymond of Capua, *The life of the blessed virgin* (Douai, 1610), 103, 185, 205–6.

[74] Wynkyn de Worde's English translation included a woodcut that replicated several aspects of di Paolo's painting: Raymond of Capua, *Here begynneth the orchard of Suon*, title page, sig. a1r.

[75] Raymond of Capua, *The life of the blessed virgin*, 183–4.

Figure 1. Giovanni di Paolo, *Saint Catherine of Siena Exchanging Her Heart with Christ* (1461–1482). The Metropolitan Museum of Art.

between whether she was experiencing something in her body or not. Thus, her claim, that she was left without an actual heart for several days, was met with understandable incredulity, even from Capua who confessed he 'laughed at her'. Equally significant is the fact that Capua carefully delineated the sequence of events, separating the visions of Christ from Catherine being ravished by God. Capua segregated Catherine's ravishment in the chapel from Christ's giving her a new heart, in both time and space.

32 EXPERIENCING GOD IN LATE MEDIEVAL & EARLY MODERN ENGLAND

Catherine's life also raises questions about the role gender played in late medieval devotion, particularly given her heavenly wedding and other intimate experiences with Christ. Much has been made of the fact that so many late medieval contemplative writers were women, and this is certainly an important point. However, Caroline Walker Bynum perhaps overstates the case for the exceptionality of female contemplatives, writing, 'women's mysticism was more historical and incarnational—more fleshly and bodily, if you will—than ordinary Christian piety. The Eucharist as body, flesh, meat, was a central focus of female religiosity.'[76] What Bynum intends by the phrase 'ordinary Christian piety' is not entirely clear. Would that be *masculine* piety? Nor is it clear by what measure the women are 'more fleshly and bodily'. It is certainly true that women, both bodily and morally, were understood to be more receptive to divine rapture, because of their perceived physical frailty and social subordination.[77] Perhaps an argument could be made that women, on the whole, employ more erotic imagery, although male writers like Rolle were comfortable using sexually charged language to describe the contemplative's relationship with Christ. For the contemplative, this relationship was experienced from a feminine point of view.[78] Whether the contemplative was male or female, they found themselves in a submissive, feminine role in their relationship to Christ. This perspective of themselves in relation to Christ was underpinned by biblical references to the Church being the Bride of Christ as well as the sensual language of the Canticles, which was understood to detail the marriage between Christ and the Church.[79] While Catherine's experiences were exceptional, and exceptionally incarnational, it seems to me that contemplative literature (written by male and female authors) drew on the imagery of Christ's body and sexualized language to express their desire to experience God. Certainly, Christ's body was a central object of such devotion, as well as the primary means by which one could experience, and communicate the sensations of, contemplation. Contemplatives kissed and embraced Christ; they expressed physical desire for him; they prepared themselves to be the Bride united to Christ the Bridegroom in a mystical union. Contemplatives meditated upon his sufferings and put themselves into an emotional frame of mutual suffering.[80] For Rolle, participation in the Eucharist and the recitation of the name of Jesus took on special devotional significance, as a means by which:

---

[76] Caroline Walker Bynum, *Fragmentation and Redemption* (New York, 1991), 66.

[77] Elliott, 'The Physiology of Rapture and Female Spirituality', 158–62.

[78] Clare Davidson, 'Erotic Devotion', *Limina*, 20 (2015), 1–13. Interestingly, Alec Ryrie makes the opposite, though equally problematic, move when observing how the language of ravishment was 'specific to men' in Protestant devotionals: Ryrie, *Being Protestant in Reformation Britain* (Oxford, 2013), 472.

[79] Ann W. Astell, *The Song of Songs in the Middle Ages* (Ithaca, NY, 1990), 73–5; Sarah MacNamer, *Affective Meditation and the Invention of Medieval Compassion* (Philadelphia, 2010), 127.

[80] Hilton, *The Scale*, I, 35.

thou shalt be fild ful of grace ni erth, and be Cristes dere mayden and spouse in heuyn. For no thynge so mych payeth God as verray loue of his name Jhesu. If thou loue hit right and lestyngly, and neuer let for no thynge that men say or do, thou shalt be rauyst in to a higher lif than thou can couait.[81]

Likewise, devotional works like Thomas Kempis's *De imitatione Christi* instructed readers who were weak in their meditative efforts to focus primarily upon Christ's humanity, particularly his wounds, and described the 'syght' of the Eucharist as a vision of heavenly glory.[82] Not only was Christ's body the object and means of contemplation, but also the ritual body in the Eucharist served as a focal point of contemplative ascent and *raptus*, as the communicants hoped to be caught up in love when they gazed upon the sacred elements.

Guides to Contemplation

Where contemplative accounts of *raptus* could soar into divine heights, providing readers with tales of heavenly bliss, more practical guides and handbooks on devotion and meditation tended to minimize the possibilities of contemplative ascent. Like the Poor Caitiff text referenced earlier, these guides focused on more realistic expectations and outcomes for the general, late medieval readership.

The anonymous, devotional manual *The chastysing of goddess children* circulated in fifteenth-century manuscripts and was the first book printed by Wynkyn de Worde in 1493. We do not know why de Worde chose *The chastysing* as his initial publication, although strangely he never reprinted it. Perhaps, as Lotte Hellinga states, it was 'circulated mainly in religious houses and among people of rank', both of which tended to prefer manuscript to printed works.[83] Regardless, it survives in fourteen full or partial manuscripts and provides readers a compilation of contemplative writers from Augustine to the fifteenth-century Flemish contemplative Jan von Ruysbroek. Like Hilton's *Scale* and *The Cloud*, *The chastysing* tempered rather than encouraged readers in pursuing *raptus*, focusing upon 'the profit to the human soul of spiritual and physical afflictions' that were expected outcomes of meditative discipline.[84] Openly critical of the more enthusiastic contemplatives, *The chastysing* provides two chapters detailing the pitfalls that even holy men and women can fall into 'by feblenese of brayne... bi dyuerse

---

[81] Richard Rolle, *Prose and Verse* (Oxford, 1998), 29. See also Denis Renevey, 'Name of Names', in *The Medieval Mystical Tradition in England, Ireland, and Wales*, ed. Marion Glasscoe (Woodbridge, 1999), 103–21.

[82] Thomas Kempis, *The folowynge of Cryste* (1504), sig. C4v. See also Ann W. Astell, *Eating Beauty* (Ithaca, NY, 2006).

[83] Lotte Hellinga, *William Caxton and Early Printing in England* (2010), 158; Julia Boffey, 'From Manuscript to Print', in *A Companion to the Early Printed Book in Britain* (Cambridge, 2014), 13–26.

[84] Anon., *The Chastising of God's Children* (Oxford, 1957), 41.

34   EXPERIENCING GOD IN LATE MEDIEVAL & EARLY MODERN ENGLAND

Infyrmytes and some by wykyd spirites'.[85] Challenging Rolle's high view of the contemplative's moral superiority, *The chastysing* dismissed divine revelation as evidence of one's own achievements: 'all thyse and suche other preue not a man ne woman holy ne perfyghte'.[86] In fact, holy men and women can be 'traueyled' with evil spirits as easily as they can be rapt up by the Holy Spirit. Being able to distinguish between evil and holy rapture should be all the more important to a lay reader. The twentieth chapter of *The chastysing* sets out a very high bar of seven tokens by which readers can measure the godliness of claims to divine revelation, including: whether the contemplative was meek and obedient, whether they were ravished in spirit, whether or not they understood the experience, whether the life of the contemplative and what was experienced conforms to 'honest and vertuous liuyng', whether the contemplative met a 'worshypful deth', and whether miracles followed the contemplative after death.[87] Interestingly, there is no hint in *The chastysing* that claims to divine revelation could fulfill only some of these tokens, suggesting the true revelation will be accompanied by all seven.[88]

Also, *The chastysing* reiterated the Augustinian division of three types of human vision: corporeal, spiritual, and intellectual. The visions of Old Testament prophets like Elisha and Elijah were corporeal and their physical eyes served as conduits. However, the visions of the apostles John and Peter, as well as the prophets Ezekiel and Isaiah, were spiritual, because the 'inward will is fulli turned away fro the bodely wyttes'. Their minds' eyes were filled with 'figures and ymages' from God, being 'ravysshed in spyryte'. It was an experience divorced from their physical bodies, even though sensory information (images and figures) from their imaginations was used in the revelation. In the spiritual vision, a translation is required for the person to understand 'what it betokened'. Using Peter's vision (Acts 10) again as an example, the author explains that 'he was holpen bi ye grace of God…afterward he vnderstoode bi ghostli feling & knoweng what it sholde betoken'.[89] Not only is the vision given by God but also God supplied the interpretative lens without which a person could not properly understand. Finally, the third kind of vision, the intellectual vision, was exemplified by the apostle Paul who had 'an inwarde and a clere vnderstondynge and knowyng…withoute ony ymage of fygure by the wonderfull myghte of god'.[90] Like the spiritual vision, the intellectual vision is accompanied by ravishment, without the need for

---

[85] Anon., *The chastysing of goddes chyldern* (1493), sig. D2v. See Steven Rozenski, 'The Chastising of God's Children from manuscript to print', *Études Anglaises* 66 (2013), 369–78.

[86] Anon., *The chastysing*, sig. E2r.   [87] Anon., *The chastysing*, sigs. E1r–v.

[88] It is not at all unusual for contemplative guidebooks to insist upon several criteria. One of the benchmarks of determining the veracity of revelation became Jean Gerson's *De distinctione verarum visionum a falsis*, wherein Gerson insisted upon five broad criteria: humility, discretion, patience, truth, and charity: Gerson, *Early Works*, 338.

[89] Anon., *The chastysing*, sig. D4v.   [90] Anon., *The chastysing*, sigs. D4v–5r.

interpretation. What is being communicated is unmediated truth: 'a sheweng of ye preuy being of god wythout ony fygure', which was immediately accompanied by 'a soden light of knowyng'.[91] These descriptions do not accompany any encouraging language to the reader that she or he should pursue such encounters with God. Rather, the author seems intent on explaining how divine revelation was able to overcome a 'feblenese of brayne', which even the biblical prophets suffered from.

The popular devotional writings of Richard Whitford offer another important example of how *raptus* became part of the larger religious culture in early sixteenth-century England. After an Oxford education, Whitford joined the Bridgettine monastery at Syon House. His books like *The pomander of prayer*, the *Jesus Psalter*, and his translation of Thomas Kempis titled *The folowynge of Cryste* went through multiple printings and provided a spiritual storehouse of prayer and devotion for several generations of Catholics and Protestants.[92] In *The pomander of prayer*, Whitford sketched out a guidebook for contemplation, where he described prayer as 'nothynge ells but an ascencyon of the soule from erthly thynges to heuenly thynges'. Later on, he reiterated this point, 'Prayer is an ascension of the mynde to god'.[93] Whitford did not elaborate any further, but instead he turned his attention to more pragmatic instructions on prayer, like whether to kneel or raise one's hands, to pray silently or out loud, and how to eliminate distractions to prayer. Elsewhere, in his translation of Thomas Kempis's *Imitatione Christi*, Whitford deployed divine *raptus* in his advice for readers. He exhorted people that a free mind is one that is kept as much as possible 'from the busyness and cares of the worlde', although Kempis did not hold such a rigid divide between the active and the contemplative as Rolle. Readers who may struggle because of 'frayltye of thy selfe' to achieve contemplation were advised to think on the Passion and Christ's 'blessyd woundes'. The wounds were thought to be spiritual havens, a 'dwellynge place' for the soul. On the following page, the text reiterates this advice, 'yf thou haddest ones entred in to the blody woundes of Jhesu and haddest there tastyd of his loue'.[94] Only when the reader prepared themselves mentally and spiritually could they enter into contemplation, for 'he that can inwardlye lyft his mynde upwarde to god and can lytel regarde outward thynges nedyth not to seke for tyme or place to go to prayers'.[95] Finally, the devout reader must remember that they cannot force contemplative ascent to happen. Ultimately, they must rest in their preparations, 'Keepe thyn intent and thy purpose alwaye hole and stronge to me and thynke not that it is an illusion', until God acts upon one's soul, when 'thou art sodenlye rauysshed in to excesse of mynde and that thou art sone after tournyd agayne to thy fyrste lyghtnesse of herte'.[96] In

[91] Anon., *The chastysing*, sigs. D4v–5r.
[92] Ian Green, *Print and Protestantism in Early Modern England* (Oxford, 2000), 346.
[93] *The pomander of prayer* (1528), sigs. A2v, D2r.
[94] Kempis, *The folowynge of Cryste*, sigs. f7v–8r.   [95] Kempis, *The folowynge of Cryste*, sig. f8v.
[96] Kempis, *The folowynge of Cryste*, sig. k5v.

other words, one must hold the line and wait. Ultimately, the contemplative pursuit according to Whitford and other such guides was one of patient resilience, pursuing something that could not be attained but by God's grace.

The differences between texts like *The chastysing* and the accounts of Catherine of Siena in the *Legenda* are not insignificant. Considering the discourse of *raptus* in late medieval England, it is important to see both ends of this spectrum to capture fully the variety of contemplative experiences that was on offer. Thus, the overwhelming flames of divine love that scorched Rolle contrast with the intellectual enlightenment of Hilton or Julian of Norwich, and all of these seem far removed from what was likely the experience of quite a few mundane readers who never moved beyond Kempis's advice to meditate upon the wounds of Christ. Nevertheless, the similarity in how the discourse of *raptus* was deployed holds these different texts together as part of a single way of thinking about divine revelation in late medieval England. Both ends of this spectrum described a powerful association between divine revelation and human understanding, that human reason was necessary but not sufficient to experience *raptus*, and that experiences of ravishment in this life were also intended as foreshadowing moments of the beatific vision after death. Not everyone would experience the former, but all Christians could rest in the hope of the latter.

The author of the Poor Caitiff perhaps set the expectation for the average lay reader quite low by concluding, with self-effacing recognition, that 'for I my silf, caitiff & wretche unworthi thoru dyvers synne before doon, beinge bynethe alle these perfect pointis, seemynge to me as fer as hens to heven'.[97] The message was clear enough: most of us will not enjoy the kinds of divine experiences of contemplative ascent. This tension between what divine *raptus* offered and the reality of most people's ordinary spiritual lives continued to impact the place of divine revelation within the religious culture, even after the Reformation began to take shape. While the Protestant reforms stripped away aspects of traditional religion, both Catholic and Protestant literature continued to emphasize many of the basic markers of contemplative devotion, as well as encouraging their readers to desire divine rapture.[98] Certainly, as we will see, Protestants generally were discouraged from seeking after visions and prophecies. Nevertheless, they were encouraged to desire an experience with the Holy Spirit within the context of *raptus*.

---

[97] MS Eng. 701, fols. 115v–116r.
[98] Liam Peter Temple, *Mysticism in Early Modern England* (Woodbridge, 2019, chs. 1–2).

2

'Wee should bee rapt vp into the third heauen'

The Reformation of Revelation

When God exhibited himself to the view of the Fathers, he never appeared such as he actually is, but such as the capacity of men could receive...whenever God grants any token of his presence, he is undoubtedly present with us, for he does not amuse us by unmeaning shapes.

John Calvin, *Commentary on Isaiah*

There shall be a glorious light, by which the soul shall not only be enlightened...but it shall be elevated and enabled to see that which else it could never see.

William Strong, *Discourse of the Two Covenants*

On Maundy Thursday 1669, in an otherwise ordinary, reformed sermon, the Scottish-episcopal priest William Annand made an important distinction between the manner in which one could ascend into heaven and Christ's Ascension (Acts 1.9). Similar to the *Cloud*-author (see Chapter 1), Annand explained that Christ 'neither was...rapt as *Paul*,...nor ravished in the Spirit as *Iohn the Divine*'. Instead, 'of His own power...[he] did Ascend, climbing up the scale of the clouds, untill He got above all Heavens'.[1] Setting aside the image of Christ bounding up into the sky with the clouds as his staircase, it is interesting that Annand felt the need to distinguish the two kinds of events in order that people listening understood that these experiences were not of a kind. Where Christ propelled himself into heaven ('under his own power'), the experience of the prophets was one of being pulled up by the power of God. Certainly, Annand would have been repelled by the suggestion that he and medieval contemplatives had much theology in common. Yet, the similarity in the way he discusses divine *raptus* and the medieval tradition is not insignificant, particularly as this similarity extends throughout much of the English Protestant theology surrounding divine revelation.

While this chapter focuses primarily upon Protestant commentaries of Revelation as a key genre representing the discourse of divine revelation, Annand's comments,

[1] William Annand, *Mysterium pietatis* (1671), 249–50.

Experiencing God in Late Medieval and Early Modern England. David J. Davis, Oxford University Press.
© David J. Davis 2022. DOI: 10.1093/oso/9780198834137.003.0003

38   EXPERIENCING GOD IN LATE MEDIEVAL & EARLY MODERN ENGLAND

despite never having written such a commentary, are relevant for a few reasons. First, as Alexandra Walsham has explained, while early modern Protestants 'did more to inhibit than encourage the appearance of popular prophets', they simultaneously 'created a climate in which the idea that rational people might communicate with God…could not be dismissed *a priori* as ridiculous'.[2] As Annand's sermon illustrates, Protestants preserved the traditional understanding of divine revelation that included a process of ravishment, in which God moved upon the human soul. Moreover, the discourse of divine revelation was interwoven into more practical concerns about Protestant belief and practice, expanding the application of the discourse from that of the medieval tradition. This chapter examines the various ways that Protestant commentators on the book of Revelation explained the process of divine revelation and how their understanding of this process impacted the ways that Protestants conceived of their own experiences with God.[3] In examining these commentaries, I want to take Walsham's point one step further, asserting that experiences of divine *raptus* generally were seen as spiritually healthy in the life of a Christian and were to be desired. In fact, one thing that sets the Protestant literature apart is just how much it emphasized the experience of *raptus* in people's regular, spiritual lives. Far from the mountaintop enjoyed by only a few medieval contemplatives, divine *raptus*, according to many Protestants, was something to be anticipated by every believer.

Before we continue, it is important to recognize the popularity of the book of Revelation in early modern England. It was by far the most illustrated and commentated biblical book, with dozens of commentaries appearing between 1547 and 1700.[4] The scholarship on this fascination with Revelation has tended to focus upon the trove of apocalyptic images in the book and the different uses that people found for these images.[5] At least one seventeenth-century commentator noted how often Revelation was abused by people attempting to unlock the book's enigmatic codes for their own ideological ends.[6] However, the much more

---

[2] Alexandra Walsham, '"Frantic Hackett"', *The Historical Journal*, 41 (1998), 49. See also Matthew Milner, *The Senses and the English Reformation* (Aldershot, 2011), 187; Walsham, *Providence in Early Modern England*, 206.

[3] Biblical commentaries were authoritative vehicles of theological interpretation, through which pastors and ministers were educated, and from which they crafted sermons, teachings, and writings. Although most commentaries, even on a popular book like Revelation, were only printed a few times, their influence extended much further than the number of editions in circulation. See e.g., Richard Bauckham, *Tudor Apocalypse* (Ann Arbor, MI, 1979); Patrick O'Banion, 'The Pastoral Use of the Book of Revelation in Late Tudor England', *Journal of Ecclesiastical History*, 57 (2006), 711–37.

[4] Bauckham, *Tudor Apocalypse*, 41; R. N. Swanson, *Religion and Devotion in Europe* (Cambridge, 1995), 177–81.

[5] See e.g., Robert Scribner, *For the Sake of the Simple Folk* (Cambridge, 1981); Helen Parish, *Monks, Miracles, and Magic* (Abingdon, 2005), Ch. 6.

[6] Richard Hayter, *The Apocalyps unveyl'd* (1676), n.p.; Warren Johnston, *Revelation Restored* (Woodbridge, 2011), 147. See e.g., Bryan Ball, *A Great Expectation* (Leiden, 1975); Paul Christianson, *Reformers and Babylon* (1978); Keith Firth, *The Apocalyptic Tradition in Reformation Britain, 1530–1645* (Oxford, 1979); Walsham, *Providence in Early Modern England*.

fundamental, and culturally central, notion of the experience of divine revelation often goes underappreciated. The basic terminology of *raptus*, often drawn from Revelation, was so popular that a Protestant minister like Annand could use it in a sermon without any need to clarify what he meant. While Annand owned at least three commentaries on Revelation, it is unlikely that all of his audience was so fortunate, and yet, Annand did not feel the need to explain these terms.[7] Although John Calvin and Martin Luther struggled to know what to do with biblical visions of heaven, many other Protestants made the most of these examples of divine revelation to encourage, exhort, and teach, often drawing connections between the biblical prophets and some of the most essential aspects and practices of early modern religious life.[8]

John Bale and Revelation

Although neither Luther nor Calvin wrote a substantive commentary on Revelation, other early reformers took up the challenge. The first of these was written by the French Lutheran François Lambert, in 1528, with even more robust commentaries coming later from Heinrich Bullinger, Theodore Beza, Augustine Marlorat, and David Pareus.[9] In England, the first Protestant commentary on Revelation was written by one of the most virulent anti-Catholic polemicists of his day. A former Carmelite friar named John Bale filled his commentary *The image of both Churches* (1545) with a barrage of attacks on the church of Rome, capitalizing upon the already established trope of a link between the papacy and the Antichrist. Despite this polemical bent, Bale's language in *The image* echoed the discourse of *raptus* found in medieval contemplative devotion, particularly when Bale described how the apostle John received the visions. Thus, when Bale considered the description of the apostle's experience in Revelation 1.10 ('I was ravished in spirit on the Lord's day'), Bale wrote, '[John was] carefully afflicted and driuen from all solase and bodily comfort, on a certayne Sunday or day of dedicate to the Lordes remembraunce, [and] was in the spirit rapte, and clearly taken vp from all worldly affects (so sweetly did the Lord releue his poore persecuted seruant)'.[10]

---

[7] More than 750 of Annand's books were sold off at auction after his death, which provides us with a reliable record of at least some of his library: *A catalogue of excellent and rare books... 25th Day of February* (Edinburgh, 1690).

[8] David J. Davis, 'Rapt in the Spirit', *Journal of Medieval and Early Modern Studies* 48 (2018), 341–64.

[9] Irena Backus, *Reformation Readings of the Apocalypse* (Oxford, 2000), 3–7. Calvin's description of divine revelation in scripture are exemplified in his comments on the visions of Isaiah and Ezekiel: John Calvin, *Commentaries on the Prophet Ezekiel* (Edinburgh, 1849), 62; John Calvin, *Calvin's Commentary of Isaiah* (Grand Rapids, MI, 1948), 198.

[10] John Bale, *The image of both Churches* (1545?), sig. C4v. Exactly how influential contemplative writings were upon Bale's thought is unclear. He was aware of the writings of Richard Rolle, and certainly would have known Kempis and likely Hilton: Allen, *Writings Ascribed to Richard Rolle*, 422–3.

40   EXPERIENCING GOD IN LATE MEDIEVAL & EARLY MODERN ENGLAND

Even in this brief comment, we can note that for Bale the vision was marked not only by temporal significance (the Sabbath) and by a separation of his body and soul initiated by divine *raptus*, but also this separation was done so that John could understand more clearly, without the 'worldly affects' of his body.

Perhaps the strong similarity that Bale demonstrates with the earlier contemplative literature should not be so surprising. The relationship between medieval contemplative literature and the early reformers continues to attract scholarly attention. On the one hand, it is easy to find Protestant condemnations of what they saw as superstition or, worse, demonic ravings in medieval writers.[11] On the other hand, strong cases have been made for intentional and unintentional use of the medieval, contemplative tradition. In Germany, Kaspar Schwenkfeld, Thomas Muntzer, and Sebastian Franck drew from this tradition.[12] Other reformers were more reserved in their acknowledgment. Luther's debt to contemplative writers is evident from studies done by Steven Ozment and Heiko Oberman.[13] Likewise, despite Calvin's disdain for the monasteries, his description of the *unio mystica* aligns quite neatly with divine *raptus* as described by Bernard of Clairvaux and Walter Hilton.[14]

In this context, it is important to keep in mind that for most reformers, experiences with God, even divine revelation of a sort, were not limited strictly to the pages of the Bible. Richard Muller explains that while reformers certainly considered the text of scripture to be the Word of God, it was 'not exclusively so'. The Word of God included the eternal self-knowledge of God, the work of God in creation (what Calvin called the *opera Dei*), the unwritten revelations 'given to the prophets', and the 'inward Word of the Spirit which testifies to the heart of the truth of Scripture'.[15] Although this broader understanding of the Word of God slowly contracted for many English Protestants during the seventeenth century (as we will see in Chapter 6), there continued to be a space, even a necessary space, for divine *raptus* in the lives of the devout.

Returning to the first English Protestant commentary on Revelation, it is interesting that while Bale's *The image* 'set the pattern' for English Protestant apocalyptic thought, it remains relatively understudied.[16] Written during Bale's exile after the fall of Thomas Cromwell in 1540, Bale created a treasure chest of scholarship

---

[11] See e.g., the seventeenth-century polemicist John Gee who mocked Catherine of Siena and other such accounts as popish inventions: *The Foote out of the Snare* (1624), 33, 40, 54–5.

[12] Steven Ozment, *Mysticism and Dissent* (New Haven, CT, 1973); Gordon Rupp, 'Word and Spirit in the First Years of the Reformation', *Archiv für Reformationsgeschichte* 49 (1958), 13–26.

[13] Steven Ozment, *Homo Spiritualis* (Leiden, 1969); Heiko Oberman, '*Simul gemitus et raptus*', in *The Dawn of the Reformation* (Edinburgh, 1986), 126–54. See also Volker Leppin, 'Luther and John Tauler', *Theology and Life*, 36 (2013), 339–45.

[14] Dennis Tamburello, *Union with Christ* (Louisville, KY, 1994).

[15] Richard Muller, *Post-Reformation Reformed Dogmatics, Vol. 2* (Grand Rapids, MI, 2003), 155. For an example, see Baxter, *The saints*, 207.

[16] Bauckham, *Tudor Apocalypse*, 22.

on the Apocalypse, citing authorities from Augustine, Jerome, and Bede to Joachim de Fiore and John Wycliffe. In addition, he drew extensively from the early Protestant commentaries by François Lambert and Sebastian Meyer. *The image*, however, was not altogether derivative. *The image* was historicist in its interpretative bent, and it was paraphrastic in its approach, restating and expanding upon the original verses rather than offering a straightforward exegesis. Also, *The image* stands out among biblical commentaries containing nineteen woodcuts alongside the text, copied from Hans Sebald Beham's popular series on the Apocalypse. While illustrations were not unheard of in some Lutheran commentaries (e.g. Lambert's *Exegeseos* had a handful), the number of illustrations in Bale's work is still striking. Although few illustrated commentaries in English were to follow, the impulse to visualize this most peculiar biblical book continued well into the next century in editions of the Bible. Popular printed images copied from the likes of Albrecht Dürer (Figure 2), Hans Holbein, and Lucas Cranach were included in English Bibles throughout the sixteenth century, making Revelation the most illustrated biblical book in early modern England.[17]

One of *The image*'s more substantive innovations was how much space Bale devoted to paraphrasing the prophet's experience of divine revelation and what it meant for contemporary faith and practice. Concerning John's experience in Revelation 1.10, Lambert commented, '*qui ante hanc visionem supra se elevatus sit*' [who before this vision was elevated above himself] and during the vision '*in spiritu ergo ad haec non usus est corporeis sensibus*' [(being) in the spirit, therefore, he did not use his bodily senses for these things].[18] Bale went further, developing a detailed description of the phenomenological aspects of divine revelation: '[John was] driuen from... bodily comfort', and he heard Christ's voice 'with mine eares'. Then, in Revelation 4, Bale expanded this description by paraphrasing Christ's instruction to John:

> Suspend thine own will, wit, study, practice, and judgment. Condemn that thou hast of nature. Lift up thyself above thyself, ascend in soul by the Spirit and power of God; and I will shew unto thee things wonderful, and such as must without fail be fulfilled... And as it had been in a thought, I was sodenly by the Lord's power taken up. I was in the spirit indeed, secluded from all carnal imaginations.[19]

Later, in Revelation 11, Bale wrote of the two witnesses, who help usher in the Apocalypse: 'they ascended vp... From worldly affects are they changed to the

---

[17] Ruth Luborsky and Elizabeth Ingram, *A Guide to English Illustrated Books*, vol. I (Tempe, AZ, 1998), 84–5; Margaret Aston, 'The Bishops' Bible Illustrations', in *The Church and the Arts* (Oxford, 1992), 280; David J. Davis, *Seeing Faith, Printing Pictures* (Leiden, 2013), 160–8.

[18] François Lambert, *Exegeseos Franciscus Lamberti* (Marburg, 1528), sig. 24v. Leslie P. Fairfield, *John Bale* (West Lafayette, IN, 1976), 197.

[19] Bale, *The image of both Churches*, sig. G4r.

Figure 2. Albrecht Dürer, *Revelation of St. John: The Adoration of the Lamb* (1511). Gift of the Print Club of Cleveland, The Cleveland Museum of Art.

'WEE SHOULD BEE RAPT VP INTO THE THIRD HEAUEN' 43

pure loue of God, and from all carnall prudence to the wisdom of the spirite. In a cloude are they rapt'.[20] Bale's comments deploy both the language of *raptus* and the stress on the intimate relationship between the knowledge and love of God that was so vital for many contemplatives.

It is difficult to know the source from which Bale derived his reading of these passages. The only citation Bale provided was to the Apostle Paul's vision of the third heaven (2 Corinthians 12), suggesting it as a kind of template for biblical experiences of divine revelation.[21] However, there are some important differences between Paul's vision and John's experiences in Revelation that Bale seems to gloss over. Paul 'was taken up' into heaven and heard things that he could not repeat, but John was instructed to write down what he saw. Also problematic is the Greek verb used in 2 Corinthians, *harpazó* [to seize, pluck, pull away by force], which was not commonly used to describe prophetic visions in the Bible but does correspond to the way that Thomas Aquinas defined *raptus*. The Greek phrase that John used in Revelation, *egenomhn en pheumati* [I was in the spirit], was more common to the biblical prophets' encounters with God. Even most English Bibles avoided the wording of rapture to describe John's revelation, translating the Greek phrase literally, which suggests an awareness that at least a linguistic difference between what Paul and John experienced was not insignificant.[22]

While the conflation of Paul's experience with all prophetic and divine revelations may seem interpretatively confusing, many Protestants offer it as a model for divine experiences in general.[23] Following Bale's commentary, according to Richard Bauckham, a 'wealth' of commentary literature on Revelation poured from the English printing presses, and with this abundance came 'increasing diversifications of approach'. There were expository commentaries, often in English, which integrated pastoral messages as well as historico-analytical commentaries, mostly in Latin, which provided limited or no pastoral application.[24] Moreover, the interest in biblical revelation cut across many Protestant dividing lines. Puritans and Anglicans, conformists and non-conformists, Royalists and parliamentarians, Arminians and Calvinists—each group had no qualms about putting Revelation to work for their own particular cause. They continued to work within, and to develop in different directions, the discourse of divine

---

[20] Bale, *The image of both Churches*, sig. C7v.

[21] Bale, *The image of both Churches*, sig. 3M2r.

[22] There are two important exceptions to this: the *Wycliffe New Testament* and the 1560 *Geneva Bible. New Testament in English*, trans. John Wycliffe (Portland, 1986), sig. 157v, 119r; *Geneva Bible* (Madison, WI, 1969), sigs. 2P3v, 2Y2v. The seventeenth century commentator William Hicks pointed this out in his explanation of Theodore Beza's Latin translation: William Hicks, *Apokalypsis apokalypseos* (1659), 32.

[23] See e.g., Henry Bullinger, *A hundred sermons vpon the Apocalipse* (1573), 139; Augustin Marlorat, *A catholike exposition vpon the Reuelation* (1574), sig. C2v; Richard Rogers, *A commentary vpon...Iudges* (1615), 297; David Pareus, *A commentary upon the divine Revelation* (1644), 19.

[24] Bauckham, *Tudor Apocalypse*, 137–9.

44   EXPERIENCING GOD IN LATE MEDIEVAL & EARLY MODERN ENGLAND

revelation. The rest of this chapter focuses upon what Protestant commentators and preachers emphasized about the experience of revelation, specifically how the discourse intersected with particular doctrinal issues relevant to the broader early modern religious culture. Evident here is not only that Protestant writers developed a way of describing divine revelation, which was based in part on late medieval paradigms, but also that the commentaries put the discourse of divine revelation to work in questions of practical theology and devotion.

Raptus in Protestant Commentaries

Perhaps the most influential work on Revelation in sixteenth-century England, following Bale's work, was Heinrich Bullinger's *A hundred sermons upon the Apocalypse*. Originally published in Latin by Jean Crespin (Geneva, 1554), the commentary provided a historicist interpretation of apocalyptic symbols, connecting them with events in church history. Bullinger also included a sermon on the persecution of the true church unfolding in the present, such as the heightened measures enacted against Huguenots in the Edict of Châteaubriant (1551) and England's return to Roman Catholicism under Mary I. Bullinger, in fact, dedicated the commentary to 'you banished men, as many of you as coming or driuen out of Fraunce, England, Italy, & other realmes and nations for Iesus Christ and the gospels sake, dwel in Germany, Swisserland, & other places', hoping that his work would bring them some level of solace and comfort.[25] Published by John Day a few years after Elizabeth I took the throne, the English translation of Bullinger's commentary proved popular for clergy and laymen who sought an accessible guide to the cryptic text of Revelation.[26]

Turning to Revelation 1.10, Bullinger, like Bale, stressed the significance of the place (the Isle of Patmos) and the time/day of John's visions (Sunday or the Sabbath). Then in Revelation 4.2, Bullinger wrote:

> Christ biddeth Iohn ascende into supercelestial places, not in body, but in minde. Therefore must our minde be lifted vp into the contemplation of Heauenlye thinges,...and the example of Iohn followeth immediatly. And incontinently I was in the spirite: that is, in a spirituall contemplation, or rauished with the spirite into the faithful consideration of those thinges whiche were shewed me.[27]

A few decades later, the Oxford divine William Fulke followed Bullinger quite closely in his *Praelections* (1573), which appeared in Latin and English simultaneously.

---

[25] Bullinger, *A hundred sermons*, sig. B6r.   [26] Backus, *Reformation Readings*, 102.
[27] Bullinger, *A hundred sermons*, 139–40. Unlike some early reformers, Bullinger insisted upon the canonicity of Revelation, providing assurances of John's authorship.

'WEE SHOULD BEE RAPT VP INTO THE THIRD HEAUEN'   45

Fulke wrote that John 'was rauished from himselfe, and that his bodely senses in the meane time rested, that his minde might be more free in beholding those thinges which the Lorde shewed vnto him'.[28] Importantly, as Randall Zachman points out, there was a reciprocal relationship between the means and the content of the biblical vision, which reinforced the individual's trustworthiness.[29] The fact that God was in control of the prophet's cognitive faculties ensured that the revelation was clearly understood, insofar as the human mind could grasp divine things. This is evident in one of the most influential Calvinist commentaries in late Tudor and early Stuart England. In *The Apocalyps*, Francois du Jon (Junius) explained, 'the rauishment in the spirit was a diuine thing and properly belonging to the seruants of God in ushc great and high reuelations as this is'. Also, this was 'a singular vocation' that was only available through 'a special grace and assistance of God, without which no man is able to behold or conceiue with profit the spirituall thinges'.[30] After 1599, Junius's commentary was printed in the Geneva Bible, as the margin notes for the text of Revelation, not only moving Junius's words from the theologian's bookshelf to the parish pew and prayer closet but also placing the discourse of divine revelation alongside the authoritative Word of God.

We can see similar language across a variety of commentaries into the seventeenth century, from the puritan Thomas Cartwright's *A plaine explanation of the vvhole Revelation* and the Bedfordshire minister Thomas Brightman's *A revelation of the Apocalyps* to the mathematician John Napier's *A plaine discouery of the whole Reuelation* and Arthur Dent's *The ruine of Rome*.[31] Likewise, the German reformed theologian David Pareus, who was popular in England, explained that John 'saw this revelation, viz. not with mortall eyes, but being ravished in spirit, his mind was carried beyond it self'. Further on, he pointed out that other commentators had followed a standard line in expounding the phrase 'in the spirit' to mean that the prophets 'did not still retain their real bodies; but being ravished, they seemed for the present to themselves, as out of the body', making one of the most definitive statements about the dissociation of soul and body.[32] What set divine ravishment apart, according to Pareus, was divine agency: 'We may hence truely conclude that neither the perspicuity of the mind, not bodelie eyes of man, can reach to heavenlie things, except the Lord doe open heaven unto him'. He went on to dissuade anyone from convincing themselves that the prophets

---

[28] William Fulke, *Praelections* (1573), sig. 4v. See also the translator of the *Praelections*, the puritan minister George Gifford, who issued his own commentary: George Gifford, *Sermons vpon the whole booke of the Reuelation* (1598), 22, 24.

[29] Randall Zachman, *Image and Word in the Theology of John Calvin* (South Bend, IN, 2007), 149.

[30] Franciscus Junius, *The Apocalyps* (Cambridge, 1596), 14, 54. For Junius's further use of ravishment, see also Franciscus Junius, *Apocalypsis* (1592), 3, 14.

[31] Thomas Cartwright, *A plaine explanation of the vvhole Revelation of Saint John* (1622); Thomas Brightman, *A revelation of the Apocalyps* (Amsterdam, 1611); John Napier, *A plaine discouery of the whole Reuelation* (1593); Arthur Dent, *The ruine of Rome* (1603).

[32] Pareus, *A commentary*, 19.

46 EXPERIENCING GOD IN LATE MEDIEVAL & EARLY MODERN ENGLAND

received revelations through dreams, 'not indeed by any locall motion', of the mind or body 'but inward illumination, the holy Ghost representing these things unto his understanding, and revealing the mysteries thereof unto him'.[33] The rector of Little Wratting (Suffolk), John Mayer, drew directly from Pareus's commentary, also employing the phrase 'local motion' to describe the movement of the soul. Mayer spent perhaps more time digesting biblical commentaries than he did pastoring his congregation, since his *Ecclesiastica interpretatio* (1627) is an encyclopaedia of authorities, with citations ranging from early church fathers like Tyconius and Ambrose to contemporaries like Brightman and Pareus. For Mayer, the Holy Spirit revealed things to John while he was 'in a transe…his soule being for the time taken out of his bodie', in order that he may clearly apprehend what God revealed.[34]

One of the most formative voices in early Stuart England was the Calvinist theologian and Cambridge fellow William Perkins. Concerning Revelation 1.10, Perkins wrote:

> This extraordinarie worke of the spirit consisteth in two actions;…First, in procuring a traunce…whereby all the sences, both inward and outward, are benumbed:…The action of the holy ghost on the mind is, to draw it from fellowship with the bodie, and al the sences, to have a neere fellowship with God that so the spirit of God may enlighten it with diuine light, that it may vnderstand the things which are reuealed to it.[35]

Perkins attended even more carefully than others to the epistemological issues latent within the discourse of divine revelation.[36] Earlier commentators mentioned that the revelations were intended to enlighten people to what Bullinger referred to as 'the contemplation of heavenly thinges'. Perkins developed what this meant. For him, the dissociation of body and soul included a loss of physical sense perception, so much so that the soul is no longer in communication with the body. Here, Perkins, more than some commentators, echoed contemplative writers like Hilton and Gerson, who described divine *raptus* as pure understanding and revelation. Furthermore, Perkins teased out the implications of this experience, anticipating the seventeenth-century debates about the reliability of such knowledge (see chapters 6 and 7). Perkins stated that John was ravished from his body for epistemological reasons, first that he might 'know that the

---

[33] Pareus, *A commentary*, 86. The insistence that divine ravishment was something akin to, but undoubtedly different from, a dream remained an important distinction throughout the period, particularly among reformed ministers and theologians.

[34] John Mayer, *Ecclesiastica interpretatio* (1627), 256. See also John Trapp, *A Commentary…the Revelation of John* (1647), 508.

[35] William Perkins, *A godly and learned exposition…of the Reuelation* (1606), 41.

[36] Perkins was not the only one to describe John's experience as a 'traunce'. See e.g., William Cowper, *The workes* (1626), 834; Trapp, *A Commentary*, 508.

things reuealed were not inuented of themselves, but giuen of God'.[37] Second, John was ravished so that:

> the things reuealed might take the deeper impression in the vnderstanding: for the mind being freed from fellowship with the bodie, and not hindered by any phantasies of the sences (they being all asleepe, and quiet) doth then most liuely and sensibly apprehend and retain the impression of things reuealed.[38]

As the connection between soul and body was loosened, the soul was able to understand more clearly and permanently. Similarly, the early Stuart minister Thomas Adams explained to his congregation that divine revelation was a kind of 'schoole... [and] Vniversitie... and God his Tutor'. The method of teaching being 'rapt vp into heauen', where the prophet can most clearly acquire 'knowledge'.[39] Only through the ravishment of the soul could a person receive such instruction.

Nor was this understanding isolated to a Calvinist theology of divine revelation. The Bishop of Galloway William Cowper's (or Couper's) commentary relied upon the Augustinian triad of *visio* to describe biblical revelation, though he used the terms 'Naturall, Prophetical, and Spiritual'. For Cowper, the prophetical and spiritual vision was experienced, '*Interna, Imaginaria, Intellectualis*', and the prophet was entirely in 'his spirit... hauing after a sort, derelinquished his body'.[40] The difference between *raptus* and relinquish is perhaps not insignificant here as Cowper may be suggesting a more participatory role for the human will (giving up rather than being ravished away). Perhaps this is not unexpected since Cowper directed his commentary against more puritan interpretations like Brightman's that tended to diminish human agency.

The language of *raptus*, so characteristic of medieval contemplative literature, was largely adopted by English Protestants; however, this adoption was not entirely straightforward. The effort that commentators expended in establishing that what the biblical prophets experienced was a kind of *visio intellectualis* seems to have been particularly Protestant. They felt a need, more acutely than most Catholics, to demonstrate that, in Perkins's words, the prophets 'apprehend and retain the impression of things reuealed'. Where medieval contemplatives deployed the discourse of *raptus* because it was understood to be the manner in which biblical prophets experienced revelation, Protestant commentators recontextualized this discourse to, at least in part, underline the superiority of those biblical models. The accounts of biblical revelation and prophecy were

[37] Perkins, *A godly and learned exposition*, 42.
[38] Perkins, *A godly and learned exposition*, 42. See also Hicks, *Apokalypsis apokalypseos*, 33.
[39] Thomas Adams, *Fiue sermons preached vpon sundry especiall occasions* (1626), 31.
[40] Cowper, *The workes*, 834.

48   EXPERIENCING GOD IN LATE MEDIEVAL & EARLY MODERN ENGLAND

trustworthy partially because the individuals experiencing them did so in a way that made the experience more epistemically secure, because they were not 'hindered by any phantasies of the sences'.

Ravishing the Sabbath

The final two sections of this chapter examine how the language in biblical commentaries was reflected in the larger early modern religious culture. In what ways did the discourse of divine revelation, which framed the Protestant understanding of biblical prophecy, correspond to and inform religious belief and practice in the period? Here, we will examine two key areas where the two intersected: the emphasis upon the Sabbath as a significant period of divine-human interaction and the role of the affections in religious devotion and divine ravishment. What will be evident in both of these areas is that Protestants were much less guarded about encouraging people toward rapturous experiences, when compared to medieval texts like the *Cloud of Unknowing* or *The chastysing of goddess children*. Although Protestants generally denounced the contemplative life, which Catholics believed was the surest path to spiritual ascent, they were much more ready to encourage the average believer to pursue an experience that was commensurate with what the contemplatives sought.

One key difference between the medieval contemplative writers, who associated divine revelation with various (and specific) holy days, and their Protestant counterparts, is that the latter tended to emphasize the weekly Sabbath. Not only did the Sabbath institute a certain amount of sacrality around divine ravishment, but it also provided a pre-packaged temporal site for godly living. Bale wrote that John received his revelations 'on a certayne Sunday or day dedicate to the Lordes remembraunce', while the prophet was at prayer.[41] Bale's qualification ('day dedicate to the Lordes remembraunce') was a reference to the difference between the Christian and Jewish Sabbath. Many commentaries following Bale stressed that the change from Saturday to Sunday had been made by the apostles, and that the specific Sabbath day was ultimately a thing indifferent, particularly when compared to the practice of setting aside one day of every week to worship God. Doing the Sabbath was more important than doing it on the correct day.

That being said, the commentators were usually quick to point out that Sunday is the best of seven indifferent options, because that is the day that Christ rose from the dead, as well as being the historical day of Christian worship. Thus, Bullinger writes:

---

[41] Bale, *The image of both Churches*, sig. C4v.

this Apostle knewe, that the faithfull on the sonday serued God in all assemblees...here we are presently taught what is the religion of the sonday, and how it is mete to obserue it. Finally worldly men are reproued, which pollute and breake it with prophane works and affaires.[42]

The popularity of Bullinger's commentary in the 1560s was part of a larger movement in Protestant practical theology, which included the publication of the Geneva Bible (1560), John Foxe's *Actes and monuments* (1562), and a standard book of homilies for preachers (1562). Bullinger's commentary fitted well into this larger effort to provide instruction and guidance for the newly established Elizabethan church. The emphasis upon 'religion on the Sonday' and Bullinger's direction for spiritual discipline served the ecclesiastical authorities striving to establish a uniformity in the larger religious culture. George Gifford and other commentators aligned readers with the 'blessed Apostles and Martyrs', who in their moments of deepest devotion were made to be 'full of glory'. Likewise, Perkins identified a 'want of priuat sanctification of this day', as the cause of some individuals' inability to benefit from public worship and religious assembly.[43] If people wanted the spiritual benefits from Sabbath worship, they must prepare themselves for it. Whatever day of the week was the Sabbath, the memorializing of it as a day dedicated to God provided an appropriate context for such extraordinary encounters.

Of course, ensuring people kept the Sabbath holy was an ongoing struggle for the clergy. The second half of the Elizabethan period witnessed an increased attentiveness to lay behavior on the Sabbath. The puritan Philip Stubbes's *The anatomie of* abuses, which is well known for its moralizing rants, stated:

> The Sabboth day, of some is well obserued, as namely, in hearing the blessed worde of GOD read, preached, and interpreted, in priuate and publique Prayers, in singing of godlie Psalmes, in celebrating the sacraments, and in collecting for ye poore and indigent...But other some spend the Sabaoth day (for the most part) in frequenting of baudie Stage-plays and enterludes...Maie games, Church Ales, Feasts, and Wakesses: in Pyping, Dauncing, Dycing, Carding, Bowling, Tennisse playing: in Beare-bayting, Cock-fighting, Hawking, hunting, and such like. In keeping of Faires, and Markets...In keeping Courts and Leets: In football playing, and such other deuilish pastimes.[44]

---

[42] Bullinger, *A hundred sermons*, 30.

[43] Bullinger, *A hundred sermons*, 140; Gifford, *Sermons*, 23; Junius, *Apocalypsis*, 3; Marlorat, *A catholike exposition*, sig. C2v; Perkins, *A godly and learned exposition*, 45. While certain scholars have treated Sabbatarianism as a 'litmus test' in determining whether someone was Anglican or puritan, Kenneth Parker rightly explains that there is a long tradition of emphasising the sacrality or, at the very least, the distinctiveness of the Sabbath across the various Protestant groups: *The English Sabbath* (Cambridge, 2002), 2.

[44] Philip Stubbes, *The anatomie of abuses* (1595), 98–9.

50   EXPERIENCING GOD IN LATE MEDIEVAL & EARLY MODERN ENGLAND

The importance of the Sabbath, for Stubbes, turned less upon any particular Sabbatarian dogma and more upon the association of the day of rest with pious living, setting the body (and the works of the body) aside in order to allow the soul to thrive. This was not simply a moralising rant about 'deuilish pastimes', which apparently included 'football'. Stubbes and his ilk lumped together honest labor and entertainment, as works unworthy of the Sabbath, for even God 'rested from all his workes'.[45] Bodily activities, virtuous or otherwise, should be renounced as much as possible, so that the life of the soul, and the things of God, may flourish.

Keeping the Sabbath was one of the most obvious applications of the book of Revelation. Protestant divines, in writing their commentaries, regularly turned the moments of the apostle's visions into opportunities to exhort readers toward Sabbatarian observance. Cartwright urged those that would model themselves after the apostle John, to 'be occupied in the study of the word of God, and in delivering the will of God unto the people'. After his comments on John's visions in Rev. 4, he wrote:

> when wee goe about holy and heauenly matters, we must be as it were in a new world, and we must separate ourselues from all worldly things, and worldly cogitations, though otherwise at other times lawfull; and addict and addresse our selues wholly to those things of our God.[46]

Likewise, Napier insisted that 'Before any accesse to heauenlie knowledge', readers must 'firste', like the apostle, 'leaue off all worldlie affections' on the Sabbath.[47] For Bishop Cowper, a requirement of every good Christian is, 'hee must bee a separate man, and after a sort, goe out of himselfe, and goe vp vnto God, to bee familiar with him, who would see the things of God'.[48] Later in the seventeenth century, the presbyterian minister Charles Phelpes used the language of 'token' in his commentary to describe the Sabbath, saying that the believer should dedicate themselves 'to the Consideration and Remembrance of what Christ hath suffered and done for us'. This, he wrote, was best accomplished when 'we do no servile work...for works of Piety, Mercy, and Necessity, they are Sabbath-day works'.[49] Likewise, University of Glasgow professor James Durham explained:

> The frame of a Sabbath should be a kind of ravishment, wherein...we do go about Prayer and other Spiritual duties in a more heavenly way, than on other

---

[45]   Davis, 'Rapt in the Spirit', 347–8.

[46]   Cartwright, *A plaine explanation*, 5, 25. See also Dent, *The ruine of Rome*, 5.

[47]   Napier, *A plaine discouery*, 102. See also Mayer, *Ecclesiastica interpretatio*, 256.

[48]   Cowper, *The workes*, 836–7.

[49]   Charles Phelpes, *A Commentary...of the Revelation of Jesus Christ* (1678), 77–8. For more on the theology of tokens, see Paul Helm, *John Calvin's Ideas* (Oxford, 2004), 167–8.

dayes, and that with a difference in our frame, being more elevated and Spiritual, we should be other men, in more divine contemplation.[50]

Durham was not satisfied with a basic exhortation to Sabbath keeping, precisely because this was a day defined in scripture by divine ravishment. In his opinion, the Sabbath should be experienced differently than other days. To assist people, Durham outlined four steps, which included abstaining from 'civil and ordinary affairs', spending the 'whole day in duties of Worship…celebrating the Communion', devoting oneself to 'duties of charity', and 'to have…a heavenly conservation, more than ordinarily taken up with God and Christ, and the things of another Life that day'.[51] Far from a day of relaxation, Durham dreamed of a Sabbath completely absorbed in spiritual pursuits. While these steps did not ensure a divine rapture into the third heaven, they (like the contemplative acts of purgation) served as important preliminary exercises.

One point that is clear is that the contemplative tradition of purgation and the Protestant stress on the Sabbath rest are not entirely of a kind. Encouragement to prayer and meditation are common among both Protestants and Catholics. In this context, however the medieval emphasis upon a purely contemplative life was roundly denounced by Protestants. Instead, Protestant writers and preachers tended to connect the biblical accounts of divine revelation to the everyday practice of piety and devotion, rather than a life of isolation and contemplation. The incorporation of *raptus* discourse into the reformed exhortations to keep the Sabbath holy indicates a significant corollary within Protestant thought between the weekly day of worship and the experiences of the biblical prophets. The discourse of divine revelation, which had been confined in contemplative literature to certain experiences (and often extraordinary circumstances), was increasingly appropriated by Protestants to exhort the everyday believer in her and his weekly devotions. The prophetic knowledge and incredible visions that John and Paul received were not the goal of this recontextualising. Rather the experience of a rapturous union with God, corresponding to that of the prophets, was believed to be a possibility for the godly life, and it was a possibility that every good Christian should be preparing themselves for with weekly regularity.

Ravishing the Affections

In an Easter service at Whitehall in 1608, one of England's most renowned preachers, Bishop Lancelot Andrewes, described the women who went to Jesus' tomb as being 'so rapt with *love*, in a kind of extasie, they never thought of the

---

[50] James Durham, *A commentarie upon the book of the Revelation* (Edinburgh, 1658), 31.
[51] Durham, *A commentarie*, 31.

52   EXPERIENCING GOD IN LATE MEDIEVAL & EARLY MODERN ENGLAND

stone'. This is not the sort of rapture that removes one's soul from the body, but Andrewes was nevertheless creating an important parallel with divine revelation, in which his listeners (and later readers) could see themselves and their love for God. The love the women had for Christ was 'a kind' of *raptus*, because 'herein is love; the very fervor of it, zeale: that word hath fire in it. Not onely diligence (as lightnesse) to carrie it upward; but zeale (as fire) to burne a hole and eate it self a way, through whatsoever shall oppose it'.[52]

The affections of zeal, joy, love, etc. were affections of the soul, and they were the natural effects of ravishment, divine or otherwise. While the women in Andrewes's sermon were not ravished by God, the interaction between divine *raptus* and the affections was an important one, since the affections were also essential in devotional practice.[53] Although most Protestant authorities discouraged people from claiming they had received divine visions, the same authorities often held up the prophets as pinnacles of godly living and affection, whose lives should be modelled and whose experiences of God should serve as sources of inspiration. Thus, Cartwright's commentary seems largely built around this approach to the lives of the prophets. He explains that Christ promises all those who follow the apostle's spiritual discipline 'he will come vnto them and Sup with them; signifying, what exceeding ioy and comfort they should receiue…yea, they should be made partakers of the ioyes of heauen'. A few pages later, Cartwright comments that the apostle's vision in Revelation 4.1, 'teacheth vs…wee must be as it were in a new world, and we must separate our selues from all worldly things, and worldly cogitations…and addict and addresse our selues wholly to those holy things of our God'.[54]

The seventeenth-century minister of St. Mary's Church (Dover), John Reading described the experience of the contemporary devotee as one that was commensurate with that of the biblical prophets. Reading's *David's soliloquie* (1627) described the power of divine ravishment upon the religious affections:

Sweet and excellent is the contemplation of things diuine and heauenly, wherby the minde is carried vp on high, a man is rauished in Spirit, illuminated with knowledge, enflamed with desire of goodnesse: all inordinate affections, wandring thoughts, and fluctuation of the minde…and distractions of the soule, are recollected into one, and the whole desire fastened in that fountaine of blessednesse, when the soule commeth to a neerer view of GOD.[55]

A Calvinist in his theology and a Royalist in his politics, Reading offers us an important example of a moderate sort of English Protestant. For Reading, this kind of immersive and overwhelming experience was accessible to all godly

---

[52] Lancelot Andrewes, *XCVI. Sermons* (1629), 407.   [53] Ryrie, *Being Protestant*, 63–95.
[54] Cartwright, *A plaine*, 23, 25.   [55] John Reading, *Dauids soliloquie* (1627), 186–7.

readers and it involved a parsing of 'inordinate affections' from a person's intellectual 'desire'. After this parsing, this intellectual desire could be filled by the 'fountaine of blessednesse' from God. In practical terms, *raptus* seems to have quieted the mind, by taking control of the soul, allowing a person to focus entirely upon divine illumination. Reading's description does not fit with what we would describe simply as a feeling, or a rush of emotional sentiment. Rather, in this experience an individual's distractions and mental wanderings fade away, their understanding and desire are united, and they develop an intense mental focus. This experience he compared to what Paul experienced, as though 'wee could see the heauens open, and Iesus standing at the right hand of GOD, though the soule, and all it affections and faculties were filled, with a sweet vision of caelestiall things, though wee should bee rapt vp into the third heauen'.[56] The ravishment of the soul, for Reading, organized the affections and the understanding, in such a way that they were capable of experiencing the beatific vision. Devotional practices of 'contemplation', 'meditation...[and] prayer' were the avenues by which 'wee are let into' this heavenly revelation by divine grace, which happens only when we are 'rauished in Spirit', to separate us from all 'wandring thoughts, and fluctuation of the minde'.[57]

Interestingly, the relationship between the affections and ravishment that Reading describes in which the experience seems to complete the process of ordering the affections correctly is not entirely commensurate with certain Catholic teachings. In his very popular *A treatise of the loue of God*, Francis de Sales warned against putting too much confidence in those 'Raptures in Praier' in which the soul 'goes out of her selfe and mounts vnto God'. If these experiences are not followed by a change in a person's affections ('calmenesse, simplicitie, humilitie'), the 'Raptures are exceedingly doubtfull, and dangerous' because these experiences tend to 'stirre vp men...but not to sanctifie them'.[58] At least for most Protestant writers, it seems that if a person were experiencing a true, divine ravishment then it was inherently a sanctifying experience, even if their sanctification was not completed during the ravishment. Although the possibility (and concern) that the memory and long-term significance of an individual's experiences with God might be corrupted by pride was certainly present in reformed devotion, it was rarely warned about in such terms as de Sales lays out.

Given this contrast between Reading and de Sales, at least on this point, it is interesting that despite the reformed emphasis upon human depravity and the human will's inability to do good, Protestant preachers and ministers continuously exhorted their audiences to act in particular ways that they might better prepare themselves for divine ravishment. For many Protestants, preparatory

---

[56] Reading, *Dauids soliloquie*, 188.

[57] The presbyterian William Bates offered similar advice: *The four last things* (1691), 382, 385.

[58] Francis de Sales, *A treatise of the loue of God* (Douai, 1630), 418.

activity often included a purgative process. Bullinger explained, 'John is prepared to receiue this vision, yea and we also are prepared in him...pourged as much as may be from earthly affections, that we may behold heauenly thynges with an heauenly contemplation'.[59] To rightly order the affections, one must discipline the soul, and Protestant ministers were ever-ready with helpful instructions. Thus, where many preachers and priests encouraged some prayerful preparation, the presbyterian Anthony Burgess insisted that preparation began with reading scripture. He asked his parishioners at Sutton Codfield, 'How can a vessel with a narrow mouth, receive all the water of the Sea into it?' Burgess instructed the people to 'suck...out' the 'divine Truth' found in the Gospel, in preparation for God's Spirit to move upon them. Reaching almost a fevered pitch at the end of his sermon, he bellowed, 'know, if Christ and holy things do not ravish thy soul, it's because thy heart is narrow!'[60]

As Alec Ryrie and others have demonstrated, there was a very active engagement with such exhortations by godly women and men.[61] Diaries, letters, and commonplace books evidence a lay culture of devotion that believed this kind of soul ravishment would provide the believer not only a glimpse of the beatific vision but also assurance of their own salvation. In one example, a late-seventeenth century Londoner, Alathea Bethell, writes that she had committed herself to 'taking my Affections from the Love of this World.' In an extended meditation on the fear of and preparation for death, Bethell comments that only through 'true Repentance...[and] Harty Submission', could she hope to 'Raise my Affections...[and] fix them on God and my Blessed Saviour'. Nevertheless, despite her best efforts, she believed that it was only through a moment of divine revelation when ('Enlighten oh Lord my / Darck Passage') that she truly could 'Glimpse...thy Glory'.[62] Indeed, John Dolben, Dean of Westminster, would have praised Bethell for her devotion. In a sermon before King Charles II, Dolben explained to his listeners that such requests and desires were the 'Scale and Standard of our Duty' to God, because only he can 'stir it up, to invite, and court, and even ravish our affections with the abundance of his favours'.[63] King Charles I's chaplain, Henry Hammond, ended one of his sermons with the moving prayer:

> O Lord...by the violence of thy Spirit, force and ravish us in our lives, as well as belief, to a sincere acknowledgment and expression of every minute part of that

---

[59] Bullinger, *A hundred sermons*, 139–40. Similarly, the late-Elizabethan Brownist preacher Henoch Clapham encouraged his English congregation in Antwerp to pursue rapture like the apostle John: *Theologicall axioms* (Amsterdam, 1597), sig. D1v.

[60] Anthony Burgess, *CXLV expository sermons* (1656), 462. See also William Foster, *The meanes to keep sinne from reigning* (1629), 27.

[61] Ryrie, *Being Protestant.*   [62] Lambeth MS 2240, fols. 18r, 19r.

[63] John Dolben, *A sermon preached before the king* (1666), 16.

Religion which is purely Christian, that we may adore thee in our hearts as well as our brains.[64]

Protestant exhortations to reform the affections were partly motivated by the pastoral concern for the people's spiritual lives and a desire to spur them on to increasingly more godly behavior. However, this does not seem to be a sufficient explanation for the direct and sustained correlation that Protestants made between the individual's life and the experiences of biblical prophets in divine *raptus*. As I have already suggested, there is very little within the commentaries, sermons, or devotional literature to dissuade someone from thinking that the kind of experience that Paul or John had had, in which their soul was ravished from their body, could be experienced by any devout Christian. Ravishment was not simply a necessity for the theology of divine revelation, it also provided a model for devout living, because it had the power to fill the soul with affection from, and for, God.

Far from discouraging any devotional modeling of the biblical prophets, Protestant commentators reframed the conversation in such a manner that their audiences were given particular ways of reading the biblical experiences. Regardless of other major differences between Protestant reformers and the Roman Catholic tradition, divine ravishment leading to revelation remained an essential form of religious understanding throughout most of the early modern period. The discourse of divine revelation that Protestant commentaries incorporated from the medieval contemplative tradition was both expanded and redirected away from the monastic, contemplative context of a life devoted entirely to prayer and toward a more secular context of the everyday Christian. The discourse maintained many of its essential elements, but it was also redeployed into contexts that further advanced the notion that divine ravishment was not the same as a divine vision, and that a soul's encounter with the divine did not necessarily entail the prophetic content evidenced in scripture.

---

[64] Henry Hammond, *Sermons preached* (1664), 257.

3

'Pictures are…not for Worship'

Images of God in Early Modern England

the holiest and highest of the things perceived with the eye of the body or the mind are but the rationale

…all that lies below the Transcendent One. Through them, however, his unimaginable presence is shown

Pseudo-Dionysus, *The Mystical Theology*

In the 1660s, a new edition of the Book of Common Prayer accompanied the Restoration of Charles II. The prayer book had been banned by Parliament in 1645, coinciding with the abolition of Anglican episcopacy, only to be revived after the ecclesiastical conference at Savoy Palace in 1661. Although the text of the Restoration Book of Common Prayer closely followed the Elizabethan 1559 edition, one innovation that followed the prayer book's revival was the inclusion of dozens of engravings that illustrated different New Testament events. To my knowledge, there is no significant scholarship dedicated to these images, even though they marked an innovation in the prayer book that extended into the eighteenth century.[1] The king's printers Christopher Barker and John Bill included a variety of representations of God in these pictures: God as an old man, as the incarnate Christ, as a ray of light, and as a symbol in the clouds. From 1664 until the end of the century, dozens of octavo and duodecimo editions were illustrated with pictures by different artists like William Faithorne, Frederick Hendrick van Hove, and Peter Paul Bouché. The small size of the books and the fact that the illustrations were unpaginated inserts made them portable and accessible. Even though different printers issued illustrated prayer books in this period, there is a startling degree of continuity in terms of the format and the design of the different pictures. Equally significant, the engravings appeared in several different Bibles in the 1670s and 1680s, setting them apart as perhaps the most widespread visual aids in Anglican devotion.[2]

[1] Even David N. Griffiths's otherwise excellent *The Bibliography of Book of Common Prayer, 1549–1999* (2002) does not make note of the illustrations. My own research has identified seventeen editions before 1701, containing ten or more engravings. The short-title catalogue numbers for these editions are: Wing B3628, B3633B, B3639, B3640B, B3647, B3649, B3650A, B3659B, B3660, B3661, B3666, B3672C, B3675, B3678variant, B3691, B3694, and B3703.

[2] *The history of ye Old & new Testament in cuts* (1671); *The Holy Bible* (1678); *The Holy Bible in Sculpture* (1683).

Experiencing God in Late Medieval and Early Modern England. David J. Davis, Oxford University Press.
© David J. Davis 2022. DOI: 10.1093/oso/9780198834137.003.0004

Images of God in early modern England are significant for our thinking about experiences of God, because the different visualizations of God offer an alternative discursive mode than the literary one found in contemplative accounts, biblical commentaries, sermons, etc. The depictions of these divine manifestations, particularly in printed works, provide some of the most widely recognized, non-literary examples of the culture of revelation in early modern England. Most importantly for us to recognize is the fact that the visual mode of divine revelation never disappeared from the English public sphere, as images of God appearing to people were never erased entirely. Certainly, the reformed distaste for what Protestants saw as Catholic idolatry curtailed image production in certain respects and reshaped it in others, but it never eliminated the visual presence of divine revelation from what people were seeing in print (and elsewhere). Instead, what we will see in this chapter is an impulse, even a cultural need, to create and disseminate images of God, specifically for the purposes of *memory* and *reflection*, even within some of the most puritan contexts. Like revelation itself, where an unknowable being becomes known, images of God exemplified the tension between the notion of a God who is beyond imagining and the signs, symbols, and representations God provided to signify himself.

The history of religious images in early modern England is hardly straightforward. Protestants both destroyed and created religious images, and while Reformation scholarship has moved away from a narrative of iconophobia, we continue to describe an incremental diminishing of religious images, charting a slow, seemingly inevitable, march toward the 'extinction' of religious images.[3] The mounting evidence over the past two decades, however, makes this narrative of incremental abolition impossible to sustain.[4] While visual representations of God were divisive, they remained one of the most commonplace religious images in early modern England and, as such, a valuable gauge for considering how people thought about and imagined the divine. This chapter examines the ways that images of God were deployed, whether the image depicted the Tetragrammaton or an anthropomorphic representation of God the Father. The chapter assesses how the visual discursive mode compares to its literary counterpart and in what ways the images of God structured and delimited people's understanding of divine revelation. Although the emphasis here is on those images that were most

---

[3] Margaret Aston, *Broken Idols* (Cambridge, 2015), 547.

[4] The narrative that the English Reformation was defined largely by iconoclasm, even iconophobia, was originally challenged in Tessa Watt's *Cheap Print, Popular Piety* (Cambridge, 1991) . Other studies followed, demonstrating that religious images survived in specific contexts: Margaret Aston, *The King's Bedpost* (Cambridge, 1993); Margaret Aston, 'Bibles to Ballads', in *Christianity and Community* (Aldershot, 2001), 106–30; Tara Hamling and Richard Williams, eds, *Art Re-formed* (Newcastle upon Tyne, 2007). More recently, scholars have presented an even more robust visual culture: Tara Hamling, *Decorating the 'Godly' Household* (2010); Michael Hunter, ed., *Printed Images in Early Modern England* (2010); Davis, *Seeing Faith, Printing Pictures*; Michael Gaudio, *The Bible and the Printed Image in Early Modern England* (2017).

widely distributed in print, I have connected, whenever possible, these popular examples with more permanent and luxurious images (e.g. paintings, household décor, etc.) in order to demonstrate just how prolific these representations of God were.

Two broad points about the religious visual culture in England will become apparent in this chapter. First, the notion that images like the anthropomorphic Trinity or the Tetragrammaton served as confessional markers is plagued by contradictions. Certainly, different groups had their favourites (e.g. the Jesuits adopted the image of the Holy Name of Jesus), and some people despised particular representations, but I have yet to identify any hard-and-fast demarcating lines in this regard. There are too many examples of Protestants and Protestant texts, of various confessional sympathies, depicting God the Father as a man (or of Catholics deploying images like the Tetragrammaton, which has often been associated with Protestantism) to fix confessional or doctrinal affiliation to a particular kind of depiction.[5] Rather than mapping confession on to iconography, I want to focus, here, upon the more evident fact that both Protestants and Catholics followed traditional visual tropes and biblical narratives in their depictions of God. A second broad point is that the line we tend to draw between the symbolic and the real, as a difference between the abstract and the substantive, was only just emerging in the seventeenth century. From what I can tell, it seems to have played little part in the image debate as a whole. That is to say, the fact that an image like the Tetragrammaton is more abstract than a picture of an old man with a beard did not offer as clear a demarcation between what was permissible and what was not. Owen Barfield reminds us that in the medieval and the early modern periods, 'hierarchical participation *per similitudinem* was the foundation of the whole structure of the universe; for all creatures were in a greater or lesser degree images or representations'. Ultimately, all things in creation, the material and immaterial, were understood to be representations of the creator. This understanding was held by church fathers like Augustine and medieval contemplatives like Richard Rolle as well as reformers like John Calvin and Richard Baxter. All things reflected aspects of God's nature, and at the same time, nothing in creation sufficiently represented him.[6]

As models and cues in devotion, visual images helped to shape (in the mind's eye) different ways of seeing divine revelation, and these ways of seeing ran a wide gamut, from the didactic and satirical to the meditative and devotional. Where the visual differs from the literary is in the ways that images engaged with the physical senses and the memory, providing what Bob Scribner described as the

---

[5] While this chapter deals largely with Protestant imagery, one example of a Catholic text deploying the Tetragrammaton is Puget de la Serre, *The sweete thoughts of death, and eternity* (Paris, 1632).

[6] Barfield, *Saving the Appearances*, 90. See also, Zwollo, *Augustine and Plotinus*, 144–55; Zachman, *Image and Word*, 25–36.

'visual vernacular which became the cultural heritage of later generations'.[7] Images drew upon the imagination in a way that mirrored the process of *visio spiritualis*, providing mental fodder for the devout soul to contemplate, allowing people to remember not only the biblical narratives but also the devotional significance attached to these accounts of divine revelation.[8] Images also provided visual platforms from which people might begin to associate their own spiritual devotion with the figures being depicted, inviting people to reflect upon their own lives and daily practice while gazing upon the picture of a prophet as the prophet sees into heaven.

Memorials and Mirrors

It is impossible to attend sufficiently to the English Reformation without acknowledging the sustained anxiety surrounding religious images for different groups. Statues and iconic images in churches were destroyed by zealous Lollards, and waves of iconoclasm, led by puritans and Anglicans alike, marked several decades of the sixteenth and seventeenth centuries. Nor were printed images immune from suspicions of idolatry, as Protestants removed images from the traditional Books of Hours and several, sixteenth-century injunctions condemned 'images in...book(s)...of the Blessed Trinity or of the Father'.[9] Printed images were ephemeral, but they were nevertheless capable of communicating the sacred as well as inspiring devotion. They certainly lacked the awe-inspiring, visual impact of a lavish altar or a ceiling painting; however, engravings and woodcuts served the more mundane devotional life of people as objects that could be manipulated, relocated, hidden, or otherwise repurposed with relative ease.[10]

Even after a century of reform, the tension between the fear of idolatry and the impulse to represent biblical events had not disappeared, and the Restoration prayer books were no exception to this tension. Thus, beneath the engraving of the Crucifixion, the printers included the line 'Pictures are made for Ornament &

---

[7] Scribner, *For the Sake of the Simple Folk*, 248. See also David Morgan, *Visual Piety* (1998), 183–4. Equally significant is Tara Hamling's analysis, demonstrating the continued devotional nature of domestic art and pictures within Protestant homes: *Decorating the 'Godly' Household*, esp. 256–86.

[8] Although there was no single, dominant theory of vision in England at the time, the culture not only recognized the differences between seeing and reading, but also people refused to reduce their religion to the purely literary and aural: Robert Scribner, 'Popular Piety and Modes of Visual Perception in Late-Medieval and Reformation Germany', in *Religion and Culture in Germany*, ed. Robert Scribner (Leiden, 2001), 120–1. See also Clark, *Vanities*, 19; Milner, *The Senses*, 177.

[9] Eamon Duffy, *Marking the Hours* (New Haven, CT, 2006), 151; Davis, *Seeing Faith, Printing Pictures*, 47–8.

[10] An important, recent study of how early modern Protestants employed domestic objects in their piety is Alexandra Walsham, 'Domesticating the Reformation', *Renaissance Quarterly*, 69 (2016), 566–616.

60 EXPERIENCING GOD IN LATE MEDIEVAL & EARLY MODERN ENGLAND

History not for Worship', to clarify the image's purpose (Figure 3).[11] Such an exhortation could have been included beneath a variety of the prayer book's images of God from the Tetragrammaton and the Holy Spirit as a dove to the Scutum Fidei, the IHS, and God the Father as a man. While the exhortation against idolatry is attached only to Crucifixion engraving, and it seems to have been removed from subsequent editions, many reformers happily would have included it on all images of God, if only to avoid offending more puritanical sentiments.

Similarly, this tension is evident in Anglican works on idolatry. In 1678, the future archbishop Thomas Tenison published *Of idolatry, a discourse*. In much of the text, Tenison followed the standard party line, condemning any image of God that served as a 'representation of the true God, and the worshipping of it as his Image', because, as Tenison explained, 'Gods infinite essence cannot be represented'.[12] A few years earlier the Cambridge philosopher Henry More made a similar remark, 'the Image being visible, & God invisible, there is manifest danger of joyning ones devotion, which is all that God can have of us, to the garish Image'. More believed that 'the true Notion' of God existed only 'in our minds', and it could not be visually represented.[13] However, such definitive condemnations were qualified by many authorities. Thus, Tenison considered 'Images of Memory', even images of God, to be acceptable, because they contained 'in them no analogy to the Divine Perfections, nor any pretended representation of them'. He explained that such memorials could be helpful in study and devotion, because they 'are apt to put us in mind of God', referring his readers to biblical accounts in which God appeared in fire, cloud, smoke, etc. Images of memory served as mental cues, allowing someone to recall what God revealed in scripture, without confusing the picture with the reality of an invisible and transcendent deity.[14]

Such efforts to draw lines between permissible and dangerous images had a long history. Elizabethan and early Stuart divines, even stalwart Calvinists like William Perkins, made exceptions for some biblical images as educational aids.[15] During the civil war, Henry Hammond, the future King Charles II's chaplain, outlined the rationale for depicting God, even in devotional contexts. In the same years that puritan iconoclasts like William Dowsing were scouring the country

---

[11] *The book of common-prayer* (1664), sigs. F6–7. Images of the Passion carried with them strong associations with Catholic devotion: Anon., *The perpetual crosse* (Antwerp, 1649). However, images of the Crucifixion were not entirely absent from Protestant contexts: Hamling, *Decorating the 'Godly' Household*, 235–7.

[12] Thomas Tenison, *Of idolatry* (1678), 268.

[13] Henry More, *An appendix to the late antidote against idolatry* (1673), 15.

[14] Tenison, *Of idolatry*, 272. This line of reasoning was a long-standing defense for the use of religious images, with roots in the apologies of the eighth-century monk John of Damascus: John of Damascus, *Three Treatises on the Divine Images* (New York, 2003), 40.

[15] William Perkins, *A golden chaine* (1600), 962.

'PICTURES ARE...NOT FOR WORSHIP' 61

Figure 3. 'The Crucifixion' in *The book of common prayer* (London: John Bill and Christopher Barker, 1664). By permission of the Rare Book and Manuscript Library, University of Illinois at Urbana-Champaign.

62 EXPERIENCING GOD IN LATE MEDIEVAL & EARLY MODERN ENGLAND

for idols, Hammond wrote that while images of God were 'prohibited', there was a space within the 'representation of a sacred story' for 'an eye, a ray, a glory &c. not to expresse the person of God the Father, but to stand for him, not to signifie any supposed likenesse of him (which is impossible)…to present him to the mind of the beholder'. These visual presentations of divine revelation did not 'expresse' the true representation of God, instead they merely 'stand for' the divine, as memorial. Rather than claiming to illustrate his essence, these memorials of God's presence were no more idolatrous, at least for Hammond, than seeing or writing the 'name of God'.[16]

In practice, many Protestants enjoyed the benefit of such distinctions. Early English Bibles contained numerous visual memorials of God's revelations to the patriarchs, prophets, and apostles, which were modelled on pre-Reformation prints by artists like Dürer and Hans Holbein. Woodcuts of divine visions experienced by Isaiah, Ezekiel, and the apostle John were standard in many editions of the Bible well into the Elizabethan period. The woodcut of Ezekiel's vision of heaven in the Geneva Bible, popular with puritan readers, depicted God as a man sitting upon a throne, and this image was reprinted in editions as late as 1616. In the New Testament, images of God (as the Tetragrammaton) and the Holy Spirit (as a dove) inspiring the gospel writers continued to appear in Geneva Bibles into the 1630s.[17] We can see similar evidence outside the pages of Protestant printing. As Tara Hamling has demonstrated, puritan domestic décor exemplifies an intentional effort to develop safe ways to represent Christ, deploying Old Testament scenes as allusions to events of the New Testament.[18] Such pictures provided people an important body of sensory data for their memories, particularly if they were going to consider biblical events in a manner other than a propositional statement or a theological axiom. This visual discourse supplemented the text, and it also provided a framework for the collective representations of divine revelation.

Of course, determining how best to portray these events, what sensory data to provide people, was never agreed upon. The need for images of God was felt across the confessional spectrum. Puritans like Thomas Cartwright condemned the Bishops Bible (1568) for its images of God as an old man but celebrated the Geneva Bible, even with its image of Ezekiel's vision. For some Protestants even small symbols, like the visual reference to the Holy Name of Jesus, was

---

[16] Henry Hammond, *Of Idolatry* (1646), 30.

[17] *The Bible* (1616); *The Holy Bible* (1631); *The Holy Bible* (1630).

[18] Thus, images like the sacrifice of Isaac served as 'types' for the Crucifixion: Hamling, *Decorating the 'Godly' Household*, 233–53. All of this visual culture was continually buttressed by the acquisition of prints and printed books from abroad, particularly from the Netherlands. See for e.g. see the illustrations by Sir Robert Peake, copied from the Catholic artist Boetius à Bolswert in *New Testament* (1638); *The vvhole book of Psalmes* (1638).

unacceptable, where others displayed it upon the walls of their homes and churches.[19] Part of the anxiety of what should and should not be portrayed had to do with the importance of human memory in religious meditation and devotion. Thinking about events a person had not experienced as well as beings that could not be perceived physically was less than straightforward. According to Augustine, it required mental access to sensations and images through which people could conjure up 'the heauen, the earth, the sea, and what-euer I can thinke vpon in them'.[20] Likewise, for Bonaventure, the memory was itself 'an image of eternity', which not only demonstrates that the soul 'is an image of God' but also helps the soul to grasp the eternal.[21] Richard of St. Victor emphasized the memory's creative potential in conjuring things 'in a blink of an eye', and the memory can 'create...a new heaven and a new earth' which is filled with 'creatures of that sort as large as you like'. Furthermore, memory was an essential faculty of the second stage of contemplative ascent, because it provided the soul a 'chamber of such immense breadth' filled with 'treasures of knowledge and jewels of wisdom', from which the understanding and the will can draw upon.[22] The memory's power extended beyond simply reminding or recording what was experienced. Memory provided a mirror, a way of seeing one's self. For Augustine, in this mirror, 'There also meete I with my selfe, I recall my selfe what, where, or when I haue done a thing; and how I was affected'. The memory allows us to replay events as well as to stand back and observe ourselves, our thoughts and actions. This reflective aspect of memory could reinforce closely held beliefs or exhort a person to change their behavior. For Augustine, the memory's function as a mirror of the self was an opportunity to 'compare' ourselves as well as 'meditate' upon our own selves, in a way that is only possible through our ability to look into past events 'as if they were now present'.[23]

In early modern England, memory's reflective power through pictures was widely recognized. Emblem book writers regularly encouraged their readers to 'behold' the pictures, by which readers could learn something not otherwise accessible in the text. Some people even believed that images were 'more powerful' than the written word, because a picture could excite the imagination and memory in a way that the written word could not.[24] The English poet John Dryden wrote that a picture 'imprints...more deeply into our Imagination and our Memory' than words can, which can inspire the soul with 'Love and

---

[19] W. H. Frere and C. E. Douglas, eds, *Puritan Manifestoes* (1972), 118; David J. Davis, 'Reforming the Holy Name: The Afterlife of the IHS in Early Modern England', *Journal of Early Modern Christianity* 8 (2021), 275–98.

[20] Augustine, *Saint Augustines confessions*, 595.   [21] Bonaventure, *The Journey*, III.2, p.19.

[22] St. Victor, *The Mystical Ark*, 252.

[23] Augustine, *Saint Augustines confessions*, 496. See also Els Stronks, *Negotiating Differences* (Leiden, 2011), 33–41; Joseph Koerner, *The Moment of Self-Portraiture* (Chicago, 1993), 136.

[24] See e.g., George Wither, *A collection of emblemes* (1635), 8, 66; R. B., *Delights for the ingenious* (1684), 55. The quotation is from Stronks, *Negotiating Differences*, 29.

64 EXPERIENCING GOD IN LATE MEDIEVAL & EARLY MODERN ENGLAND

Admiration'.[25] Nor was this reflexive capacity entirely a conscious effort; the picture gazed back into the viewer whether or not they actively reflected upon its virtues. This is why devotional literature exhorted readers to look upon, or think about, godly pictures in their prayers and meditations, so that their minds would be filled with holy thoughts. Thus, Thomas Bentley's book of private devotions, *The monument of matrones*, which contained several illustrations of Christ, formed this notion into a prayer: 'Let thine holie memorie…possesse my whole soule, and rauish me…Let my soule, I beseech thee, passe from visible vnto inuisible, from terrestriall vnto heauenlie'.[26]

Francis Quarles's popular book *Emblemes* (1635) offers many good examples of devotional reflection using visual representations. The work was a Protestant revision of the popular Catholic emblem book *Pia Desideria* by Herman Hugo and contained eighty-one engravings that were intended to show to 'sense what faith alone could see'. Further on, Quarles elaborated on this sentiment, explaining that *Emblemes* provided the reader an experience of what in reality only 'our ravish't eye shall see / Great ELOHIM, that glorious One in Three'.[27]

In one example from Quarles's book, a picture of the human soul (as a female figure) sits at the base of a tree, which serves as a cross for the Crucifixion (Figure 4). Illustrating the verse from Canticles 2.3 ('under his shadow had I delight, and sat down'), Quarles's text describes the Crucifixion as a shade-tree for the 'sweltring Soule':

> Looke up, my soule; advance thy lowly stature
> Of thy sad Thoughts; advance thy humble eye:
> See, here's a Shadow found; The human nature
> Is made th'Vmbrella to the Deity,
> To catch the Sun-beames of thy just Creator;
> …
> A Cloud of dying flesh betwixt those Beames and thee.

Quarles was not satisfied simply with a visual and literary reminder of Christ's death and sacrifice. The reader should reflect ('Looke') upon Christ, examining herself or himself in this reflection. Gazing upon the image should be, in one sense, like gazing at a mirror, in which one looked at the state of their own soul. Both text and image encouraged a memorial reflection upon the soul's need and

---

[25] John Dryden, 'To the Reader', in Charles Alphonse Du Fresnoy, *De arte graphica* (1695), 102.

[26] Thomas Bentley, *The monument of matrones* (1582), 438. See also Joseph Hall, *The arte of diuine meditation* (1606), 160.

[27] Quarles, *Emblemes* (1639), 302. Such experiences seem to have been very popular, as *Emblemes* was one of the bestselling collections of its kind, and the illustrations served as models for domestic art later in the century. See e.g., Hugh Adlington, et al., 'Beyond the Page', *Huntington Library Quarterly*, 78 (2015), 521–51.

Figure 4. Francis Quarles, *Emblems* (London: M. G. and W, 1696), 240. The Huntington Library, San Marino, California.

66   EXPERIENCING GOD IN LATE MEDIEVAL & EARLY MODERN ENGLAND

limitations ('lowly stature') as well as the solace it can find beneath the 'Vmbrella' of the Crucifixion.

Of course, one danger was that if pictures could inspire self-reflection leading to a more virtuous lifestyle, the opposite was also true. Wanton pictures were believed to lead to vice if gazed upon too long. Similarly, ugly pictures, according to at least one physician, even could deform unborn children in their mother's wombs, as the soul of both mother and foetus would be affected by the awful sight.[28] Equally dangerous, according to many Protestants, were idolatrous images or images in inappropriate contexts that could be misconstrued or, worse, abused by unholy reverence.

What we want to consider in the rest of this chapter are three different contexts in which certain images of God garnered widespread appreciation among most English Protestants. As Quarles reminded his readers, different depictions could have different purposes: some blind and scorch with divine 'Sun-beames' of God's presence, others threaten providential judgment from a 'just Creator', and still others comfort the godly in their weakness and suffering, serving as a symbol of the divine 'Vmbrella' of God's grace. Each of these—images of God's presence, images of providence, and images of consolation—mediated different opportunities to remember different moments of divine revelation as well as meditate upon one's relationship to a God who reveals himself to his people.

Tokens of Immanence

One context where we can find God being depicted with regularity is what I will refer to as images of divine immanence. While Protestant reformers often emphasized God's transcendence, particularly as it related to the image debate, this did not diminish the belief that God was everywhere present. The word *immanence* was not in popular usage in early modern English; however, its meaning—God's presence in the created world—was not foreign to either Catholics or Protestants.[29] Christ was named 'Immanuel' (God with us), and biblical verses like Psalm 139.7 ('whither shall I flee from thy presence?') were well known. John Calvin began his *Institutes* with a statement about God's immanence: 'our very being is nothing but subsistence in the one God', arguing God maintains every aspect of the natural, and supernatural, world. Likewise, the Dominican priest Luis de Granada, popular among English Catholics, explained that 'God is present euery where, not only by his power, but also by his essence'.[30]

---

[28] Matthew Scrivener, *The method and means to a true spiritual life* (1688), 177; James MacMath, *The expert mid-wife* (Edinburgh, 1694), 15.

[29] 'immanence, n.'. *OED Online*. Oxford University Press. https://www.oed.com/view/Entry/91796 (accessed February 9, 2022).

[30] John Calvin, *Institutes* (1970), I.i.1; Luis de Granada, *Granados deuotion* (1598), sig. 2C3v. For Calvinists, the reality of God's immanence was proof that the greater sacrality of particular places and

In this section, I want to consider those images that did little more than represent the presence of God, for images of divine immanence served as 'tokens' of God's presence. Such tokens, according to the Catholic priest Nicholas Sander, put 'us in the mind of' God's revelation by bringing to mind a biblical, or otherwise authoritative, representation of God's self-disclosure.[31] While these tokens can be easy to dismiss as visual formalities, or mere decoration, there is evidence to suggest that their significance stretched beyond mere convention.

The 1664 Book of Common Prayer contained a representation of the Holy Name of Jesus, symbolized by the letters IHS, surrounded in glory above the scene of the Circumcision of Christ (Figure 5). Created by William Faithorne, the image of the Holy Name in the engraving represented both Christ's humanity and his divine identity.[32] In this illustration, the IHS highlights the fact that the Circumcision was Christ's initiation into the Hebraic covenant.[33] However, the representation of the Holy Name is not an essential element in communicating this message. One defining aspect of divine immanence we can see demonstrated in this engraving is that the visual representation of God's presence could be auxiliary to the larger narrative. The image suggests no interaction between God and the other figures in the scene, nor is it absolutely necessary to the theological significance of the Circumcision. While it certainly accentuates the message, the symbol could be removed without losing the meaning. This is evidenced by the fact that after 1681, the IHS was removed from the picture in subsequent editions, leaving readers only an empty space of light above the scene.

One popular location for images of divine immanence was a book's title page, where the image provided a kind of authentication of the text, alongside other authoritative markers (e.g. the printer's name, stamps of official approval, etc.). Before the Reformation, Bible title pages included scriptural writers (e.g. Moses, Paul, etc.), translators like Jerome, or papal symbols (e.g. the papal tiara, the cross-keys, etc.). For Protestants, biblical scenes or symbols of divine revelation became common fare.[34] These tokens of God's presence, in various forms, stood apart from any other visual narrative on the page. Like the Holy Name above the Circumcision, there is rarely any interaction between God and the other figures, making such images of God more static than other representations and inviting viewers to pay them little attention. That is not to say that these images did not

---

objects was foolishness, because all creation was equally sacred. See e.g., William Perkins, *Lectures vpon the three first chapters of Reuelation* (1604), 68.

[31] David J. Davis, *From Icons to Idols* (Eugene, OR, 2016), 110.

[32] Very similar images were created by European artists Heironymous Weirix and Boetius Bolswert. For the popularity of the Holy Name, see James Clifton, 'A Variety of Spiritual Pleasures', in *Jesuit Image Theory* (Leiden, 2016), 318–52.

[33] *The book of common-prayer* (1664), sigs. D7–8. For Calvin, the Circumcision formally initiated the process by which Christ would serve as a substitute for Israel's perennial sacrifices: Calvin, *Institutes*, IV.xvi.7–12.

[34] Luborsky and Ingram, *A Guide*, vol. I, 83–93. See my chapter 'The Visual Culture of Reformation Bibles', in *The Oxford Handbook of the Bible and the Reformation* (Oxford, forthcoming).

Figure 5. 'The Circumcision of Christ' in *The book of common prayer* (London: John Bill and Christopher Barker, 1664). By permission of the Rare Book and Manuscript Library, University of Illinois at Urbana-Champaign.

matter, as some readers clearly took tokens of divine immanence very seriously. For example, Tenison condemned a frontispiece printed in Lyons for a 'Roman Pontificall' because:

> on the Top…is pictured an old man with a Globe in his hand, and a glory streaming from all parts of him. On his head there is a Triple Crown, or Miter, and over it this Motto, Holy-Trinity, one God, have mercy upon us. At the bottom, the Pope is plac'd, in a like Garb, with Miter, and Key; and a glory about his head.[35]

While Tenison specifically takes issue with the anthropomorphizing of God the Father, I cannot imagine he was concerned that people might worship a title page in the same way that they would kneel before a statue. After all, a book's title page is not the most obvious devotional object. Like many images in stained glass windows, these images of God were intended less for a person to gaze upon in any devotional way and more to remind them that God is gazing upon them. Here, the memorial is not about remembering what God had done or revealed in scripture but that he was still continuously present. The fact that Protestants like Tenison took issue with the way in which this memorial was fashioned tells us, at least to some extent, how much they paid attention to these tokens of divine representation.

Other examples of this sort, which Tenison and other Protestants found less offensive, included the Holy Spirit as a dove, which decorated a variety of title pages, either alone or as a member of the Trinity.[36] Also, the Tetragrammaton was a widely accepted representation of God's immanence. Reformed households from Kent to Devon and north to Edinburgh were decorated with the Tetragrammaton, and churches like St. Mary Abchurch in London, known for its puritan preaching, had altarpieces and ceilings decorated with the Holy Name of Jesus.[37] Another popular token of divine presence was the Scutum Fidei (the triangular shield of faith, signifying the doctrine of the Trinity). A woodcut of the shield accompanied by a three-faced figure of the Trinity could be found on

---

[35] Tenison, *Of idolatry*, 266.

[36] Although Margaret Aston pointed to the destruction of the dove image in things like the Cheapside Cross, the figure was nevertheless ubiquitous in print, baptismal fonts, and domestic décor throughout early modern England: Aston, *Broken Idols*, 593–604; Hamling, *Decorating the 'Godly' Household*, 160–2; Davis, *Seeing Faith, Printing Pictures*, 184–6. For sixteenth-century woodcuts of Christ's baptism and the Day of Pentecost containing the Holy Spirit as a dove, see Luborsky and Ingram, *A Guide*, vol. II, 171, 177.

[37] Hamling, *Decorating the 'Godly' Household*, 164, 193, 224; Clare Haynes, *Pictures and Popery* (2006), illustrations 28, 31, 38. Aston describes the Tetragrammaton as a 'verbal emblem' (*Broken Idols*, 583) , which strikes me as something of a misnomer, since I cannot imagine most early modern English readers were pronouncing the Hebrew letters. The Tetragrammaton was more pictorial, or pictographic, than verbal, insofar as the shapes when arranged together represented the idea of God rather than the sound of a word.

English psalters before the Reformation, and while the three-faced God was eventually prohibited by the papacy, the symbol of the shield remained a popular one (Figure 6).[38]

In the 1664 prayer book, the Scutum Fidei illustrated Trinity Sunday, alongside the collect which read, 'Almighty and everlasting God, who hast given unto us thy servants grace…to acknowledge the glory of the eternal Trinity, and in the power of the divine Majesty to worship the Unity'.[39]

Here, the Scutum Fidei provides us with an excellent example of the ambiguity inherent in the visual discursive mode, as the potential ways of seeing this image varied from person to person, based upon the intellectual lens a viewer brought to the text. The tradition of the image as representative of the triune God would have made the essential meaning of the image apparent to most early modern people; however, not everyone would have made the interdiscursive connection with 1 John 5.7 without the accompanying text that frames the engraving ('And these three are one'). Some may have associated it with Eph. 6.16 ('take the shield of faith'), or some other similar verse about divine protection. However, it is unlikely that more than a minority of people knew the rich symbolic tradition behind the image, dating back to the twelfth century. As Bob Scribner notes, the 'rhetorical power' of pictures, like the texts they often accompanied, was partially contingent upon their audiences bringing a necessarily basic understanding of the imagery with them.[40]

One final point is that while certain images of God served a more totemic role, I do not think we can dismiss them as mere marketing devices. For one thing, there were many editions of bibles and prayer books—in fact most of the surviving editions—that did not contain such images, suggesting that the pictures were not necessary to make money. Also, the fact that the images of God were deployed when they were not essential to the picture speaks to their desirability in early modern culture. Although such representations of divine manifestation could authorize a text as well as indicate, to some degree, confessional or theological content, their popularity suggests an underlining cultural inclination toward not only visually memorializing divine revelation but also affirming the belief that God was continually present in the created order. Images of immanence presented a deity that could ravish an individual's soul and could be experienced in more subtle ways that did not rely upon an extraordinary encounter. God could be seen, if only by a visual analogy, in a variety of tokens to stir one's memory and spiritual fervor.

---

[38] Aston, *Broken Idols*, 584–6.

[39] *The book of common-prayer* (1664), sig. G5v. The Scutum Fidei was first popularized by the twelfth-century apocalyptic writer Joachim de Fiore, and it could be found in windows, baptismal fonts, missals, books of hours, and heraldic coats of arms.

[40] Scribner, *For the Sake of the Simple Folk*, 244, also see 245–50.

Figure 6. 'Trinity Sunday' in *The book of common prayer* (London: John Bill and Christopher Barker, 1664). By permission of the Rare Book and Manuscript Library, University of Illinois at Urbana-Champaign.

72 EXPERIENCING GOD IN LATE MEDIEVAL & EARLY MODERN ENGLAND

Providential Pictures

Closely related to images of divine immanence are those that represented divine providence. While there is no definitive line between these categories, I will be considering providential images of God that depict God's ordering of the cosmos, his protection over the church and/or the godly, and his judgment of sin. Images depicting God's providence tend to represent greater activity on the part of the divine figure than do images of immanence, as the latter generally are intended to communicate the mere presence of God.[41]

For example, a popular biblical image of divine providence was the conversion of Saul (Paul) on the Damascus road (Acts 9), when Saul was thrown to the ground by a revelation of Christ, who asked the future apostle 'why persecutest thou me?' (9.4). In the 1664 prayer book, an engraving depicts heavenly light blinding Saul as he falls from his horse (Figure 7), which was reprinted in several editions of the Restoration prayer book. The image connected the reader to the biblical figure with the accompanying prayer: 'Grant, we beseech thee, that we having his wonderful conversion in remembrance, may shew forth our thankfulness unto thee', not only providing a token of what God had done but also calling upon the reader to respond ('shew forth').[42]

Visualizing the scene had a long history in late medieval and early modern Europe, and depictions were included in Lutheran Bibles and English New Testaments.[43] Continental artists popular in England, from Dürer in 1490s to Jean le Clerc in the 1680s, depicted Christ appearing in the clouds.[44] Also, the purpose of the conversion scene provided a popular story with which to visualize God's intervening power in the normal course of space and time. Leading voices like Richard Baxter referred to the event as a primary example of the disclosing of 'Gods unrevealed Will', in which 'The Power of God went forth with that Light...[to] lay proud Prosecutors on the Earth, and tame them and make them fear and hear'.[45] The imagery of light was commonplace in depictions of providence. Perhaps the most obvious examples of this were representations of the Annunciation, where the Virgin Mary has a ray of light (often accompanied by an angel or a dove) shining down upon her. Despite the Protestant aversion to Marian devotion, the Annunciation was one of the exceptions to the general avoidance of her picture.[46] Illustrated Restoration prayer books contained an

[41] Alexandra Walsham has demonstrated that providence was understood not as 'hasty improvisations', where God is counteracting events and decisions outside his control, but instead as interventions that were part of an ordered 'programme for history': *Providence in Early Modern England*, 13.

[42] *The book of common prayer* (1676), sig. I1v.

[43] *Das newe Testament* (Basel, 1523), title page; Luborsky and Ingram, *A Guide*, vol. I, 175–6.

[44] *Figures des histoires de la Sainte Bible* (Paris, 1688), 267.

[45] Richard Baxter, *A paraphrase on the New Testament* (1685), sigs. I3v, K1r.

[46] Between 1534 and 1603 Annunciation images appeared in no fewer than twenty printed books: Luborsky and Ingram, *A Guide*, vol. II, 170. See also David J. Davis, 'Images on the Move', *The Journal of the Early Book Society* 12 (2009), 99–132.

Figure 7. 'The Conversion of Paul' in *The book of common prayer* (London: John Bill and Christopher Barker, 1664). By permission of the Rare Book and Manuscript Library, University of Illinois at Urbana-Champaign.

74   EXPERIENCING GOD IN LATE MEDIEVAL & EARLY MODERN ENGLAND

Annunciation engraving, which followed closely behind the image of Saul's conversion, providing an important comparison of two people whose experiences with divine providence were instrumental in the history of Christianity.[47]

More than memorializing these biblical events, other visual representations used the divine light of providence in contemporary contexts. Images of particular individuals, as well as generic images of devout people in prayer, regularly appeared in similar positions as the Virgin, with heavenly light shining down upon them.[48] Also, popular representations of the discovery of the Gunpowder Plot in 1605 became idealized examples of providential protection, as divine light, sometimes depicted emanating from a divine eye, reveals Guy Fawkes's foiled conspiracy. Even earlier, an anti-papal image replaced Saul with the pope on the Damascus road, with divine light and the Holy Spirit knocking the pope from his horse. These popular images commemorated God's favouritism by visually reminding readers that divine providence thwarted England's enemies.[49]

Not to be outdone, Roman Catholics deployed divine revelation to illustrate the providential protection of the papacy. As part of the larger polemical debates with Archbishop James Ussher, the Jesuit priest William Malone challenged Ussher's efforts to undermine the Roman Catholic claim to papal primacy. His book, *A reply to Mr. Iames Vssher*, included a fascinating title page illustration of the anthropomorphized Trinity above the pope (probably Urban VIII) along with his clergy and the saints, all playing harps (Figure 8). In this depiction, the Roman Catholic hierarchy joins the choir of angels in worship around the heavenly throne of God, and below, Protestants like John Knox blare a cacophony of noise and smoke from horns and trumpets, signifying their religious discord.[50] The order of divine providence serves as evidence of the truth of Roman Catholicism, as it is more aligned with the harmony of creation. Along with answering Ussher's criticisms, Malone explained his intent was to demonstrate how Catholicism was 'diuinely vnited together by a miraculous harmony...throughout the world'. Malone contrasted this harmony with the 'horrid dissonance and vnreconcileable

---

[47] *The book of common prayer* (1664), sigs. I2–3. Miri Rubin's analysis of the Annunciation in late medieval devotion provides an interesting contrast to Saul's encounter with God: *The Mother of God* (New Haven, CT, 2005), 342–5.

[48] For the sixteenth century, see Davis, *Seeing Faith, Printing Pictures*, 202–10. Seventeenth-century examples, echoing the position of the Virgin, include: Augustine, *Saint Augustines confessions*, title page; William Brough, *Sacred principles* (1659), title page; Edward Wettenhall, *Enter into thy closet* (1676), title page. BPI 6113.

[49] See e.g., *Guy Fawkes holding a lantern outside Parliament* (seventeenth century), BPI 5717; *A Plot of Powder*, (1605), BPI 702. The Restoration prayer books included an engraving of the discovery of the Gunpowder Plot to commemorate November 5th: *The book of common prayer* (1668), sigs. R8–S1. See also the image of Christ printed in Thomas Scot's *Vox Dei* (1624), as discussed in Walsham, *Providence in Early Modern England*, 277–8.

[50] William Malone, *A reply to Mr. James Vssher* (Douai?, 1627), title page.

'PICTURES ARE ... NOT FOR WORSHIP' 75

Figure 8. William Malone, *A reply to Mr. Iames Vssher his ansvvere* (Douai?: Permissu superiorum, 1627), title page. By permission of the Huntington Library, San Marino, California.

discord' of the different Protestant confessions, which ultimately fails to disturb the eternal concord between Roman Catholicism and heaven.[51]

Images of God's providence offered multiple paths for reflection. The images could bring to mind the abundant goodness and power of God. They also could

---

[51] Malone, 'The Preface to the Reader', in *A reply*, sig. *1v.

assure people of the orderliness of Creation. Providential images of God's revelation as the Creator were familiar to Protestant readers, perhaps most popularly in the image of the Garden of Eden first printed in the Geneva Bible (1583), which was reproduced in quarto and smaller bibles into the 1600s. The centrality of the Tree of the Knowledge of Good and Evil in the image emphasizes the Protestant stress on human corruption; however, the gravity of the Fall is understood within the larger divine order, as the Tetragrammaton hovers above.[52] Similarly, Peter Heylyn's mid-seventeenth century *Cosmographie* depicted God's order and provision across the entirety of human history and global geography. God's active intervention could be traced in events from Noah's ark to the Roman Empire. In at least six editions before 1700, the title page of *Cosmographie*, engraved by John Fillian, contained the Tetragrammaton and the Holy Spirit as a dove in control of the four known continents: Europe, Asia, Africa, and America. The scroll below the Tetragrammaton is a definitive statement of God's providence: 'DIXIT ET FACTUM EST'.[53]

While it may seem reasonable to assume that the substitution of the Tetragrammaton for an anthropomorphic God was part of the decline of religious images in England, for many Protestants, the name of God communicated much more than the decline of traditional imagery. The Anglican convert Solomon Franco described the Tetragrammaton as an abbreviated means to describe God's very nature: 'Here was revealed to Moses the mystery of the Tetragrammaton, the proper name of the absolute Creatour, the Cause of all causes, a Name which denotes him to be the onely true Being, absolute and independent in himself, without either beginning or end'.[54] More than other figures of God, the Tetragrammaton communicated his absoluteness as the being that transcended all being, and at the same time, an absolute being who could step into the course of historical events.

For example, the Tetragrammaton had an active role in the title page for George Hakewill's *An apologie or Declaration of the povver and providence of God in the gouernment of the world* (Figure 9). In the text, Hakewill refuted the notion that the world, in both its material and civil orders, existed in a state of decline, promoting an anti-entropic theology rooted in the Calvinist emphasis upon divine sovereignty. For Hakewill, God was not only the 'Disposer of all things', but also 'He holdeth backe the Sythe of Tyme from destroying or impairing the Vniverse'.[55] That is to say, until God determines the time for the final judgment,

---

[52] Davis, *Seeing Faith, Printing Pictures*, 192–4.

[53] Peter Heylyn, *Cosmographie in four bookes* (1652), title page. BPI 5271.

[54] Solomon Franco, *Truth springing out of the earth* (1668), 10. See also the frontispiece for Francis Bacon, *Sylva sylvarum* (1627). BPI 1851.

[55] George Hakewill, *An apologie or Declaration of the povver and providence of God in the gouernment of the world* (1630), opp. title page. BPI 1931. Hakewill's text seems to have been a popular one, as Edward Dering, Lady Ann Clifford, and Mary Dudley Sutton owned copies (PLRE).

'PICTURES ARE...NOT FOR WORSHIP' 77

Figure 9. George Hakewill, *An apologie or Declaration of the povver and providence of God in the gouernment of the world* (Oxford: William Turner, 1635), title page. By permission of the Rare Book and Manuscript Library, University of Illinois at Urbana-Champaign.

78   EXPERIENCING GOD IN LATE MEDIEVAL & EARLY MODERN ENGLAND

a topic which absorbed the last chapters of *An apologie*, then the universe was indestructible because it rested comfortably on God's providence. On the title page, the print maker Thomas Cecill created a collage of scenes of the Tetragrammaton directing Father Time and Death in their ravaging of Creation. God both holds back the march of Time and he dictates the destruction of one city over another.

This ordering of the macrocosmic order was also true for the lesser order of the human body. The popular medical text *Mikrokosmographia* by Helkiah Crooke went through multiple editions in the 1600s. Crooke's medicine was traditionally Galenic and Pythagorean, conceptualizing the human body as a microcosm of the universe. The title page of the 1631 edition (reprinted in 1651) conjoined natural philosophy with divine providence, depicting the Tetragrammaton and the eye of God surrounded by the circles of the created order. Below the male and female anatomical forms appear alongside small depictions of physicians going about their profession. Similar representations of divine providence appeared in works on surgery and pharmacology, recognizing a transcendent governor who ordered the physical world with omnipotent power to intervene at will.[56] Interestingly, however, the works themselves rarely developed the theme of God's providence in the context of medical practice. As Jennifer Evans explains, despite the fact that physicians operated under 'the implicit understanding that their effectiveness was governed by God's providence', they tended to focus upon the natural, rather than venture into the supernatural, in their writings.[57] It would seem then that visual representations of divine providence in medical treatises stood apart from the text, serving as a kind of paratext that augmented but did not directly engage. They served as reminders of a transcendent reality in which the physician participated.

In many respects, the belief in divine providence shored up the doctrine of divine immanence, presenting a world in which divine agency was continuously present and omnipotent. Pictures of biblical events provided models from which one could contemplate God's agency in the world as well as frame and understand contemporary events. Although it seems unlikely that most people expected God to appear in the clouds, the pictures served to remind people that he had done so in the past and continued to direct space and time in the same manner, even if he did so invisibly.

Images of Consolation

The final group of images of revelation we will examine are those that were intended to comfort the devout. While many different images of God could offer

---

[56] Helkiah Crooke, *Microkosmographia* (1631), BPI 2270; John Woodall, *The Surgeons Mate* (1639); *Pharmacopoeia Londinensis* (1618), BPI 2283; John Gerard, *The Herball* (1633), BPI 670.

[57] Jennifer Evans, *Aprhodisiacs, Fertility, and Medicine in Early Modern England* (Woodbridge, 2014), 61.

consolation, for our purposes here, images of consolation will fall into two groups. First, those images that directly linked the reader and a pictured person receiving a divine revelation. The second group includes images that invited the reader to gaze directly upon God, usually by stripping away most, or all, of the surrounding narrative, leaving little more than the divine presence.

An important and popular example of the first group is the image of Stephen's revelation of God during his martyrdom in Acts 7 (Figure 10). Most often in early modern England, the scene was depicted with heavenly glory shining down upon Stephen as he is stoned. On rare occasions, images following examples from the continent contained anthropomorphic figures of Christ and God the Father, looking down upon the martyrdom, which more accurately illustrate Stephen's own testimony, 'I see the heavens opened, and the Son of man standing on the right hand of God' (Acts 7.56). In the 1670s, one example of this scene, created by van Hove following an earlier print by Aegidius Sadeler, was included in several Bibles and at least one edition of the prayer book (1676).[58] In the latter, a corresponding prayer connected the reader and the martyr:

> Grant, O Lord, that in all our sufferings here upon earth for the testimony of thy truth, we may stedfastly look up to heaven, and by faith behold the glory that shall be revealed...(as) Stephen being full of the holy Ghost, looked up stedfastly into heaven, and saw the glory of God, and Jesus standing on the right hand of God.[59]

This is an important example of what Francis Quarles described as an impulse to provide to the bodily eyes 'what faith alone could see'. Based upon the account in Acts 7, it is clear that no one else saw what Stephen saw, and yet, the prayer book encouraged believers to 'stedfastly look up to heaven', following the faithful martyr in his beholding of divine glory. Also interesting is the fact that Stephen, while understood to be experiencing ravishment, seems to have been in control of his body, at least enough to say to the crowd, 'Behold, I see the heavens open' (Acts 7.56), and it is not insignificant that later in the seventeenth century Stephen's example will be used to question the separation of the soul from the body during ravishment (see chapters 6 and 7).

Although most images in Protestant works did not provide a picture of what Stephen actually saw, this example from the 1670s was not completely unusual in depicting God the Father. For example, Hans Holbein's popular *Icones* was

---

[58] These rarer anthropomorphic depictions included: *The history of ye Old & new Testament in cutts* (1671), New Testament #70; *The Holy Bible* (1678), New Testament sigs. I5v–I6r; *The book of common-prayer* (1676), sig. D6r. Due to the closure of most libraries and archives during the Covid-19 pandemic, I was unable to acquire a reproduction of the somewhat rare van Hove copy of Sadeler's original.

[59] *The book of common-prayer* (1676), sigs. D5–6.

Figure 10. Aegidius Sadeler, *Steniging van de heilige Stefanus* (1580–1629). Rijksmuseum, Amsterdam.

translated into English, with a series of woodcuts that had been used in a variety of continental Bibles. Among other images of God, Holbein's series included a picture of the Trinity illustrating Psalm 109, which was intended to console the reader and inspire devotion. The motto above the woodcut reads: 'Christ sittyth at the right hand of his father. God the father gyuidh vnto his son a preystly dignitye vuhyce shal luer in due for the benefice of his passion'.[60]

The copy of Holbein's Trinity shown here suffered iconoclastic attack, with pen ink scratched through the depictions of God the Father and the Holy Spirit (Figure 11). While this sort of religious violence exerted on printed images was not unheard of, it was rarer than one might think.[61] Such activity put into practice the multiple denunciations of printed images of God, like the puritan Thomas Adams's rant about the idolatrous image of 'An old man, sitting in a chaire, with a

Figure 11. Hans Holbein, *Drieëenheid* (1538). Rijksmuseum, Amsterdam.

---

[60] Hans Holbein, *The images of the Old Testament* (Lyons, 1549), sig. K4r. Rijksmuseum, RP-P-OB-4511II(V). Similar images appeared in the English Catholic *Manual of prayers* (Douai, 1613), 204 and again *A Manual of prayers* (1686), 30.

[61] Thus, Margaret Aston concedes that even after decades of reformed iconoclasm, 'God the Father as a bearded ancient was a fossilized mental icon' who was 'hard to unseat': *Broken Idols*, 575.

82 EXPERIENCING GOD IN LATE MEDIEVAL & EARLY MODERN ENGLAND

triple Crowne on his head, and Pontificall robes on his backe, a Doue hanging at his beard, and a Crucifixe in his armes'. He very easily could have been referring to the illustrations in the popular *A manual of prayers*, most recently printed in 1619.[62] In response to such attacks, English Catholics reminded people that the figure of the Ancient of Days (Daniel 9) was the biblical support for depicting God as an old man. Thus, the Catholic priest Thomas Godden (Tylden) responded to Protestant accusations of idolatry:

> God himself was no less adorable when he appeared to Daniel like the Ancient of Days, than when he gave the *Law* to *Moses* without any *Similitude:* To conclude, to be *Supremely-Excellent* is *Proper* to God alone; *Not-to-be-representable* by an Image, is Common to Him with Angels, though in a higher degree: and however it enter materiall.[63]

Godden saw little difference in intent between representing God as a blank space in the clouds or the Tetragrammaton and images of the Ancient of Days. All biblical memorials provided a similar aid to the imagination, but no image fully expressed that which is 'Not-to-be-representable'. Similarly, Abraham Woodhead asked, 'why may not the same reverence be given to such figures recommended to us by such sacred Scripture-Apparitions, as is to other representations of sacred Persons'. Echoing a standard Catholic argument about reverence that Protestants gave to figures of apostles, martyrs, and even contemporary divines, Woodhead could not understand the Protestant refusal to show the same reverence to God, particularly when Catholics acknowledged that they should 'imagine no true resemblance of the Person'.[64]

For Protestants who were unmoved by such arguments, other images of divine revelation could be turned to consolatory use. Thus, in his sermons, Bullinger said that the Tetragrammaton was the 'most excellent' means of communicating the character of God. Similarly, the Elizabethan clergyman Thomas Rogers, known for his translation of Thomas Kempis, wrote, 'That name I loue and reuerence and feare:/…That name which Angels laude and furies dreade,…That name which flesh is to impure to name, / My sinfull soule with sacred zeale inflame'.[65] If the name of God could 'inflame' people to worship and love for God, then the representation of that name could have a similar effect. In early modern England, the Tetragrammaton became a commonplace image of visual consolation.[66]

---

[62] Thomas Adams, *The temple* (1624), 19; Anon., *Manual of prayers* (1613), 204–5.

[63] Thomas Godden, *Catholicks no idolaters* (1672), 67.

[64] Abraham Woodhead, *Concerning Images and Idolatry* (Oxford, 1689), 10.

[65] Henry Bullinger, *Fiftie godlie and learned sermons* (1577), 608; Thomas Rogers, *Celestiall elegies* (1598), sig. C6v.

[66] For example, see Hieronymus Wierix's engraving *Christ en Maria geknield op de wolken Aanbidding van de maagd Maria door heiligen* (Rijksmuseum, RP-P-1904–794).

In the Restoration prayer books, the Tetragrammaton was depicted, surrounded by heavenly saints, while a hand reaches down to the godly on Earth who kneel in devotion (Figure 12). The consolatory image connected the terrestrial saints with the 'household of God', offering comfort to readers during the liturgy for All Saints Day. The accompanying collect asked God, 'Grant us grace so to follow thy blessed Saints', with whom the elect are 'in one communion and fellowship, in the mystical body of thy Son Christ our Lord'.[67] The engraving immediately follows several portraits of Christ's disciples, who, in the image of God's household, now wear crowns and royal gowns. The image invites the devout reader to imagine themselves as part of this glorious assembly. As the Anglican divine Jeremy Taylor preached:

> when God the Father was pleased to pour forth all his glories, and imprint them upon his holy Son in his exaltation, it was by giving him his *holy Name*, the *Tetragrammaton* or *Jehovah* made articulate;...Gods name is left us here to pray by, to hope in, to be the instrument and conveyance of our worshippings.[68]

It is no mystery that visual and textual references to Christ served as some of the most obvious consolatory images.[69] For John Owen, Christ was the absolute manifestation of divine revelation, the 'Glorious Image and Representation' of God that was 'a Real Representation' of God's properties and attributes.[70] Even Christ, in the gospel of John, affirmed this understanding of himself saying, 'he that hath seen me, hath seen my Father...I am in the Father, and the Father is in me' (John 14.9–11). In fact, many Protestants believed that any revelation of God in the Old Testament was an appearance of God the Son (not the Father).[71] This interpretation did not provide authorization to depict Christ visually; instead, it seems to undermine the narrative that the Ancient of Days (a concept advanced by early modern Catholics) was a beneficial memorial of God. Thus, the Geneva Bible's image of God in the Book of Ezekiel depicted a younger man, without a long beard, clearly indicating which member of the Trinity was on display.[72] Also, efforts were made to explain how one might fashion an image of Christ without creating an image of God, attempting to parse out the human and the divine natures of Christ's incarnation.[73]

---

[67] *The book of common prayer* (1664), sigs. I7–8, quote on sig. I7v.

[68] Jeremy Taylor, *XXV sermons* (1653), 308.   [69] John Brinsley, *Two treatises* (1656), 16, 32.

[70] John Owen, *Christologia* (1679), 59–61.

[71] Carl L. Beckwith, ed., *Reformation Commentary on Scripture* (Downers Grove, IL, 2012), 197–8.

[72] Davis, *Seeing Faith, Printing Pictures*, 161–5. Interestingly, a close copy of the Ezekiel image was included in the Reina-Valera Spanish Bible with the slight difference that a triangle is included behind God's head, a symbol more commonly associated with God the Father: *La Biblia* (Basel, 1569).

[73] Peter Vermigli, *The common places* (1585), 340–1. See also William Perkins, *A reformed Catholike* (1597), 169–72. The justification for depicting Christ in profile came from the supposed first-century portrayal of Christ by Publius Lentulus: Richard Williams, 'The Reformation of an Icon', in Hamling and Williams, eds, *Art Re-formed*, 71–86.

Figure 12. 'The Household of God' in *The book of common prayer* (London: John Bill and Christopher Barker, 1664). By permission of the Rare Book and Manuscript Library, University of Illinois at Urbana-Champaign.

While not all images of Christ were intended to console, images of the Passion served as some of the most consistent images of this kind. English Catholics enjoyed a steady flow of texts and images focusing on Christ's suffering, as a means of encouraging the reader in their own struggles.[74] The mid-seventeenth century *The Perpetval Crosse, Or Passion of Iesus Christ* by Judocus Andries was printed in Antwerp, Brussels, and Munich, with forty engravings by Jan Christoffel Jegher. The English edition, printed by Cornelis Woons, explained to readers that Christ 'was neuer without his Crosse, both outvvard and invvard', encouraging them to follow in his example. The text even included a simple path to the forgiveness of sins via a printed pardon from the Bishop of Mechlin (Mechelen), on the final page for anyone willing to recite the prayers daily.[75] Among the images in Andries's book, the perpetuality of Christ's suffering included an image of the pre-incarnate Christ with God the Father and the Holy Spirit in heaven, as Christ lays aside his divine crown to take up the cross (Figure 13). The image suggested that the Passion and Crucifixion exist in some sense outside of space and time, as an eternal reality that could be drawn upon for devotional purposes.[76] Such representations memorialized what Christ did as well as invited people to hold up the image as a mirror, encouraging them to participate in a sympathetic way with Christ's sufferings by reciting the prayers in exchange for the forgiveness of sin.

Among Protestants, of course, such pardons were not acceptable. Moreover, some images of Christ's Passion and the crucifix were hotly contested, as many people saw them as obvious markers of popish corruption.[77] Nevertheless, reformed devotionals like *A bryefe summe of the whole Byble* illustrated the sufferings of Christ, even including scenes of Christ accepting the cross from God the Father.[78] Likewise, along with the Restoration prayer books, Caroline Bibles also contained engravings of the Passion. *The history of ye Old & new Testament in cuts* (1671) included eleven such engravings, and the 1678 Authorized Bible included five of the Passion series, although the actual Crucifixion was illustrated much more rarely. The 1678 Bible contains an engraving of Christ as a child kneeling

---

[74] Davis, *Seeing Faith, Printing Pictures*, 87–102; Alexandra Walsham, *The Catholic Reformation in Protestant Britain* (2014), 107; Eamon Duffy, 'Praying the Counter-Reformation', in *Early Modern English Catholicism* (2016), 206–25.

[75] *The perpetval crosse*, 48.

[76] *The perpetval crosse* (1649), quote at sig. A2v, the image is at, sig. A4v. For similar Catholic images of Christ's suffering, see *The New Testament of Iesus Christ* (Douai, 1633), title page; Bonaventure, *Stimulis diuini amoris* (Douai, 1642), title page.

[77] Bernard Garter, *A Newyeares gifte* (1579), sig. H2r; John Vicars, *Gods arke* (1645), 128, 185; Antonio Gavin, *The frauds of Romish monks and priests* (1691), 194.

[78] *A bryefe summe of the whole Byble* (1549), sigs. E2v, F6r, F7v. Interestingly, one of the only religious oil paintings created for an English audience around 1600 was of the Crucifixion: *The Crucifixion with Moses, David, St. Paul, and St. John the Baptist* (Victoria and Albert Museum, P.1–1938). See Tara Hamling's thorough analysis in *Decorating the 'Godly' Household*, 236–8.

Figure 13. Jan Christoffel Jegher, *Heilinge Drie-eenheid* (1649). Rijksmuseum, Amsterdam.

before the instruments of the Passion, imagery that was very familiar in Catholic visual culture but rarely seen in Protestant contexts.[79]

Such representations were visual models intended to stir up spiritual passion. Protestant devotionals like Richard Vennard's *The right way to heaven* (Figure 14) depicted Christ with a wounded side and a crown of thorns, alongside the prayer to the 'Paine perced Shepheard' to 'seeke mee Christ...seeke thine owne, thine owne whom thou hast bought'.[80] Others like William Austin's *Devotionis Augustinianae flamma* contained entire woodcut series of Christ's life, and each woodcut was titled 'a meditation' for a different holy day (e.g. the Crucifixion for Good Friday, etc.). Austin described the sufferings from Christ's perspective, inviting the readers to hear God speaking to them: 'See my Armes,...While sharpe Nailes...Rend my pale-Hands, where I hang'.[81] For James Barry, an English dissenting minister at the end of the seventeenth century, these devotional passions came upon him with such force that he 'thought I had the Person of Christ claspt in my Arms in the Bed'. Apparently, these experiences became a 'frequent Practice' for Barry, until a particular moment when 'I made to know (Experimentally)...While I was Wakeing, I was entertained with strange variety of Interlocution (or Discourse) which Passed between Christ and me', in which Christ enlightened his soul about the meaning of certain scriptures.[82]

The consoling images of Christ's suffering also could bring to mind accounts of contemporary martyrs. Both John Foxe's *Actes and monuments* and the seventeenth-century *Antiquitates Christianae* (a combined volume of William Cave's *Antiquitates apostolicae* and Jeremy Taylor's *The life of Christ*) provided pictures that associated the suffering Saviour and the martyrs with the contemporary reader.[83] Taylor's work connected several, large engravings by Faithorne depicting the Passion with the readers' own devotional lives: 'The Soul of a Christian is the house of God...but the house of God is the house of Prayer...Prayer is the ascent of the mind to God, and petitioning for such things as we need for our support and duty'.[84] Memorials of God's self-disclosure provided opportunities for such reflection, not only by bringing to mind what had been revealed in the past, but also by aiding the imagination and better preparing the individual for prayer and the potential for divine ravishment.

---

[79] *The history of ye Old*, 39–50; *The Holy Bible* (1678), sigs. New Testament C2–3, F7–8, G1–2, Q1–2.

[80] Richard Vennard, *The right vvay to heauen* (1602), sigs. E2v–E3r (image on sig. E3v). See also the cheap pamphlet Anon., *Fire from heauen* (1613), sig. A2r.

[81] William Austin, *Devotionis Augustinianae flamma* (1635), 138, 117. See also Graham Parry, *Glory, Laud and Honor* (Woodbridge, 2006) 63, 69, 78; Kenneth Fincham and Nicholas Tyacke, *Altars Restored* (Oxford, 2007), 262.

[82] James Barry, *A reviving cordial* (1699), 95–7.

[83] For more on Foxe's book in this regard see Deborah Burks, 'Polemical Potency', in *John Foxe and His World* (Aldershot, 2002), 263–76.

[84] Jeremy Taylor, *Antiquitates Christianae* (1684), 261. The title page was first created by Faithorne for Jeremy Taylor's book *The Great Exemplar*. BPI 7677.

88 EXPERIENCING GOD IN LATE MEDIEVAL & EARLY MODERN ENGLAND

Figure 14. Richard Vennard, *The right vvay to heauen* (London: Printed by Thomas Este, 1602). The Huntington Library, San Marino, California.

Equally important was the emphasis Protestants placed upon Christ's victory over death, particularly since images of the Resurrection seem to have been much more popular among Protestants than images of the Crucifixion.[85] The widely printed woodcut 'Christ Jesus Triumphant' first appeared in works of theology and devotion in 1578 and was recycled in at least twenty different works into the early seventeenth century. The wounds of Christ's crucifixion are on display in the

---

[85] Davis, *Seeing Faith, Printing Pictures*, 219–20.

image; however, Christ holds a palm frond (rather than a cross) and stands victorious atop Death and the Devil.

Of course, the traditional image of Christ's victory was the Salvator Mundi, which Renaissance artists from Jan van Eyck and Fra Bartolomeo to Titian had recreated. In England, Thomas Tallis, the Elizabethan composer, popularized the Salvator Mundi in his *Cantiones* (1575), and poets like Francis Quarles memorialized the consoling image of the almighty Christ as well.[86] Although images of the Salvator Mundi were not as popular in Protestant England (e.g. the minister Richard Culmer boasted of attacking one such image in his church), the imagery did not disappear entirely.[87] For the Dean of St. Paul's Cathedral in London and renowned English poet, John Donne, there were few images that could console the believer like the Salvator Mundi, because the image represented, 'that which he did, and suffered, was sufficient in it selfe, and was accepted by the Father, for the salvation of the world'. During the Interregnum, a copy of the prayer book was heavily amended by an unknown reader, who added engravings, including a new frontispiece of the Salvator Mundi which was originally produced by Faithorne.[88] It would seem that, even before the English prayer book came equipped with illustrations from the print shop, readers were devising ways to have their liturgy visually represented.

Another Faithorne creation of the Salvator Mundi was printed in Samuel Wesley's poetic work *The Life of Christ*, at the end of the seventeenth century (Figure 15). Father of the influential ministers Charles and John Wesley, Samuel Wesley's poem was perhaps the bestselling version of a popular genre which put to verse the last days of Christ's life. The engraving, positioned opposite the title page, depicts Christ staring directly out at the reader with a startlingly intimate gaze.[89] The picture demonstrates an important tension embedded within many consolatory images. Having the saviour of the world gaze at the reader could provide comfort and assurance of salvation, reminding them of what Christ has done. At the same time, Christ's gaze might create anxiety about the fact that the same Christ was watching everything a person says and does.[90] While it is difficult to know how much influence the illustrations had on the book's success, Wesley captured the power of such a gaze in his description of Christ's transfiguration: 'The Sun shrunk back his Head but newly shown, / Eclips'd with stronger

---

[86] Peter Le Huray, *Music and the Reformation in England* (Cambridge, 1978), 194; Francis Quarles, *Diuine poems* (1633), 62.

[87] Richard Culmer, *A parish looking glasse* (1657), 11.

[88] John Donne, *LXXX sermons* (1640), 529. See also Henry Valentine, *Private devotions* (1654), 274; Thomas Watson, *A body of practical divinity* (1692), 118. For the earlier Salvator Mundi image created by Faithorne, see Posey Krakowsky, 'The Ecclesiology of Prayerbook Illustrations', *Anglican and Episcopal History*, 83 (2014), 244–7.

[89] Faithorne's engraving seems to be a close copy of a *Salvator Mundi* print created by Schelte a Bolswert (Rijksmuseum, RP-P-1950–189).

[90] See also Hamling, *Decorating the 'Godly' Household*, 267–8.

Figure 15. Samuel Wesley, *The life of our blessed Lord & Saviour Jesus Christ* (1697), opposite title page. The Huntington Library, San Marino, California.

Splendor than his own…Too big or to be stifl'd or exprest: / Reason at Revelation must expire'.[91] Although human reason must expire at the point of revelation, the ability to memorialize visually the revelation remained something that was desirable, if not necessary, for Catholics and many Protestants.

[91] Samuel Wesley, *The Life of Christ* (1693), 6.

Whether the image represented God's providence or his suffering, there remained a need to depict God in such a way that might console and comfort people. The visual discursive mode of divine revelation was part of a continuous compulsion in English religious culture to depict and meditate upon the ways that God appeared to people. Late medieval and early modern images of divine revelation served as memorials of God's manifestations recorded in scripture. The visual memorials provided mental exemplars for understanding divine rapture, and they offered a pictorial platform from which people could reflect upon themselves and their own experiences. The fact that different groups and religious identities enjoyed representing God in different ways is important. Perhaps even more important is the continued impulse, across the confessional divides, to depict God, who was by definition transcendent and incomprehensible.

One of the organizing features of this chapter has been the overlooked engravings that accompanied many Restoration prayer books. While these books of the established church do not represent the entirety of English Protestantism, they do offer important benchmarks for any notion of a religious visual culture. The illustrations in the prayer books were not only permissible but also engineered to be part of the episcopal forms of belief and practice. While the prayer book engravings of God followed standard norms for such depictions, the images, when taken together, present an encyclopaedia of early modern ways to depict the divine.[92] Perhaps the inclusion of so many different images of God reflected both the religious fissures of the time and a visual culture that never settled upon a single way to represent the divine. As a refusal to deploy only one image, the prayer books negate the ability of any image to serve fully as a depiction of the incomprehensible deity, leaving people to meditate on something that cannot be comprehended but must be remembered.

---

[92] Certainly, many English men and women cast off attending the established church, but we should not forget that demand for Book of Common Prayer was not insignificant. In many parishes, it represented the preferred form of Protestantism: Tim Harris, *London Crowds in the Reign of Charles II* (Cambridge, 1987), 59–60.

PART II
RAPTUS AS PRAYER AND POETRY

4

'A love-token of Christ to the Soul'

Prayer and Devotion after the Reformation

It is the heart that perceives God and not the reason.

Blaise Pascal, *Pensées*

Thunder forth thy Lightening-bolt, and disperse my worldly thoughts…Turn my senses unto thee, O my dear Father, and make me to forget all earthly things.

John Colet, *Daily devotions*

Before he was governor of the Massachusetts Bay Colony, John Winthrop grew up among the landed gentry in Sussex. Trained in the law like his father, Winthrop inherited the family home at Groton Manor in 1613 and spent the next several years as a typical, puritan gentleman. Like others among the godly, Winthrop kept a detailed journal of his spiritual life, offering some valuable insights into the interior devotions of a lay, educated puritan. In February 1616, shortly after the death of his first wife Mary, Winthrop recorded a spiritual struggle that he endured following a trip to London. After returning from his trip, which was itself filled with spiritual enrichment and blessing, Winthrop bemoaned the fact that he quickly adopted an 'appetite' for 'earthly things'.[1] His backslide into temptation was followed by 'a light ague', which afflicted him with a lethargy toward prayer and devotion, a tedium persisting for several days. Finally, after reading two popular devotional writers and speaking with a close friend about his spiritual state, Winthrop was inspired by God to read some of the love letters that he and Mary Winthrop had written to one another during their courtship.

Echoing Paul's vision of the third heaven, Winthrop wrote that this was a 'sweet meditation of the presence and power of the Holy Ghost', which 'I am not able to express the understanding which God gave me in this heavenly matter'.[2] It is unclear whether Winthrop was unable to put into words 'the understanding' or if he thought he was prohibited from expressing it. Either way, he shared what he could. Winthrop described an overwhelming love for Christ that 'brought' him

---

[1] John Winthrop, 'Experientia', *Winthrop Papers* (Boston, 1929), 197.
[2] Winthrop, 'Experientia', 196.

Experiencing God in Late Medieval and Early Modern England. David J. Davis, Oxford University Press.
© David J. Davis 2022. DOI: 10.1093/oso/9780198834137.003.0005

in to suche a heavenly meditation of the love betweene Christ and me, as ravished my heart with unspeakable ioye…I desired no other happinesse but to be
embraced of him; I held nothing so deere that I was not willing to parte with for
him; I forgatt to looke after my supper, and some vaine things that my heart lin-
gered after.[3]

Winthrop's experience fits into the larger discourse of ravishment discussed in
previous chapters. Not only did he undergo physical and spiritual trials before-
hand, but also Winthrop believed that the Holy Spirit was the agent of this experience. Winthrop's description emphasized the neglect, and dissociation, he had for
his physical body, not even desiring food. What Winthrop described was not
entirely unique among English Protestants, particularly those of a puritanical
leaning, even though the intensity and sensuality of the account may ring dis-
cordantly with our contemporary notions of puritan culture. The basic framework that informed the *raptus* of medieval contemplatives gave shape to much of
the devotional literature, Protestant and Catholic, of the sixteenth and seventeenth centuries.

Keeping in mind the important differences that Alec Ryrie describes between
Protestant and Catholic meditative practices, this chapter explores the similarities
in how the language of *raptus* was appropriated in English devotion, across the
different confessional divides.[4] One major difference between late medieval and
early modern usage of *raptus* is just how much more prolific and widespread the
discourse was in the sixteenth and seventeenth centuries. This chapter charts the
adoption of divine rapture as a means of speaking about revelation in more popular works of devotion and personal piety. Practical books on prayer and spiritual
praxis, across a variety of confessional camps, placed the discourse of divine revelation at the heart of sincere meditation and devotion, encouraging their readers
toward an experience that was, at least in certain respects, commensurate with
the biblical prophets. These works not only borrowed the basic terminology of
raptus and ravishment, but also developed corresponding descriptions of the
early modern Christian's prayer life that reflected key biblical experiences. Here,
we will examine some of the more popular works of prayer and devotion in
England following the Reformation, cutting as wide a swathe as possible across
the terrain of devotional literature. While commentaries and sermons were often
only printed a handful of times, private devotionals occupied a much greater per-
centage of what early modern readers could access, as many devotional titles were
printed dozens of times over several decades, flooding the public sphere with
accounts, practical meditations, and exhortations for people to desire divine
revelation.

---

[3] Winthrop, 'Experientia', 202.   [4] Ryrie, *Being Protestant*, 113–14.

Praying for *Raptus*

Winthrop's account of his reliance upon devotional books to assuage his spiritual anxiety is one example of the importance of such works in many people's lives.[5] Readers annotated their favourite books of prayer and devotion. They expressed displeasure with authors and passages by crossing them out. They lavishly decorated their most treasured volumes with elaborate bindings and jewellery, removing and inserting illustrations, and binding different devotional works together into a single volume.[6] For example, one seventeenth-century reader of Julian of Norwich's *XVI Revelations of Divine Love* extensively marked up the book, not only identifying relevant biblical verses, but also correcting the text and even offering mild criticism of Julian.[7]

One of the more important of these devotional books, at least in English Protestant circles, came from the Suffolk minister Joseph Hall, the future Bishop of Exeter and Norwich. Although Hall's *The arte of diuine meditation* (1606) was not a bestseller, it exerted incredible influence by providing 'a comprehensive theory of meditation for an English-speaking Protestant audience' and introducing seventeenth-century readers to late medieval and continental devotional writers.[8] According to Ian Green, 'no other vision of prayer came near to having the same degree of penetration' into Protestant devotion as these 'collections of supplementary prayers'.[9]

In Hall's devotional, readers could get practical advice on the times and places for meditation, mental exercises to strengthen one's meditative abilities, as well as different set devotions and prayers. Hall described meditation as the means by which 'we are rauished with blessed Paul into Paradise; and see that heauen which we are loath to leaue, which we cannot utter'. Meditation, he went on to say, was not intended only for 'hidden Cloysterers' who were bent on 'nothing but contemplation'. Even though he cites medieval monastic authorities, like Bernard of Clairvaux, Hall thought of meditation as 'the pastime of [all] Saints' and 'the best improvement of Christianitie', regardless of whether they led an active or contemplative life.[10] *The arte of diuine meditation* prescribed a disciplined regimen of

---

[5] For an exhaustive catalogue documenting the popularity of Protestant devotional works, see Green, *Print and Protestantism*.

[6] Alexandra Walsham, 'Jewels for Gentlewomen', in *The Church and the Book* (Woodbridge, 2004), 123–42; Anthony Wells-Cole, *Art and Decoration in Elizabethan and Jacobean England* (New Haven, CT, 1997); David Cressy, 'Books as Totems in Seventeenth-Century England and New England', *Journal of Library History*, 21 (1986), 92–106. As William Sherman has demonstrated, the bindings remained a cherished location for personalizing religious books, even using traditional iconography: *Used Books* (Philadelphia, 2008), 71–86.

[7] Julian of Norwich, *XVI Revelations of Divine Love* (1670), Huntington Library copy, call# 482732.

[8] Ryrie, *Being Protestant*, 114.   [9] Green, *Print and Protestantism*, 277.

[10] Hall, *The arte*, 24, 4.

98   EXPERIENCING GOD IN LATE MEDIEVAL & EARLY MODERN ENGLAND

daily meditation to prepare people for spiritual ascent because 'profane' feet cannot climb the 'hill of Meditation'.[11]

Even before Hall's book, the language of divine rapture was evident in Protestant devotional writing. *The pomaunder of prayer* by Thomas Becon described the 'heauenly life' of devotion as one in which 'am I rauished and rapt with thy loue with the ardaunt desire of the...remembrace of thee'.[12] Other examples engaged both the literary and visual modes of ravishment discourse, providing the reader with images with which to inspire their devotion. The influential printer John Daye issued two books attributed to St. Augustine. *Certaine select prayers* went through five editions in fifteen years, and it recommended readers recite the following: 'my whole spirite being kindled with desire to see thee, findeth it selfe rauished with thel oue of things inuisible'.[13] Alongside this prayer, and every other in the collection, Daye printed small woodcuts of biblical saints kneeling in prayer, gazing up at the Tetragrammaton. Similarly, the layman Thomas Bentley tailored his *The monument of matrones* toward female readers, decorating his compendium of prayers and meditations with similar illustrations of women kneeling in prayer. In one of these prayers, Bentley wrote:

O most mightie God,...do thou O father of light, from whome all good gifts doo come and proceede, vouchsafe to powre downe plentifullie of thy principall spirit vpon me, and so rauish my hart with the flame of the loue of thee and thy people, & with an earnest zeale of thy house.[14]

Other works provided contemporary examples of people's ravishing experiences with the Holy Spirit. One seventeenth-century bestseller, Philip Stubbes's *A cristal glasse for Christian women*, described the spiritual exercises of Philip's late wife Katherine. To commemorate Katherine's pious life, her husband wrote that her 'whole heart' continuously 'bent to seeke the Lord', meditating constantly upon the scriptures. More than once, Philip wrote, Katherine was 'rauished with the same spirit that Dauid was', during her daily devotions, directly associating his wife's experience with that of psalmist's.[15] Outside of her private devotions, Katherine regularly discussed scripture, extolling other people to speak and act in a godly manner, remaining in all situations a paragon of grace and integrity. At Katherine's death, Stubbes describes her as smiling because she saw 'a vision of the ioyes of heauen, and the glory that I shal go too', which she afterward

---

[11] Hall, *The arte*, 49.   [12] Thomas Becon, *The pomaunder of prayer* (1561), sigs. 94v–95r.
[13] Augustine, *Certaine select prayers* (1574), sig. N7r.
[14] Bentley, *The monument of matrones*, 271. For more on Bentley's book see e.g., Patrick Collinson, *Elizabethan Essays* (1994), 104–5; John N. King, *Tudor Royal Iconography* (Princeton, NJ, 1989), 243–56.
[15] Philip Stubbes, *A cristal glasse* (1592), sig. A2v. Thirty editions of Stubbes's pamphlet were printed between 1591 and 1688.

described to him.[16] It is important to note, however, that Philip never details what Katherine experienced during her divine ravishings. His account, and perhaps what Katherine explicitly reported to Philip, remained abstract ('the glory') and generic ('ioyes of heauen'). Unlike medieval contemplatives, Protestant, and particularly puritan, accounts of *raptus* tended to avoid detailing any specific sights, sounds, etc.

Another important difference between some Protestant practices and the Catholic tradition of ravishment that Katherine's biography highlights is the safe space that the deathbed, or sickbed, seems to provide for Protestant accounts. While Catholic contemplatives could experience divine *raptus* following a serious illness, Protestants often experienced such things while they lay dying. Thus, the vicar of Preston (before he was ejected in 1662 for nonconformity) Isaac Ambrose recorded that Edward Gee (a presbyterian minister in north England) experienced a deathbed 'ravishing', which filled Gee with such 'heavenly joys as, I thought, his heart could hold'.[17] Again, Gee, via Ambrose, did not report any particular message or vision from God. Rather, such Protestant examples spoke of receiving a kind of understanding that activated a variety of emotional responses, which ran across a spectrum from consolation and joy to dread and fear of divine judgment.

At the same time, we can see a similar de-emphasis upon the content of divine revelation during *raptus* in early modern Catholic devotionals. The very successful *Of prayer and meditation* written by the Spanish Dominican Luis de Granada (Grenada) generally avoided discussing divine visions and voices, even though Granada encouraged people in their desire for ravishment. Printed in at least a dozen editions between 1582 and 1634, Granada focused upon many of the practical issues of meditation and ravishment. The 'place of praier', he wrote, is 'that misticall ladder that Iacob sawe, which ioyneth heauen with the earthe...and men doe ascende vnto almightie God'.[18] The illustrations of the English edition printed in Paris emphasized connections between Christ and those that follow him.[19] The title page depicted men and women dressed in monastic robes following Christ, all carrying crosses, suggesting that one need not join a holy order to enter into contemplative living. Similarly, Gaspar Loarte's *Instructions and advertisements* tended to be much more instructional in the virtues and means of meditative practice, rather than descriptive of the things one might experience during

---

[16] Stubbes, *A cristal glasse*, sig. A4v.

[17] Isaac Ambrose, *War with Devils* (4th edn, 1769), 168.

[18] Luis de Granada, *Of prayer and meditation* (Paris, 1582), sig. 97r. The fact that eight of these editions were printed in London, and among several different printers, speaks to both its popularity and acceptability in England. Copies of *Of prayer* can be found across the religious spectrum, in the private libraries of recusants like Thomas Tresham as well as Protestants like Edward Pearson, the churchwarden of Howden (Yorkshire) (PLRE).

[19] These included Christ washing the disciples' feet, the Last Supper, the Crucifixion, the *pietà*, as well as contemporary illustrations of the Catholic mass: Davis, *Seeing Faith, Printing Pictures*, 81–94.

ravishment. Although the text began with St. Dominic's vision of the Virgin, Loarte tended to describe the devotional virtue of meditation, 'as a mirror, wherein, by eftsons lookyng & taking view, we may with the eies of our soule see'.[20] Stories like the Annunciation of the Virgin, the Virgin's visit to her cousin Elizabeth, and Jesus in the Garden of Gethsemane, along with scriptures like Mary's *magnificat* (that 'most mystical' prayer), should be foremost in the reader's mind.[21]

It is important to note here what other scholars have already attended to: the intersections between Protestant and Catholic devotional literature during this period. Scholars have long recognized the debt that English Protestant devotional writings owed to the Catholic tradition. One important example of this is Edmund Bunny's Protestant revision of the Jesuit priest Robert Parsons's *The First Booke of the Christian Exercise*. Although much has been made of Bunny's edits, Bunny kept several passages pertaining to the discourse of *raptus*.[22] After rigorously stripping the soul of sin and temptation, the 'accomplishment and perfection of all happiness', according to Bunny, is 'called by deuines Visio Dei beatifica'. This beatific vision of God, as Richard Baxter wrote in 1650, is where the soul finds fulfilment and rest, where the devout reader is 'rauished' and what is experienced is 'glasse to our eyes: music to our eares: hony, to our mouthes: most sweet and pleasant balme...light, to our understanding'.[23] Then, Bunny followed immediately with a warning against any works-based theology that might convince the reader that such experiences are proof of salvation.

Another important example of this Catholic-Protestant intersection, and a model that Bunny followed in his editing, is Thomas Rogers's translation of Thomas Kempis's *Of the imitation of Christ*. Rogers, an Elizabethan minister, was not timid in his editing for a reformed readership (first published in 1580), even to the point of removing the entire fourth book on Purgatory.[24] In book two, Rogers's translation reads, 'If thou canst not meditate on deepe and heauenlie mysteries, rest thy self in the paines of Christ, and abide willinglie in his wounds...healthful wounds, and stripes of Christ'. Spiritually weak readers could find solace in a basic meditation on the Passion, while the devout reader was encouraged to pursue a more significant encounter: 'I saie the true spiritual man, which is voide of inordinate desires, and loueth Iesus unfeinedlie, can both turn himselfe freelie vnto God, and rauished in spirit aboue himselfe, quietlie enioie him'.[25]

[20] Gaspar Loarte, *Instructions and advertisements* (1597), sig. A1r.
[21] Loarte, *Instructions and advertisements*, f. 17r.
[22] Brad S. Gregory, 'The "True and Zealouse Service of God"', *Journal of Ecclesiastical History*, 45 (1994), 238–68.
[23] Edmund Bunny, *A book of Christian exercise* (1586), 131–2.
[24] Elizabeth Hudson, 'English Protestants and the *imitatio Christi*, 1580–1620', *Sixteenth Century Journal* 19 (1988), 541–58; Green, *Print and Protestantism*, 306.
[25] Thomas Kempis, *Of the imitation of Christ* (1580), 72, 74.

'A LOVE-TOKEN OF CHRIST TO THE SOUL' 101

Despite the spiritual passion that runs through Kempis's book, there is something particularly cerebral in his meditative style. The emphasis is on quiet meditation, dismissing any rude noises or frenetic gestures. Rogers would have identified such infelicities with papist mysticism, but the truth is that he would have been echoing criticisms that were outlined by late medieval texts like the *Cloud of Unknowing* and *The chastysing of goddess children*. In book three, Kempis's emphasis reaches its most prescriptive, saying,

> blessed are the eares, which listen not to the outward sound…Blessed are the eies which are close from seeing outward…Blessed are they who pierce vnto spiritual things, and prepare themselues more and more dailie meditations to come vnto the knowledge of Gods heauenlie mystieries.[26]

Interestingly, the disassociation of the soul from the body during divine *raptus* was preceded by a silencing of the bodily senses. Certainly, part of this silencing might require the use of the senses to gaze upon memorials of revelation, to read particular scriptures, or to listen to sermons on the Sabbath; however, the goal was to move, or be moved by God, beyond these 'dailie meditations'.[27]

From these early works, then, it is perhaps not surprising that seventeenth-century devotionals did not diminish the language of divine rapture/ravishment, although it is a rapture that emphasises restraint, in certain respects. One of the most frequently printed books in Stuart England, Arthur Dent's *The plaine-mans pathway to heauen* (1601), connected the idea of spiritual ravishment with the Calvinist doctrine of election. While anti-Calvinists attacked what they saw as a brutal, even deterministic, view of salvation, Dent assured his readers that God's election provided the godly 'strength and comfort', for it is 'the banner of Christs loue displaied vpon her, forthwith she was rapt and inflamed with a desire for him'.[28] In other words, the doctrine freed the soul to experience ravishment more easily, without the inhibiting fears surrounding one's salvation. Similarly, another popular source of spiritual solace was the collection of prayers *The garden of spiritual flowers*. *The garden* instructed, 'let thy heart be taken up' on the Sabbath. Later on, the soul is described as having 'fiery winges sublime', so that it can 'Mount to the throne'.[29] As discussed in Chapter 2, the Sabbath provided a useful context for Protestants to advocate for contemplative practices. Thus, Lewis Bayly in *The practise of piety* required a cessation from work on the Sabbath in order for

---

[26] Kempis, *Of the imitation*, 110–11.

[27] It is also worth noting that the contemplative tradition that Kempis represents, and seems to have attracted Protestants like Rogers, strongly discouraged people from working themselves into an ecstatic state. A seventeenth-century Jesuit example of this restraining advice is Robert Bellarmine: Bellarmine, *Jacob's Ladder*, 211.

[28] Arthur Dent, *Plaine-mans pathway to heauen* (1607), 299.

[29] Anon., *Garden of spirituall flowers* (1609), sigs. F4v, I2v.

102 EXPERIENCING GOD IN LATE MEDIEVAL & EARLY MODERN ENGLAND

God to ravish the soul: 'For our studie must be, *to bee rauished in spirit vpon the Lords day*. In a word, Thou must on that day cease in thy calling to doe thy worke: that the Lord by his calling, may doe *his* worke in thee'. Bayly went on to link divine ravishment to humanity's *telos*: 'blisseful and glori|ous obiect of all intellectuall, and reasonable creatures in heauen, is the God-head'. This experience was 'a beatificall vision of God', very much like the one Moses had when he encountered the burning bush.[30]

It is difficult to know what early modern readers would have expected or anticipated in regard to their own devotional lives. Did they anticipate a beatific vision or an experience with God commensurate with Moses, David, or Paul? The accounts of those who reported such an experience were a self-selecting bunch, representing a small minority of the larger reading public. However, as we have seen already, *raptus* was no longer considered an experience reserved only for prophets, hermits, and contemplatives. It had practical application for the average Christian, Protestant and Catholic. Thus, Lorenzo Scupoli's popular *The spiritual conflict* identified divine revelation as the ultimate weapon against sin, going so far as to encourage people to 'use violence to thy selfe, and vanquish thine own affections' in order to prepare themselves. While only God could 'expel this darkness from my soul, drive off these clouds from my understanding', a person could situate themselves appropriately.[31] Similarly, Joseph Hall instructed people to develop a longing for a 'perpetual rauishment of spirit, till beeing freed from this clog of earth', because in 'rauishment' the soul is united to Christ, which was the *telos* of a person's faith, and this union could be found in different degrees within the everyday lives of the believer. Such unions included those found in the corporate worship of the members of the church (the body of Christ) as well as participation in communion.[32]

The rest of this chapter charts the emphasis upon spiritual unification in the context of divine revelation in both Protestant and Catholic contexts. Looking at different examples of divine ravishment in scripture and the history of the church encouraged a camaraderie with Christians of ages past. Second, early modern Englishwomen and men were encouraged to meditate upon the unification of the mystical Bride (the Church) and the Bridegroom (Christ), particularly as represented in the Canticles. Finally, the sacrament of communion offered one of the

---

[30] Lewis Bayly, *The practise of piety* (1613), 565, 186–7. Among private libraries of the time, Bayly's book far outstrips many of the other popular devotionals, with sixteen different copies in various collections (PLRE).

[31] Lorenzo Scupoli, *The Christian pilgrime* (Paris, 1652), I.8, II.5. See also Gaspar Loarte, *The exercise of a christian life* (1579), 33–4; de Granada, *Of prayer*, sig. 296r.

[32] Joseph Hall, *Holy Raptures* (1654), 160; Ryrie, *Being Protestant*, 90. See also Joseph Hall, *The devovt soul* (1650), 69, 112, 130. Far from being a people isolated to their prayer closets, recent scholarship has attended to the fact that English Protestants were people of corporate devotion, wary of the dangers lurking in spiritual seclusion: see e.g., *Private and Domestic Devotion in Early Modern Britain*, eds Jessica A. Martin and Alec Ryrie (Abingdon, 2016).

most regulated opportunities to remember and reflect upon the unification of all three—the individual, the body of Christ, and Christ—which was very often framed in the language of *raptus*.

The Union of All Believers

In March 1555, the London weaver Thomas Tomkins was tortured by Bishop Edmund Bonner for his Protestant beliefs. According to John Foxe, Bonner burned Tomkins's hand to give him a taste of what the heretical pyre, as well as his subsequent eternal damnation, would feel like. However, Bonner's twisted plans were foiled by divine *raptus*, as Foxe explained, '[Tomkins] reported...that his spirit was so Rapt vp, that he felt no payne. In the which burning he neuer shronke, till ye vaines shronke and the synewes brast, and the water did spyrt into M. Harpesfieldes face'.[33] To spare Tomkins, God rapt him in the spirit, cutting him off from the torments of his physical body, allowing him to experience heavenly joy.

Such stories of people who experienced divine *raptus* at crucial moments were important in early modern religious discourse. People who suffered for true faith were among the more powerful models for godly behavior, and their stories encouraged, exhorted, comforted, and terrorized readers. They were not merely fodder for sermons and puritan polemic to chastise ungodliness; stories of the martyrs were common reading in devotional and contemplative contexts.[34] The ejected minister Thomas Mall's *The great cloud of witnesses* (1664) abbreviated such accounts from various martyrologies into just over two hundred octavo pages. In his introductory 'To the Reader', Mall invited his readers to 'converse' with those individuals who have accomplished 'rare exploits of Faith...before being swallowed up in the beatifical vision'.[35] For Mall, and other martyrologists, these stories had the power to unify the early modern reader with other members of the historical church in a kind of vicarious experience in which one could imagine themselves alongside heroes of their faith. The stories did not necessarily instruct people to follow the martyr's footsteps into physical torment but rather reminded readers that other people who shared their beliefs had suffered, willingly and bravely. Also, the stories inspired people to godly living, as well as providing certain assurances of what people believed to be true, as the experience of divine ravishment marked the martyrs, along with the devout reader, as members of the household of God (see Figure 12).

---

[33] John Foxe, *Actes and monuments* (1570), 1750.

[34] See e.g., *Martyrs and Martyrdom in England, 1400–1700*, eds Thomas S. Freeman and Thomas F. Mayer (Rochester, NY, 2007); Brad S. Gregory, *Salvation at Stake* (Cambridge, MA, 1999); Ryrie, *Being Protestant*, esp. 422–7.

[35] Thomas Mall, *A cloud of witnesses* (1665), sig. A6v.

104 EXPERIENCING GOD IN LATE MEDIEVAL & EARLY MODERN ENGLAND

Thus, Joseph Hall pointed his readers to the example of the apostle Stephen's martyrdom in Acts, as both a model and a focus of meditation, explaining that devout readers 'could be rapt vp thither in desire' in the same manner as the first Christian martyr.[36] In a Paul's Cross sermon on Easter Sunday 1593, the preacher Thomas Playfere told the crowd that the church father St. Ignatius went boldly 'to his martyrdome', so overcome with a love for Christ that he 'was so strangly rauished with this delight'. Similar examples, like the second-century martyr Blandina, who was gored by a bull, gave reassurance to early modern people suffering for Christ, because she felt no pain 'so filled [was she] with ravishing joys of the Holy Ghost…during all her torments'.[37] While many writers considered one such example sufficient to make the point clear, the ejected minister Christopher Ness seemed committed to including everyone in scripture who experienced divine ravishment. Ness's book *A Christians walk and work* referenced many of the popular examples as well as more obscure prophets like Malachi and Amos. Repeatedly in the text, Ness drew direct parallels between biblical models and the life of the early modern Christian. Thus, he commended readers that it was 'your duty and priviledg to take a few turns daily' at 'Divine Contemplation', by meditating upon the lives and deaths of Christ's first followers. In this practice, Ness encouraged people to be 'an Anchorite' on the Sabbath following Moses, who was 'ravished in Spirit all the 40 days he conversed with God'.[38] However, the anchoritic mindset was not meant to be a permanent one. Pointing to King David, whose active life prohibited him from full-time contemplation, Ness believed that being 'ravished in Spirit' in times of meditation along with the psalmist was much more appealing than being trapped inside a monastery.[39]

Although James Harrington's *Horae Consecretae* was written in a context of isolation and seems to be a work for private devotion, the idea of being united with rest of the body of Christ runs throughout the book. Relatively unattended to in contemporary scholarship on devotion, Harrington was a Parliamentarian soldier during the civil war as well as the third baronet of Ridlington. Following the Restoration, he was stripped of his lands and title, and after being exiled, Harrington found comfort in the knowledge that 'the whole mystical body of Christ…and every Member thereof, is said to be *joyned to the Lord, and is one Spirit*…as by an unmeasurable, and everlasting Ligament'.[40] This everlasting link to the rest of the body of Christ extended to the biblical prophets, whom Harrington found to be ideal models for his own devotion. In the *Horae*, he expressed a desire for ravishment 'with holy Stephen' and elsewhere 'let me with holy Paul' go up into the third heaven.[41] He asked God to 'make me a second

---

[36] Hall, *The arte*, 160.
[37] Thomas Playfere, *Hearts delight* (1603), 54; Samuel Clarke, *A generall martyrologie* (1660), 44.
[38] Christopher Ness, *A Christians walk* (1678), 45.   [39] Ness, *A Christians walk*, 210.
[40] James Harrington, *Horae Consecretae* (1682), 179.
[41] Harrington, *Horae Consecretae*, 72, 175.

Elias', and like John and Peter, he longed for 'ravishing and transporting' that would nourish his understanding and bless his affections.[42] Harrington does not expect a new revelation, clarifying several times that such visions and extra-biblical knowledge were ceased, but he does speak of desiring an experience with God similar to those of the biblical prophets. However, unlike other puritans (e.g. Richard Baxter), Harrington does not frame his understanding of such heavenly experiences in the context of the soul's rest but rather in a context of being perfected. For him, even the physical senses will undergo a perfection, allowing them to experience the wonders of heaven even more clearly.[43] Finally, it is important to note that Harrington believed ravishment comes in various forms. Love, music, intellectual apprehension—all can ravish the soul, and the soul seems to have the power to ravish itself in a way. Nevertheless, it is clear in the text when Harrington is speaking of the kind of divine *raptus* that only God can initiate.[44]

Although Catholics had their own bevy of martyrs and martyrologies, their models for rapturous devotion came more from the large congregation of saints at their disposal. In England by 1580, a great deal of the material evidence of the cult of the saints had been erased by iconoclastic zealots; however, the cultural presence of the cults remained strong into the seventeenth century in Catholics who celebrated the lives of ancient and more recent saints. In his *Exercise*, Loarte offered up the seventh-century Greek saint John Climacus's account of 'a religious man, whom he both saw and knew...[who] was in such sort rauished in spirite, as he saw the dreadful rigour, and such thinges as passe in the time of judgement, and doome of euery soule'[45] The Jesuit work *Fuga saeculi* pointed to St. Anthony and St. Bernard who had experienced numerous moments of *raptus*. The Jesuit writer Henry Hawkins celebrated the life of the thirteenth-century St. Elizabeth of Hungary, daughter of King Andrew II, who spent most of her life 'alwayes dig-ging in the wounds of her Sauiour in his Passion, where shee attayned at last the highest points of Contemplation, and was frequently rapt in spirit'.[46] The English Catholic College at Douai printed a new translation of St. Catherine of Siena's life in 1609, and then in 1621, the Catholic community at St. Omer published an English version of St. Catherine of Bologna's life and visions. A subsequent edi-tion in the next year included a translation of Marcos de Lisboa's life of St. Clare, which exhorted readers that on Maunday Thursday, Clare was 'so absorpt and rapt out of herselfe, that her eyes being open and without motion, she...remained so insensible, being conioyntly crucifyed with Iesus Christ'.[47]

---

[42] Harrington, *Horae Consecratae*, 164, 155.

[43] See e.g. Hans Boersma, *Seeing God* (Grand Rapids, MI, 2019), 329. One of Harrington's more sustained comments on this perfection is *Horae Consecretae*, 209–20.

[44] Harrington, *Horae Consecretae*, 69, 74, 81.   [45] Loarte, *The exercise*, f. 157v.

[46] Giovanni Pietro Maffei, *Fuga saeculi* (St. Omer, 1632), 196, 304; Henry Hawkins, *The history of S. Elizabeth* (Rouen, 1632), 361.

[47] Clare of Assisi, *The Rule of...S. Clare* (St. Omer, 1621), 101, 105–8; Lisboa de Marcos, *The life of...S. Clare* (St. Omer, 1622), 104.

More contemporary examples of the ravishing of saints also were on offer. Several different lives of St. Francis Xavier were printed in St. Omer, retelling Francis's raptures during his times of contemplation.[48] The seventeenth century Carmelite contemplative Caterina de' Pazzi (Mary Magdalene de' Pazzi) received a series of contemplative revelations, which were recorded by her confessor Vincenzo Puccini. His book was translated by the English College at Saint-Omer, and the book was dedicated to Lady Mary Percy, abbess of a Benedictine monastery in the southern Netherlands. During an extended illness on May 27, 1584, 'the morning of the most holy Trinity', Caterina, 'was rapt into heauenly contemplations'. During this rapture, Pazzi underwent a beatific vision where she first was physically healed, and then in each of the subsequent forty days she 'receaued the food of Angells, the same wonder was seene; she remaining abstracted from her senses, and immersed in diuine contemplations'.[49] Importantly, a significant difference between these models and most of the Protestant examples we explore in this book is that the accounts of the Catholic saints regularly detailed what was seen and heard during their divine experiences. Beyond the analogical and affectionate language that speaks of the glories of heaven and the overwhelming emotions that accompany such divine encounters, Catholic accounts seem much less tongue-tied in describing precisely what the individual perceived.

One of the more important exceptions to this difference was Father Augustine Baker's *Sancta Sophia*, which synthesized much of the earlier Catholic contemplative literature. Baker stressed the individual pursuit of an encounter with God, outlining what was certainly by this time a well-worn regimen of mortification, solitude, and devotion (reading and prayer). It was only 'By meanes of a continuall conuersation' with God, Baker wrote, that contemplatives could reach 'an absolute, internall solitude, a Transcendency & forgetfulness of all created things, and especially of them selues'.[50] His views on ravishment, however, are not nearly as clean cut. Not only does he conflate ecstasies and raptures, both of which he described as more sensual than rational, but also like some earlier contemplative writers, Baker seems more concerned with discerning the experience's legitimacy. Rather than elaborate on the experience of divine ravishment, he instead sets out twelve 'rules' for discerning whether or not an experience is actually from God.[51]

Perhaps the other significant figure who looms large over English Catholic contemplative thought in the seventeenth century is Hugh Paulinus (Serenus) Cressy. In a thirty-year career as a Catholic priest, Cressy became responsible for the preservation of large portions of the late medieval English contemplative

---

[48] See Orazio Torsellino, *The admirable life of S. Francis Xavier* (St. Omer, 1632), 256.

[49] Vincenzio Puccini, *The life of the holy and venerable mother Suor Maria Maddalena De Patsi* (St. Omer, 1619), 22–3. See also Francisco de Losa, *The life of Gregorie Lopes* (Paris, 1638), 111.

[50] Augustin Baker, *Sancta Sophia* (Doway, 1657), sig. C3v. For more on Baker see Temple, *Mysticism*, 21–32.

[51] Baker, *Sancta Sophia*, 265–72.

tradition, providing an important point of union between contemporary and past devotees. Cressy became popular not only with English Catholics at home and abroad but also with Protestant sectarian groups who latched on to writers like Julian of Norwich.[52] Cressy was responsible for editions of both Walter Hilton's and Norwich's writings. Cressy dedicated the 1670 edition of Julian of Norwich to Lady Mary Blount, a powerful Catholic aristocrat in Worcestershire who promoted Catholic literary culture. In his letter to Lady Blount, he summarized the purpose of such examples of ravishing piety:

> afford Her a place in your Closet,...you will enjoy her Saint-like Conversation...She recounts to you the Wonders of our Lords Love to Her, and of his Grace in Her. And being thus employed, I make no doubt but you will be sensible of many Beams of her Lights, and much warmth of her Charity, by reflection darted into your own Soul.[53]

Evidence of handwritten marginal notes suggests that such advice was taken to heart, at least by some readers. Whether in prayer closets or in sitting rooms, such accounts of divine revelation were 'darted' into the souls of devout readers, with the intent, at least in part, to unify them and their devotional practice with past and present saints and martyrs.[54]

Uniting the Bride and the Bridegroom

On May 20, 1641, the minister Isaac Ambrose was:

> cast...into a spiritual, heavenly ravishing love-trance;...[in which he] tasted the goodnesse of God, the very sweetness of Christ, and was filled with the joys of the Spirit above measure...a love-token of Christ to the Soul, a kisse of his mouth whose love is better than wine.[55]

From Bernard of Clairvaux and Bonaventure to seventeenth-century Calvinists, religious writers seized upon the mystical union of the Bride of Christ and the Bridegroom to express divine ravishment in terms that were both amorous and

---

[52] Temple, *Mysticism*, 122–7.

[53] Serenus Cressy, 'To his most Honoured Lady', in Norwich, *XVI revelations*, sig. A2v.

[54] For example, beside one of Julian's ravishments, the reader of the Huntington Library copy, call # 482732, commented in the margin 'Oh! Sweet Love! Eternal Prayse': Norwich, *XVI Revelations*, 57.

[55] Isaac Ambrose, *Media* (1657), 183, see also 214, 465, 499–500. For a thorough assessment of Ambrose's theology see Tom Schwanda, *Soul Recreation* (Eugene, OR, 2012), 166–96. In his three-volume devotional, *Prima, Media, and Ultima*, Ambrose provided readers numerous instances of heavenly raptures.

108 EXPERIENCING GOD IN LATE MEDIEVAL & EARLY MODERN ENGLAND

overwhelming.[56] For Ambrose, Christ's kiss was better than wine and no other experience measured up to being ravished by the Holy Spirit in such a manner.

The covenantal union of the church (Bride) and Christ (Bridegroom), alluded to by Ambrose's comment about the 'love-token', was referenced several times in the New Testament, and for both Catholics and Protestants, this mystical marriage was understood to be analogous to human marriage. In *Of prayer*, Granada explained, 'This heauenlie bridegrome desired also, to be loued of his spouse, with a passing great loue, and therefore he ordained this diuine misticall morsel...worthie to be engraued euen in the innermost parte of our hartes'.[57] Loarte's *Exercise* begged Christ to 'burn me', so that he may be 'perfectly united' to the Bridegroom in the bedchamber.[58] Likewise, from the early reformers on, the imagery of Christ as the Bridegroom inhabited an important space in Protestantism. Theodore Beza's sermons on the Canticles elaborated on the bridal relationship saying that even while on earth the bride will be 'rauished with the consideration & contemplation of those heauenly blessings, as if they were already dwelling in, and inhabiting the heauens'. Comparing every Christian's experience with that of Paul's visions of the third heaven, Beza went on to say, 'we should cry out at this most high, most great, and most profound secret of secrets'.[59] Thomas Playfere referred to God as 'our heauenly husband', explaining that we should 'set God alwaies before our eyes, and not once look aside, or be enamored with any gaud of worldly glorie, but despise euery blaze of beautie whatsoeuer' that would distract us from him. Then, working himself up into an agitated pitch, 'why are we not euen nowe, in the name of God, inflamed with the loue of God: and wholly rauished with delight in the Lord?'[60]

The spiritual affections, discussed in Chapter 2, were critical in the deployment of such marriage imagery. More than many other contexts of divine revelation, the union of the Bride and Bridegroom conjured up sensual and erotic overtones that reminded readers that these experiences were not merely intellectual. Arthur Dent pointed to the example of Mary Magdalene, when she was ravished in spirit for Christ, whose 'affections were kindled with the love and obedience of Christ'. Likewise, Hall explained that 'Gods Schoole is more Affection, than Vnderstanding', pointing to overwhelming sensations of joy and sorrow as typical examples of what people can encounter when they are moved by divine ravishment.[61] It was not that the intellectual faculties ('Vnderstanding') did not play a role, but rather that the education to which Hall refers went beyond what the understanding could grasp.

---

[56] Erica Longfellow, *Women and Religious Writing in Early Modern England* (Cambridge, 2004), 18–58; Elizabeth Clarke, *Politics, Religion, and the Song of Songs in Seventeenth-Century England* (2011).

[57] Granada, *Of prayer*, f. 60r.   [58] Loarte, *The exercise*, 442.

[59] Theodore Beza, *Master Bezaes sermons vpon...the canticle of canticles* (1587), 11, 30.

[60] Playfere, *Hearts delight*, 53, 57–8.   [61] Dent, *Plaine-mans pathway*, 299; Hall, *The arte*, 9.

The puritan minister Francis Rous's devotional *The Mystical Marriage* (1631) provides one of the most elaborate expositions of the marriage analogy written in English, serving as an example of how passionate the experience of divine ravishment could be. Much like Winthrop's account at the beginning of this chapter, Rous described a spiritual experience with God that was spiritual and sensual:

> Cleare vp thine eye, and fixe it on him as upon the fairest of men, the perfection of spirituall beautie, the treasure of heauenly joy, the true object of most fervent love, and inflamed affections: and accordingly fasten on him, not thine eye only, but they mightiest love, & hottest affections. Looke on him so that thou maist lust after him, for here it is a sinne, not to looke that thou maist lust, and not to lust hauing looked. For the spirit hath his lust also.

Only after someone had appropriately prepared themselves would Christ enter into 'the chambers of thy soule'.[62] The Christian is instructed to act ('Cleare', 'fixe', and 'fasten'), and the affections that are stirred here are every bit as visceral as the medieval contemplatives. Not only does Rous put forward a devotional that has all the passion of Richard Rolle, but he also crafts the metaphor of the marriage around his Calvinist doctrine, regularly returning his reader to the benefits of ravishment in the election of the godly: 'that she may cheerfully run the race, and performe the service set before her'.[63] The Bride of Christ is transported in such an 'extasie and ravishment', that 'she is too narrow and feeble to containe and beare a joy that is too large and strong for her; and therefore having filled her to the utmost capacity, it goes beyond and runnes over'.[64] Nor was it sufficient for Rous that divine ravishment occurred once or twice in a lifetime: 'Let her often goe out of the body, yea out of the world by heavenly contemplations...where her treasure, her joy, her beloved dwelleth'.[65] Although the true fulfillment of this uncontainable joy was delayed until the Bride and Bridegroom were permanently united in heaven, the godly, according to Rous, could experience a foretaste of the union through *raptus*.

Nor was this solely a puritan way of speaking about Christ within English Protestantism. The Arminian bishop John Cosin disagreed with Rous on several theological points; however, both men found the mystical Bride and Bridegroom to be a powerful site for devotional attention. In a prayer that was essentially a

---

[62] Rous, *The mystical marriage* (1631), 13–14. Robert Bolton made it clear that this lust should be distinguished from the lusts of the flesh, which he describes with the phrase 'the Siren's Song': Robert Bolton, *Instructions* (1631), 484–5.

[63] Rous, *The mystical marriage*, 64.

[64] Rous, *The mystical marriage*, 48. Ryrie has explored the theology of joy that Rous develops here, and the spiritual rapture that is concomitant with this joy is compared to bodily drunkenness (*Being Protestant*, 85–7). In the same passage, drunkenness that derives from wine is described as 'grosse, heavie, dull, and earthy', but the drunkenness of the Spirit is 'pure, piercing, and full of activity'.

[65] Rouse, *The mystical marriage*, 266–8.

wedding vow, Cosin wrote, 'Lord Jesu, I giue thee my bodie, my soule, my substance, my fame, my friends, my liberty, and my life: dispose of mee and of all that is mine, as it seemeth best to thee and to the glory of thy blessed Name'.[66] In this life, part of the believer's move toward the mystical marriage included an abandonment (or a willingness to abandon) anything that might interfere with the ultimate union of the Bride and Bridegroom. For Cosin, this was everything that was not Christ. Similarly, Bishop Cowper described an encounter with God as amorous: 'Sometime he will kisse vs, with the kisses of his mouth, and as it were, vvith the Apo|stle, *rauish vs vp to the third heauens'*. However, 'other times' are characterized by periods of spiritual purgation, even if that meant God 'casts downe his angry countenance vpon vs…and permits *Sathan also to buffet vs least wee should be exalted out of measure'*.[67] It would seem then that the preparation of the Bridegroom was not all affection and passion; it involved both the delights of ravishment and mourning over sin.[68]

Although the sexualized language latent within such devotional writing can make some people uncomfortable, the mystical Bride and Bridegroom were not completely dissociated from ideas about early modern marriage. Certainly, late medieval figures like Margery Kempe strictly delineated between the two relationships, even sacrificing her physical sexuality for a closer connection to Christ. However, as examples like Winthrop's remembrances of the desire he shared for his wife suggest, a person's human marriage and their mystical marriage could benefit one another. Erica Longfellow has demonstrated that these benefits included learning how to attend to human spouses with strength, humility, charity, and, most importantly, long-suffering.[69] Focusing upon Christ in devotion and preparing one's self for spiritual intimacy with him were habits that could translate into being a better spouse. Thus, the popular nonconformist minister Edward Reyner went so far as to celebrate the 'Conjugal relation' between man and woman because through sexual union people could 'promote the Communion of…souls with Christ'. Reyner exhorted his male readers to think of their relationship as the Bride of Christ, when their own wives needed more physical affection than they were interested in giving.[70] This kind of role-reversal was almost certainly more effort than many men would manage, but the ideal scenario Reyner set out (treating one marriage like the other) provides some insight into just how unambiguously real, and serious, the notion of the mystical marriage was. This union of the soul with Christ was no mere metaphor meant to console and exhort people to godly living.

---

[66] John Cosin, *A collection of priuate deuotions* (1627), 78.
[67] William Cowper, *The triumph of a Christian* (1608), 78–9.
[68] For more on the importance of spiritual mourning see Ryrie, *Being Protestant*, 49–59.
[69] Longfellow, *Women and Religious Writing*, 32–3.
[70] Edward Reyner, *Considerations concerning marriage* (1657), 41–2.

Finally, it is important to make note of the role that the language of space played in this context. Protestant reformers despised the cult of the saints and the worship of relics, but at the same time, the language of a sacred space and place is very much present in the devotional literature.[71] Even Calvin struggled in this regard. As Randall Zachman points out, Calvin sacrality was rooted in 'the ministry of the Church' (i.e. sermons, prayer, hymns, sacraments, etc.) not in any space or place, so sacredness could be found anywhere the Church was at work. At the same time, 'Calvin insists' the physical spaces of churches 'have the same kind of alluring beauty as did the Temple in Jerusalem'.[72]

Of course, for Catholics, the emphasis upon sacred space was much less problematic. Even after the Reformation, traditional worship at and of material sites continued, albeit more sporadically and often surreptitiously.[73] Despite the best Protestant efforts, shrines like Saint Winefride's Well in Holywell (Wales) continued to attract the faithful on pilgrimage to honour the seventh-century saint who was killed by her suitor Caradog. In the seventeenth century, the English Jesuit John Falconer pointed to Winifred's death as an example of mystical marriage because Winifred chose Christ as her husband over a mere man. Falconer recounted that Winifred meditated: 'through her eares to her soule, the vitall breath of his heauen|ly discourses…as in her spouses bed-chāber, raised by amourous thoughts of his wonderfull Perfections, and rapt with pure delights, freshly euery day communicated vnto her'.[74] The place where the holy saint offered herself up to God could become a place for anyone's ravishment, where the individual member of the Bride of Christ could meet with the Bridegroom.[75]

Communion as *Raptus*

Both the union of the members of the household of God and the mystical marriage of the Bride and Bridegroom were realized, to a certain degree, by regularly participating in the sacrament of communion. One of the most widely used illustrations in Restoration prayer books and bibles was 'The House of Prayer', depicting a group of clergy and laypeople kneeling in prayer, asking God for forgiveness ('Spare thy People O Lord') (Figure 16). This request was part of the regular

---

[71] Scholarship on Protestant worship spaces only has begun to scratch the surface of this topic. See e.g., Will Coster and Andrew Spicer, eds, *Sacred Space in Early Modern Europe* (Cambridge, 2005); Martin and Ryrie, eds, *Private and Domestic Devotion*. For avant-garde conformity see Fincham and Tyacke, *Altars Restored*, Ch. 3.

[72] Zachman, *Image and Word*, 346.

[73] Alexandra Walsham, *The Reformation of the Landscape* (Oxford, 2011), 264–7.

[74] John Falconer, *The admirable life of Saint VVenefride* (St. Omer, 1635), 31–2.

[75] Walsham, *Reformation of the Landscape*, 52. As Walsham describes here, the site became a Tudor 'dynastic icon' after the chapel was constructed by Lady Margaret Beaufort, which is possibly one of the reasons why it was never dismantled.

Figure 16. 'The House of Prayer' in *The Preaching Bible* (Cambridge: John Field, 1668). By permission of the Dunham Bible Museum, Houston Baptist University.

'A LOVE-TOKEN OF CHRIST TO THE SOUL' 113

Anglican liturgy, preceding the administration of the Lord's Supper, in which believers joined together with each other in the communal act of partaking in the body and blood of Christ. That the clouds open up above the people kneeling in prayer illustrates this heavenly union, as the faithful are drawn in spirit to the object of their devotion, and the reader is invited to join in this spiritual sight.

This association between communion and *raptus*, which brought the discourse of divine revelation into the normal progress of the Christian week, was also evident in popular devotional works. *The garden of spiritual flowers* encouraged people:

> let thine heart be rapt with heauenly meditation when thou seest the Bread and Wine deliuered, let thine heart within thee meditate so zealously and fervently vpon the Passion of our blessed Lord and Sauior for thy redemption, as if with thine own eyes thou didst then behold his bodie nayled on the Crosse and his precious blood shed for thy sake.[76]

The language here reflects Calvinist sacramental theology, which was predominant in much of English Protestantism. Calvin's conception of communion as a kind of *unio mystica* stressed that Christ remained in heaven during the sacrament, and the individual's soul ascended.[77] The unification of the members of the body of Christ with Christ in the celebration of communion was shot through with the fundamental language of spiritual ascent. Because of the centrality of the sacrament to the Christian faith, as Julie Canlis argues, the *unio mystica* offered an 'interpretative grid for the ongoing Christian life' in its entirety.[78]

This ordering was also important in Calvin's critique of the Catholic doctrine of transubstantiation. In the *Institutes of the Christian Religion*, Calvin explained, 'they think they only communicate with it [the body of Christ] if it descends into bread; but they do not understand the manner of descent by which he lifts us up to himself'.[79] A few sections later, he continued, 'they leave nothing to the secret working of the Spirit, which unites Christ himself to us...As though, if he should lift us to himself, we should not just as much enjoy his presence!'[80]

It is difficult to overstate Calvin's influence upon English Protestantism in regard to communion.[81] We can hear his criticism of transubstantiation in George

---

[76] *The garden of spiritual flowers*, sig. G6r.

[77] Zachman, *Image and Word*, 339. Throughout his career, Calvin continually revisited this point of his sacramental theology, deepening his commitment to the idea of the *unio mystica* as the process by which a person encounters Christ through partaking in the sacrament.

[78] Julie Canlis, *Calvin's Ladder* (Grand Rapids, MI, 2010), 118. See also Lee Palmer Wandel, *The Eucharist in the Reformation* (Cambridge, 2006), 165.

[79] Calvin, *Institutes*, IV.xvii.16.

[80] Calvin, *Institutes*, IV.xvii.31, see also IV.xvii.24. Hans Boersma's analysis is helpful here *Seeing God* (Grand Rapids, 2018), 261–5. Also see Milner, *The Senses and the Reformation*, 262–4.

[81] This is not to say that English Protestantism did not enjoy internal disputes over sacramental issues. See e.g., Judith Maltby, *The Prayerbook and the English People* (Cambridge, 1998), 46–52; Anthony Milton, *Catholic and Reformed* (Cambridge, 1995), 498–9.

114   EXPERIENCING GOD IN LATE MEDIEVAL & EARLY MODERN ENGLAND

Gifford's commentary on Revelation, when Gifford focused upon the location of Christ's body in Revelation 4: 'He is not now by his bodily presence in the earth, no not inuisibly as the Papists would haue it in the sacrament'.[82] In fact, regardless of the brand of Protestantism, as Horton Davies has demonstrated, the doctrine that the 'presence of Christ is mystical and spiritual, not carnal or local, and it represents, presents, and applies to believers the benefits of the covenant of grace' remained central to English reformed thought.[83] Calvin's sacramental theology can be seen even in the language of the Book of Common Prayer, the Elizabethan catechism, and popular homilies, so perhaps it is not surprising that the communion table was a site for ravishment.[84]

Although accounts of such ravishing experiences during communion are not abundant, they were by no means abnormal. The early Stuart puritan Samuel Fairclough reportedly was overcome with 'raptures' while administering the sacrament to the congregation in Haverill (Suffolk). The experience was so overwhelming that, as one account described him, he seemed to be 'one of the heavenly Quire', because the Holy Spirit had filled him with such 'enlargements of the Soul'.[85] Similarly, in the middle of the seventeenth century, Isaac Ambrose related a story of a 'godly woman' who suffered a demonic attack, where the devil discouraged her from partaking in the sacrament. In response to her prayers, the woman was filled with 'soul-ravishing joys', and 'the Lord was pleased to bring into her mind' verses from the Canticles, which helped her fend off the temptation.[86]

In *Meditations on the Lords Supper* (1638), Edward Reynolds compared the *unio mystica* in the Lord's Supper with the 'hypostaticall' union of Christ's deity and humanity, insisting that the agency of the experience belongs entirely to God: 'the Spirit of God, ever raiseth up the affections from earth, fastneth the eye of Faith upon Eternity, ravisheth the soule with a servent longing to bee with the Lord'.[87] Going through six editions in the 1640s, the *Meditations* seems to have been popular with a readership looking for guidance on how to prepare for communion. Reynolds explained that godly people must prepare for communion in the same manner as someone prepares to experience God, 'first hewed, and fitted by

---

[82] Gifford, *Sermons*, 27. Immediately following his description of John's soul journey into heaven, Gifford concluded that 'we receiue the very flesh and bloud of our Saviour in the Sacrament but mystically, and after a spiritual and heauenly manner.'

[83] Horton Davies, *Worship and Theology in England* (Grand Rapids, MI, 1996), 311–12. Also, Brian Spinks, *Sacraments, Ceremonies, and Stuart Divines* (Aldershot, 2002), 22–3.

[84] *The Book of Common Prayer*, 1559; *The Elizabethan Prayer Book*, ed. John E. Booty (Charlottesville, VA, 2005), 258; Alexander Nowell, *A Catechism* (Cambridge, 1853), 215; Thomas Cooper, *A Briefe homily* (1580), sig. A2r.

[85] Samuel Clarke, *The lives of Sundry eminent persons* (1683), 137.

[86] Ambrose, *War with Devils*, 286. Also see Richard Hooker, *Works of Richard Hooker*, eds Georges Edelen and W. Speed Hill (Cambridge, MA, 1977), I.iv.45–8; Lancelot Andrewes, *Responsio* (1610), 12–15.

[87] Edward Reynolds, *Meditations on the holy sacrament* (1638), 196.

repentance, and other preparatory works before he should approach to incorporate himself into that spirituall, and eternall building'. Communion was a two-fold event, where in the action of imbibing the bread and the wine, was a physical experience that mirrored the spiritual movement, and transformation, of the soul being taken up and incorporated into the body of Christ ('eternall building').[88]

We can see how the absence of such experiences with God during communion could be indicative of spiritual maladies. The nonconforming minister Edmund Trench complained that in 1685, he found himself in 'Apprehensions of my own Condition', as he was riddled with 'impertinent Thoughts, wandring Imaginations, inordinate Affections'. Certainly, this exemplifies the sort of intense spirituality that often characterized puritan devotion; however, Trench's crisis seems to have reached a new level when he experienced absolutely nothing during communion on Christmas Day. He explains that the service 'afforded so little sweetness and benefit, that I receiv'd no more from the infinite Fountain, ascended no higher towards him, and had not much larger Communications from him'.[89] Clearly, Trench's expectations for what he should be experiencing during communion are rooted in the discourse of divine *raptus*. Perhaps more important is the fact that Trench seems to understand the soul's ascent and divine 'Communications' to be normative, at least for the godly, and to go so long without such ravishing experiences during communion alarmed him.

Nor was this association of *raptus* and communion a generally puritan or staunchly Calvinist one. The popular devotional writer Christopher Sutton, who seemed to prefer Bonaventure to Calvin, combined divine ravishment with the metaphorical imagery of the wedding feast and instructions upon receiving the sacrament.[90] In *Godly meditations upon the most Holy Sacrament*, which had been through thirty editions by 1677, Sutton exhorted readers:

But mark, my soul, that all cannot ascend to this hill, but only, as the kingly Prophet speaketh, the harmless and pure in heart; and not after every sort, but with a wedding garment, wherewith we ought to be decked at Christ's feasts.[91]

A few pages later, Sutton explained, 'The fruit of this meditation is, to lift up ourselves above ourselves', and, like the enlightenment given to the biblical prophets, the sacrament provides to the communicant 'understanding...by this holy Sacrament, that it easily cometh unto the knowledge of God'.[92] Likewise, William

---

[88] Reynolds, *Meditations*, 28, 179.

[89] Edmund Trench, *Some remarkable passages* (1693), 88–9. These sorts of experiences seem to be why Alathea Bethell is encouraged to 'Receive as often as you can / the Holy Sacrament' (MS 2240, fol. 52r).

[90] Fincham and Tyacke refer to him as an 'anti-Calvinist': *Altars Restored*, 109.

[91] Christopher Sutton, *Godly Meditations upon...the Lord's Supper* (Oxford, 1866), 17–18.

[92] Sutton, *Godly Meditations*, 22, 31. See also John Owen, *Of communion* (1657), 157.

Brough, a supporter of Archbishop William Laud, wrote the popular book *Sacred principles* with the stated purpose of preparing and describing the experience by which Christ 'brings us to those Heavenly spheares'.[93] Following many of the preparative practices we have seen in other texts, Brough gave his readers 'An Holy Rapture' to be recited after taking communion. Then, afterward, one should celebrate the 'Mysterious Incorporation!' by reciting, 'Thou hast Entred Thy Body and Blood into me, by Thy spirit', which was in effect God taking 'possession of me'.[94]

In a final example, following the Restoration, the young Anglican priest Simon Patrick's *Mensa Mystica* continued to promote this understanding of communion. After he was preferred to St. Paul's church in Covent Garden, Patrick became a celebrated London preacher (and later bishop), and his *Mensa* went through three editions in a single year. Despite this celebrity in his own day, Patrick has been largely underappreciated in modern scholarship.[95] Nevertheless early on in the *Mensa*, he defined the sacrament of communion in seven ways: a remembrance of Christ's sacrifice, a celebration of thanksgiving, a holy 'rite-covenant' with Christ, a solemn oath, a sign and seal of salvation, a means of union with Christ, and a means of union with the rest of the body of Christ. The wine, or what Patrick called 'the blood of God', had the power to 'send up our Souls in Songs of praise to Heaven', where we would desire to 'evaporate our spirits in flames of love, and that our Souls were nothing but a harmony'.[96] Comparing the experience to inebriation, Patrick wrote, 'celestial drunkenesse, when the Soul…is indeed out of itself…above it selfe'. Like alcoholic inebriation, 'celestial drunkenesse' is accompanied by forgetfulness and loss of self-control; however, it is this state of mind, he insisted, 'we must long for when we are at the Supper of the Lord'.[97] Of course, one important difference was that, unlike inebriation, a person could not work themselves into the state of celestial drunkenness. At the communion table, 'The holy Spirit' became both the provider and what was provided. The Holy Spirit must be 'conferred on us in larger measures', because it was the Spirit 'which is the very bond and ligament that ties us to him'.

Here, Patrick moves from the metaphor of drunkenness to the language of *unio mystica*, which he argued is greater than the 'moral union…between Husband and Wife'. It is closer in certain respects to 'a natural union as between head and members, the Vine and Branches, which is made by one spirit or life dwelling in the whole'.[98] Christ was considered to be the energy, the source and

---

[93] William Brough, *Sacred principles* (1659), title page. The book went through eight editions between 1650 and 1679.

[94] Brough, *Sacred principles*, 310.

[95] One of the few modern studies of his life and work is the recent book by Nicholas Fisher, *Symon Patrick (1626–1707)* (Newcastle upon Tyne, 2019).

[96] Simon Patrick, *Mensa Mystica* (1684), 21.   [97] Patrick, *Mensa Mystica*, 24.

[98] Patrick, *Mensa Mystica*, 90.

root, of the individual and corporate life of the church. The sacramental celebration both remembered and participated in that union, because in the partaking of the sacrament:

> Christ comes down upon us by the power of the Holy Ghost, moving by his heavenly virtue in our hearts, though he remain above…it doth both quicken us to his service, and tie us to him, Body and Blood, because we sensibly feel the virtue and efficacy of them in our selves.[99]

The point of this chapter is not to collapse all such experiences of devotion into a single kind. There are clear differences between the sort of divine encounter described by the likes of John Winthrop and Isaac Ambrose and the revelations of someone like Julian of Norwich. The former two spoke in terms of joys and ecstatic sensations overwhelming the soul, while the latter described visions and full-blown conversations with God and the saints. This is no small difference, and the fact that very few Protestants ever attest to such experiences is important to recognize. Nevertheless, the medieval and early modern individual could turn to a common discourse of ravishment when attempting to explain what was being experienced in their encounters with God. In this regard, in the way that divine revelation was understood as a process of ravishment, medieval contemplatives and reformers had more in common than they might have liked to admit. The transmission of the discourse of divine revelation into early modern devotional literature went much further than simply continuing the proliferation of a late medieval trope. Certainly, one reason for this transmission had to do with the commonly held belief that the church was the body of Christ, and the unity of this relationship was exemplified and confirmed in various contexts from the mystical marriage to the practice of communion. However, the adoption of ravishment and rapture as a means of describing the goal of devotional and meditative practice did more than transfer from one confession to another. It was diffused into a much broader spectrum of social and cultural contexts. By placing divine revelation into a decidedly popular context, devotional literature recontextualized the medieval discourse, inviting people to prepare and pray for God to move upon their souls in such a way that was commensurate with the divine experiences of the biblical prophets and Christian saints. In this regard, the Reformation helped spread a very medieval understanding of Christian faith and practice, dislodging it from a largely cloistered context, and insisting that all Christian believers should pursue the divine *raptus* of the soul.

---

[99] Patrick, *Mensa Mystica*, 96.

5

'Language of the Angels'

The Poetics of Divine Ravishment

> What dost thou of the Lord thy God desire
> …when with uplifted eyes,
> And mind quite rapt with a celestial fire,
> Thou dartest thy petitions to the skies?
>
> Rhys Pritchard, 'The Lord's Prayer'

John Donne's death was a drawn-out affair. Donne's friend Izaak Walton tells us that Donne lay in bed for fifteen days, after having prepared his funeral urn and shroud. In Donne's final moments in March 1631, Walton recounts that Donne experienced a 'beatifical vision', in the manner of St. Stephen, seeing the same heavenly figures as the New Testament disciple. Donne's 'soul' finally 'ascended' once he was 'satisfied with this blessed sight'. William Winstanley, who included Donne in his *England's vvorthies* (1660), added that Donne was 'in a serious contemplation of the mercies of my God', and God revealed to Donne the providential acts in Donne's life that led him to the deanship of St. Paul's. Such deathbed revelations were not unheard of, but it was not an everyday occurrence in early modern England.[1] Donne's vision stands out among many Protestant ravishments because of who Donne was and his description of what he saw and learned; however, in terms of the process of *raptus*, the account was relatively orthodox. While the elder Donne's vision presents a more tranquil experience of revelation from the younger Donne's well-known holy sonnet 'Batter my heart three-person'd God', both sonnet and experience echo the traditional discourse of *raptus*:

> Take mee to you, imprison mee, for I
> Except you'enthrall mee, never shall be free,
> Nor ever chaste, except you ravish mee.[2]

---

[1] Izaak Walton, *The lives of Dr. John Donne* (1670), 78; William Winstanley, *England's vvorthies* (1660), 306–7. Neither Walton nor Winstanley record a similar experience for any of their other biographies, giving an indication of how uncommon such experiences were. An early copy of the image of Donne in his shroud can be found in: BL Add MS 71474, f. 164. Other such accounts can be found in Peter Marshall, *Beliefs and the Dead in Reformation England* (Oxford, 2002), esp. pp. 8, 71, 134.

[2] John Donne, *Poems* (1633), 38.

Experiencing God in Late Medieval and Early Modern England. David J. Davis, Oxford University Press.
© David J. Davis 2022. DOI: 10.1093/oso/9780198834137.003.0006

'LANGUAGE OF THE ANGELS' 119

Perhaps it is fitting that the cleric and literary giant who meditated on the beatific vision for his sermons and deployed its imagery in his poems should be granted such a moment before his death.[3]

The importance of poetry to early modern English culture is difficult to over-state. Erin McCarthy refers to poetry as an 'ubiquitous cultural phenomenon' in early modern England, which characterized England's expression of the larger Renaissance. While certainly not all English poetry was good poetry, English readers seemed to enjoy a steady flow of it, good or bad. Along with entire books of poetry, poems were embedded in works of romance and devotion as well as political polemic, social commentary, law, science, and philosophy. As for divine poetry, there are more than a few dozen collections recorded in the English Short Title Catalogue, representing a variety of confessional positions. Several of these collections went through more than five editions, making them some of the more popular poetic works appearing in print.[4] Second to devotional works, poetry contained the most examples of divine ravishment in early modern literature.

Donne's sonnet not only deploys the discourse of divine revelation, but also plays an important role in a much larger academic conversation about all divine (or sacred) poetry in early modern England.[5] As part of Donne's series of holy sonnets, the poem circulated widely in the early decades of the seventeenth cen-tury in manuscript and was printed in at least six editions of the sonnets between 1633 and 1670.[6] 'Batter my heart...' was among the more popular of the holy son-nets in manuscript, and it remains one of the more controversial among scholars. Some scholars follow Barbara Lewalski's famous 'Protestant poetic' quite closely in their reading of the poem, while others hear echoes of Ignatius of Loyola and earlier Catholic influences in Donne's verse.[7] The fact that Donne was born into a recusant family and later converted to Anglicanism only stokes the debates around the theology embedded in the sonnet's lines. While R. V. Young rightly warned against 'too precise theological categorizing' of early modern poetry and poets, some scholars have taken this as an exhortation to read 'Batter my heart...' through a variety of other lenses, as suppressed homoeroticism or sadism or even

---

[3] For more on Donne's theology of the beatific vision, see Boersma, *Seeing God*, 302–13.

[4] Erin A. McCarthy, *Doubtful Readers* (Oxford, 2020), 1. Some of the most widely printed collec-tions were George Herbert, *The temple* (Cambridge, 1633); Quarles, *Diuine poems*; George Sandys, *A paraphrase vpon the divine poems* (1638); William Prynne, *Mount-Orgueil* (1641); Henry Vaughan, *Silex scintillans* (1650) ; William Crashaw, *Steps to the Temple* (1670).

[5] Helpful in this regard is Tina Skouen, 'The Rhetoric of Passion in Donne's Holy Sonnets', *Rhetorica*, 27 (2009), 159–89.

[6] For the substantial manuscript tradition of the Holy Sonnets, see John Donne, *The Variorum Edition...The Holy Sonnets*, ed. Gary A. Stringer (Bloomington, 2005), LX–LXVII, as well as *Digital Donne: The Online Variorum* http://digitaldonne.tamu.edu/index.html

[7] Lewalski, *Protestant Poetics*, 271–2. Earlier summaries of the literature can be found in R. V. Young, *Doctrine and Devotion* (Woodbridge, 2000), 2n3–4; Donne, *The Variorum Edition*, 178–86.

psychological depression.[8] Unfortunately, these interpretations tend to desensitize us to the writers' abilities to work in a variety of ways and traditions, to borrow from different theologies and synthesize them into a work of beauty.[9] Certainly, poems should not be stripped of all doctrinal intent, which seems to me an equally egregious error. Rather, I want to steer the conversation away from ferreting out whether poets were Calvinist, Arminian, crypto-Catholic, Jesuit, or what have you. The profound anxiety Calvinists expressed about their own sinfulness certainly emerged in their poetry, as did the visceral anguish that Catholics felt about Christ's passion. However, anxiety over sin is not isolated to Calvinism any more than anguish about the Passion is strictly a Catholic sentiment. Also, such expressions can be indicative of doctrine without being determinative of dogmatic association. Instead, my argument here is that Donne's invocation for God to move violently upon him, the insistence that divine ravishment is necessary for the individual Christian, was part of a larger poetic move that considered revelation to be an essential aspect of the soul's relationship with God, whatever the poet's confessional background.[10]

Also important for this chapter is what Joad Raymond refers to as 'a figurative mode' that allowed people to speak about divine revelation according to 'visible patterns', which 'denoted with imperfect transparency higher truths'.[11] This chapter demonstrates that the poetic deployment of divine ravishment communicated in figures and imagery closely fits these kinds of patterns that Raymond recognizes as an accommodating language. Rather than diminishing the significance of this language as some scholars have done, likening the poetic language of ravishment to a metaphor, it is apparent here that early modern poetry was echoing the language of divine *raptus* that we have been examining thus far.[12] For one thing, figurative accommodation most often connects two things that are similar but of different qualities or degrees. In terms of the discourse of divine revelation, the basic figures were borrowed from scripture and then expanded by the poets, broadening how the experience of divine *raptus* was understood and offering

---

[8] Young, *Doctrine and Devotion*, 17; Gary Kuchar, *Divine Subjection* (Pittsburgh, 2005), 235; Ramie Targoff, *John Donne, Body and Soul* (Chicago, 2008), 108, 123; Brian Cummings, *The Literary Culture of the Reformation* (Oxford, 2007), 397; David L. Edwards, *John Donne* (Cambridge, 2001), 236.

[9] We should also be conscious of the fact that early modern readers of poetry read across confessional lines, as commonplace books bear out. See e.g., Brotherton Collection MS Lt 91, fols. 23r, 37r, 56r.

[10] Very helpful in this regard is Paul Cefalu's notion of 'Johannine devotional poetics' which he develops in *The Johannine Renaissance* (Oxford, 2017).

[11] Joad Raymond, *Milton's Angels* (Oxford, 2010), 165. Although I have opted not to include an analysis of *Paradise Lost* in this chapter, John Milton's work *De doctrina Christiana* is relevant here, as he argues that the only way to speak of God is in the language of accommodation: *A Treatise on Christian Doctrine* (Cambridge, 1825), 16–20. I am very grateful to my colleague Dr. Emily Stelzer for pointing me to Milton on this point.

[12] An example of this sort of scholarship that would diminish the value of ravishment language in poetry is Cummings, *The Literary Culture of the Reformation*, 276.

readers a body of literature intentionally crafted to assist people in desiring divine revelation. Focusing on the more popular works of divine poetry, as well as a few examples that are further off the beaten path, this chapter argues that there was an early modern understanding of poetry as a preparative for divine ravishment that gave people a way of thinking and approaching revelation that could not be found in the same way in works of devotion or theology. The aesthetic quality and concerns of poetry offered people something not always present in other kinds of devotional writings: an expression of worship that attempted to reflect in form and content the heavenly beauty being described.

Poetry as Preparation

In Chapter 3 we discussed Francis Quarles's *Emblemes*, in which Quarles attempted to show 'sense what faith alone could see'.[13] Part of this showing was pictorial and part of it was poetic. Alongside his emblematic engravings, Quarles provided meditative verses to be read with the images. Like images, sacred and divine poetry offered a way to communicate the spiritual reality of ravishment in a different way than theologies, sermons, devotionals, and commentaries. Interestingly, Quarles's high view of divine poetry was not unusual. It aligned quite closely with the presbyterian Edward Reynolds, who, in his treatise on the soul, singled out the poets' power to move the soul in such a way that it would be more ready for divine ravishment. Reynolds's book is an interesting source, for not only was it one of the more popular of such treatises, but also Reynolds was a moderate sort of presbyterian, serving as a member of the Westminster Assembly and then conforming to episcopacy following the Restoration (eventually becoming Bishop of Norwich). In his treatise, Reynolds explained that the soul's will relied upon the imagination and 'Fancie', to provide appropriate devices that would 'quicken, allure, and sharpen its desire towards some...object'. Inspirational works like Quarles's *Emblems* were ideal in equipping the imagination with such devices. Rather than a 'severe and sullen argument', the human soul could be moved through more indirect means, by the 'sweetnesse of Eloquence'. Reynolds specifically singled out poets as possessing the ability to create images that stirred the imagination, which could move the human will with delight, joy, terror, etc., to 'quicken and rayse' the soul with 'a kind of heat and rapterie', or what the 'Philosophers called Extasie'.[14] He even cited the apostle Paul's vision of the third heaven, as an example of the goal of all godly souls to be so 'transported' by divine ravishment. Poetic language offered an important medium through which people could ready their souls for such divine movement. Reynolds stressed the power of

---

[13] Quarles, *Emblemes*, 302.   [14] Reynolds, *A treatise...of the soule*, 18–21.

122   EXPERIENCING GOD IN LATE MEDIEVAL & EARLY MODERN ENGLAND

beautiful words to heighten the soul's senses, encouraging the soul toward 'actions extraordinarie' without the body, including 'Assent, Faith, Invocation...wherein the Soule is carried beyond the Spheres of Sense, and transported unto more raysed operations'.[15]

What set poetry apart was its power, without any divine agency, to ravish the soul in a lesser way. Poetry could dissociate the internal senses from the physical senses, allowing a person to experience something that had nothing to do with an individual's temporal or spatial contexts. In *The defence of poesie* (1595), Philip Sidney described the power of poetry as providing a 'hart-rauishing knowledge', in which the poet wields a power to create 'a perfect picture...an image of that whereof the Philosopher bestoweth but a wordish description, which doth nei-ther strike, pearce, nor possesse, the sight of the soule'.[16] Similarly, Sidney's con-temporary Barnabe Barnes described divine poetry as a 'spirituall Pegasus' that 'in divine harmonie of spirite' can lift up the mind to 'that maiesticall Throane'.[17] All poetry could ravish the soul's senses; however, only divine poetry harmonized the soul with heaven, nurturing and inspiring in the human soul a readiness for divine *raptus*. Only divine poetry could both immerse the soul in such accom-modating imagery that reflected biblical truth and excite the soul's senses toward a more intense desire for God.

When we turn to some of the more significant collections of divine poetry in the period, we see a similar awareness that divine *raptus* and poetry's influence on the soul were closely intertwined. Perhaps the most popular collection of divine poems was George Herbert's *The temple* (1633).[18] In a commendatory poem 'An Epitaph upon the Honourable GEORGE HERBERT', one 'P.D. esq' exhorted *The Temple*'s readers to 'Go thaw your hearts at...[the] celestial fire' of Herbert's verse.[19] Likewise, readers of the Catholic-convert Richard Crashaw, who was described as a second Herbert, were assured that sacred poetry helped to 'meas-ure the soul into that better world', because it was the 'Language of the Angels; it is the Quintessence of Phantasie and discourse center'd in Heaven; tis the very out-goings of the soul'.[20] While it was understood that divine grace was necessary for

---

[15] Reynolds, *A treatise...of the soule*, 8, 36.

[16] Philip Sidney, *The defence of poesie* (1595), sigs. B3v, D1v.

[17] Barnabe Barnes, *A divine centurie of spirituall sonnets* (1595), sig. A3v. Almost a century later, we still see this sentiment in poets like Edward Phillips, nephew of John Milton: *Theatrum poetarum* (1675), sig. *5r.

[18] References to and quotes from *The temple* abound in the seventeenth century. Perhaps the most telling for our purposes is the fact that Richard Baxter printed Herbert's 'Home' at the end of his popu-lar treatise *The saints everlasting rest*, with the prayer, 'O shew thy self to me, / Or take me up to thee': Baxter, *The saints*, 853–4.

[19] Herbert, *The temple*, sig. A6v. The readership of *The temple* has been studied most recently in Joel Swann, '"In the hands and hearts of all true Christians",' *Journal of Medieval and Early Modern Studies*, 50 (2020), 115–37. My thanks to Dr. Swann for allowing me to read a pre-published version of his article.

[20] Crashaw, *Steps*, sigs. A2v–3r.

both salvation and divine ravishment, it is important that we do not neglect the space for human participation created by divine poetry. Herbert did not believe that the reader could light the 'celestial fire', any more than they could redeem themselves from sin. In 'Trinitie Sunday', the speaker asks God to 'Enrich my heart…With faith, with hope, with charitie; / That I may runne, rise, rest with thee'.[21] As Constance Furey argues, there is an unmistakable 'dynamism…not a self lost or transcended' in early modern divine poetry, which is too often neglected. The relational exchange between the soul and God can be found in the language of 'emulation…unrequited longing, and through interest in difference as well as the pleasure and reassurance of unification'.[22] The reliance upon divine agency was very much present, in fact it was essential. Equally essential was the reader's willingness to take and read, to meditate, and otherwise devote themselves to preparing their souls for encountering God.

The poet also was drawn into this relational exchange. Often the poets expressed a reliance upon God to ravish them in order that they might produce godly verse, which in turn might aid their readers. Thus, in Quarles's *Divine Poems*, the poet compares himself to the classical pagan poets and boasts that he writes about the greatest mythic hero, the 'King of Kings', which was both exciting and daunting. In his poem, 'To the Most High', Quarles invited God to 'Ravish my stupid Senses' and to only 'Take the Bayes that lift'. The 'Bayes' referred to the Roman laurel crown of poets and victors, so Quarles longed for God to ravish his soul so that his poems ('Bayes') may lift or ravish his readers in return. In another example, George Sandys, among the few divine poets who was not also a cleric, wrote popular paraphrases of scripture in verse. In a commendatory poem for Sandys's *A Paraphrase vpon the Divine Poems*, his friend Wintoure Grant wrote,

> Truth in Poesie so sweetly strikes
> Vpon the Cords, and Fivers of the Heart;
> That it all other Harmony dislikes,
> And happily is Vanquished by her Art.
> These God-like Forms, inspir'd with Breath divine,
> Blest in themselves, and maketh others Blest.[23]

There was a poetic kind of ravishment that could play on the heart's 'Fivers' (fibers), but divine poetry also prepared the soul to experience 'God-like Forms'. The soul's affections could be stirred and in stirring be 'inspir'd with Breath divine'.

---

[21] Herbert, *The temple*, 59. Also, in 'Easter Wings': 'O let me rise' (p. 34).
[22] Constance Furey, *Poetic Relations* (Chicago, 2017), 91. Too often scholars have tried to square such language within a strict doctrinal framework. As an example, see Cummings's analysis of *The temple*, in which he reduces such language to a 'trope for the gift of grace': *The Literary Culture of the Reformation*, 323–7.
[23] Sandys, *A paraphase*, sig. ***v.

124   EXPERIENCING GOD IN LATE MEDIEVAL & EARLY MODERN ENGLAND

Perhaps this is why one of the most formidable female intellects of the seventeenth century, Lady Margaret Cavendish, warned that while 'Divine Poets are Heaven's Birds, that Sing to God' the Bible, in her opinion, should not be paraphrased into verse. Cavendish explained 'so Holy a Truth ought not to be Express'd Fabulously', with the romanticized language of poetry, unless they were given in 'Divine Poetical Raptures…Inspired with Divine Influence' like the Psalms. She worried that one form of divine inspiration (in poetry) would be conflated with the purest form (in scripture).[24] Poetry, very much like sensual stimuli, blended truth with 'Feignings', making the Bible the most 'Unfit' text to paraphrase into verse, because one ran the risk of misrepresenting, and violating the sanctity of, holy scripture.[25] However, the evidence suggests that Cavendish was in a small minority on this point.

Early, and authoritative, examples of paraphrasing scripture in verse included Theodore Beza's drama *Abraham sacrifiant* (Geneva, 1550), translated by Arthur Golding in 1577. One of the most influential poetic paraphrases of scripture was Guillaume de Salluste Du Bartas's *Les Semaines*. A Huguenot at the court of King Henri of Navarre (Henri IV of France), Du Bartas was popular for his poetic rendition of the early chapters of Genesis. Cited by leading English writers, Du Bartas was a favourite of King James I, who translated some of Du Bartas, and the translation *Divine Weeks* by Joshua Sylvester (Sylvestre) in 1605 went through at least six editions before 1642.[26] One of the translation's commendatory poems by John Davies of Hereford, described Du Bartas's poetry as 'Sacred Raptures on the Muses Hill', which Du Bartas fashioned by going 'out of thy Body with thy Minde', so that he could 'More freely…vse thy Wit and Will'.[27] Turning to the sixth day of creation, Du Bartas explained that the human soul is what set humanity apart from the beasts, because God

> Did not extract out of the Elements
> A certain secret Chymick Quint-essence:
> But, breathing, sent as from the lively Spring
> Of his Diuineness som small Riuerling,
> …a portion
> Of the pure lustre of Coelestiall Light.[28]

---

[24] Lady Margaret Cavendish, *CCXI sociable letters* (1664), 263–4. For more on Cavendish's poetry and philosophy in this regard, see Stephen Hequembourg, 'The Poetics of Materialism in Cavendish and Milton', *Studies in English Literature* 54 (2014), 173–92.

[25] Cavendish, *CCXI sociable letters*, 263.

[26] For Du Bartas's popularity in England, see Peter Auger, *Du Bartas' Legacy in England and Scotland* (Oxford, 2019).

[27] Guillaume de Salluste Du Bartas, *Du Bartas. His Deuine Weekes* (1611), 816–17.

[28] Du Bartas, *Deuine Weekes*, 164.

'LANGUAGE OF THE ANGELS' 125

This 'portion' was the essential ingredient that allowed humans to commune directly with God, because the soul was, in part, composed of 'his Diuineness'. Much later, the poem explained that even the first man Adam 'mounted on the burning wings / Of a *Seraphick* loue' during his conversations with God in the Garden of Eden. As such, Du Bartas requested, 'O God, behold me, that I may behold…Ravish me Lord, O (my soules life) reviue', which he distinguished from false raptures that the devil induced, 'like the Bedlam *Bacchanalian* froes, / Who, dauncing, foaming, rowling furious-wise / Vnder their twinkling lids their torch-like eyes.'[29] Divine ravishment did not have such physical disturbances. Not only did Du Bartas believe that ravishment depended upon a divine movement toward the soul, as God must 'behold me' first, but also Du Bartas desired a particular kind of ravishment, the combination of love and reason, which was epitomized by the beatific vision.[30]

While other forces could ravish the soul, only music came close to poetry's power. Authorities from scripture and Augustine to Dante and John Milton characterized the celestial spheres and the heavenly realms as being filled with music. William Shakespeare described poetry and music as siblings, both of whom can 'ravish human sense.'[31] According to Sidney, music and poetry essentially were equals in their powers over the soul; poetry demonstrated how close human beings were, in their abilities and composition, to the 'heauenly maker', for 'nothing he sheweth so much as in Poetry; when with the force of a diuine breath, he bringeth things foorth surpassing her (nature's) doings'. At the same time, for Sidney, 'Musicke' is 'the most diuine striker of the senses', and words, set to a rythmn, can strike both one's reason and one's internal senses.[32] We see a similar appreciation of music's power in Richard Crashaw's 'Musick's Duel': 'Thus high, thus low, as if the Silver Throat…Her little soul is ravisht; and so poured / Into loose extasies, that she is plac't / Above her self, Musicks Enthusiast'. The Jesuit poet Henry Hawkins, in his *Parthenia Sacra* (1633), attached ravishment to music describing it as an experience in which we 'loose our selues' and 'rest our senses.'[33]

It is perhaps not surprising then that the popular London diarist Samuel Pepys confessed his affectionate reaction to a particular piece of moving 'wind-musique':

---

[29] Du Bartas, *Deuine Weekes*, 292–3.

[30] Robert Aylett believed that Du Bartas experienced divine ravishment: *The brides ornaments* (1625), 112. The distinction between kinds of poetic ravishment, one that leads to God and one that 'dulls the wit', can be found in Milton's *Paradise Lost*: David Ainsworth, *Milton, Music, and Literary Interpretation* (New York, 2020), 17.

[31] Psalm 19; Augustine, *Saint Augustines confessions*, 675–7; William Shakespeare, *Poems* (1640), sig. B6v. See also Sandys, *A paraphrase*, sig. g3r, p. 70; Quarles, *Diuine poems*, 150. For Milton, see Ainsworth, *Milton, Music, and Literary Interpretation*, 18–32.

[32] Sidney, *The defence*, sig. F3v. See also Anon., *The praise of musicke* (Oxford, 1586), 41.

[33] Crashaw, *Steps*, 84; Henry Hawkins, *Parthenia Sacra* (Rouen, 1633), 139. See also the Catholic collection of poems by John Abbot, *Jesus praefigured* (Antwerp, 1623), 106. For the power of religious music see Jonathan Willis, *Church Music and Protestantism in Post-Reformation England* (Aldershot, 2010).

126 EXPERIENCING GOD IN LATE MEDIEVAL & EARLY MODERN ENGLAND

it ravished me, and indeed, in a word, did wrap up my soul so that it made me really sick, just as I have formerly been when in love with my wife; that neither then, nor all the evening going home, and at home, I was able to think of any thing, but remained all night transported.

So entranced by this experience, Pepys insisted that he and his wife immediately begin practicing with wind instruments.[34]

While few divine poets shared Cavendish's trepidations about turning scripture into verse, it was well known that the ravishing talents of music and poetry could be turned to profane purposes. Such works ran a wide gamut of bawdiness from the refined verse of Donne's 'The Extasie', which used the essential features of divine ravishment (e.g. 'Our souls...gone out') to describe sexual intimacy, to the coarser poems of Jane Barker's *Poeticall Recreations*. In one verse, Barker described the lover of a woman named Graciana, who attended weekly church services not for sermons (given by the 'thick-skull'd Parson') but for a chance to kiss the girl. In fact, the eventual kiss moved him so much that he was 'transported so, / That perfectly I do not know, / Whether my ravish'd soul be fled, or no'. Even more scandalous was the ravishing power of a lover's tongue and Robert Gould's description of 'a Convulsive Rapture' of two bodies, which climaxed in a 'Bliss...Rapt up to the Third Heav'n of Extasie!'[35]

To be sure, divine poets complained of such debasing of their art. John Davies of Hereford pointed to poetry's decline, going all the way back to ancient Greece when poets 'mingled Humane praises with Divine'. As a remedy Davies suggested, poets must purify verse, so that the human soul can hear 'The Praise of him which made the Heav'n'.[36] The difficulty, of course, lay in the fact that there were two kinds of beauty—one physical and one divine—being described, and one kind brought on affections and sensations that were very similar to the other. Robert Burton explained that the 'Saints of God' experienced 'a Diuine furie, a Holy madnesse, euen a spiritual drunkennes', when confronted with God's beauty, which were similar to that 'diuine taste of that heauenly Nectar...which Poets deciphered by the sacrifice of Dionysius, and in this sence with the Poet *insanire lubet*'.[37] Both the saints and the pagan poets were ravished because of the beauty they experienced and, subsequently, expressed: 'One Beauty ariseth from God, another from his creatures'.[38]

---

[34] Samuel Pepys, *The Diary of Samuel Pepys*, ed. Henry B. Wheatley (1893), 27 February 1668. See also the experience the year before when Elizabeth Mercer, a family friend, sang to him: 24 January 1667.

[35] Donne, *Poems*, 278–9; Jane Barker, *Poeticall recreations* (1691), 10, 21; Robert Gould, *A satyrical epistle* (1691). See also Thomas Carew's 'A Rapture' in *Poems* (1640), 83–9.

[36] John Davies, *The...immortality of the soul* (1697), sig. b3v, p. 21. See also George Herbert, *Select hymns* (1697), sig. A2v.

[37] Robert Burton, *The anatomy of melancholy* (Oxford, 1621), 42–3.

[38] Burton, *The anatomy*, 500. See also the printer William Godbid's comments in the preface to Francis Cockin, *Divine blossomes* (1657), sig. A8v.

'LANGUAGE OF THE ANGELS' 127

That the same language was used for divine revelation and a sexual encounter was no secret, nor was it to be taken lightly. At the same time, the language of ravishment was not avoided, even though this similarity might create confusion for readers. In fact, some poets seem to have steered directly into the ambiguities implied by such language. Joshua Sylvester's translation of Du Bartas provides one of the most startling examples: 'O sacred flight! sweet rape! Loues soueraign bliss! / Which very loves deer lips dost make vs kiss'.[39] It is important to note that this was the first of three points in the book where Sylvester chose to employ the middle English word ('rape') rather than the English word that directly corresponded to Du Bartas's French 'rauissement', so it is worth attending to a few things about Sylvester's word choice here.[40] First, the *Oxford English Dictionary* identifies eleven different definitions in use before Sylvester's translation, confirming the ambiguity already embedded in the word. Second, Sylvester is clearly aware of this ambiguity, because he used 'rape' several times in the same book to refer to sexual assault, distinguishing it with words like 'profane', 'detested', 'ruthless', and 'wanton'.[41] Elsewhere, the ravishment of the soul (which is also named 'rape') is 'blessed' and 'sacred'.[42] One of the clear distinctions apparent in Sylvester's different uses of the word is that examples carrying negative qualifications were violations of an individual's will; whereas those examples described as 'blessed' and 'sacred' expressed the individual's desire for God. With this in mind, it is somewhat easier to reframe our understanding of the terminology, in certain places, as an expression of relationship and attraction between two people, rather than one of despicable violence. While Sylvester's use of the word means 'to take or seize by force', denoting a kind a violence, such violence is not necessarily a violation of a person. As Donne's holy sonnet exemplifies, the human speaker desires to be ravished by the divine and would gladly be the active agent if they could ('Never shall be free, / Nor ever chaste, except you ravish me').[43]

Although some scholars devalue the language of ravishment in their readings of divine poetry, often reducing it to a sexualizing trope, it seems to me that a great deal more intellectual freight accompanied the language than a singular understanding of sexual violence.[44] At the very least, it is important that scholars do not anachronistically hold early modern writers to our very specific definitions

---

[39] Du Bartas, *Deuine Weekes*, 226.

[40] For the other two times he used 'rape' to compare the prophet Elijah's being taken into heaven, comparing it to the soul's experience of divine *raptus*, see Du Bartas, *Deuine Weekes*, 606, 607. The French original reads: 'O doux rauissement, sainct vol, amour extremé, / Qui fais que nous baisos les leures d'Amour mesme!'; see Guillaume de Salluste Du Bartas, *La Seconde Semaine* (Paris, 1584), 14.

[41] Du Bartas, *Deuine Weekes*, 370, 409, 546. Helpful here is Kathryn Gravdal's analysis of the language and law of rape in medieval France: *Ravishing Maidens*, esp. pp. 1–20.

[42] Du Bartas, *Deuine Weekes*, 606, 607.   [43] Furey, *Poetic Relations*, 92–3.

[44] An unfortunate example of this devaluation is Noam Flinker's analysis, which reads all such literature as an objectification of women: *The Song of Songs in English Renaissance Literature* (Cambridge, 2000), 117.

128   EXPERIENCING GOD IN LATE MEDIEVAL & EARLY MODERN ENGLAND

of words, which poets would not have understood so narrowly. The word choice is certainly shocking and ill-advised, at least given our perspective; however, it seems evident enough that there was a recognized and respected difference in what was meant when the same word was used in other contexts. The difference between these meanings was so profound that Sylvester described one as 'profane' and the other as 'sacred'.

The rest of this chapter will explore the different ways that poets unpacked such accommodating imagery in order to demonstrate how the poetic impulse to portray experiences with God further expanded the well-established discourse of *raptus* and the larger culture of divine revelation.

Passion and Place in Divine Poetry

One of the most bountiful storehouses of poetic accommodation came from the Canticles and its imagery of the Bride and Bridegroom. In *Divine poems*, Quarles expressed the Bride's love in her own words as she stands in the bridal chamber: 'O How I'm ravisht with eternall blisse! / Who e're thought heaven a joy compar'd to this? / How doe the pleasures of this glorious Face / Adde glory to the glory of this place', which is accompanied by an instructional marginal note '*by heavenly contemplation*'. A few pages later, the Bride and Bridegroom come together with kisses that are 'apt to ravish, able to allure / A frozen soule, and with thy secret fire, / T'affect dull spirits with extreame desire'.[45] The kiss, as a union of body and soul, was an important feature of Neoplatonic thought, particularly in humanist literature like Baldassare Castiglione's *Book of the Courtier* (translated by Thomas Hoby in 1561). Following Plato's *Symposium*, Castiglione described the lovers' kiss as 'a joining of souls rather than of bodies, because it has such a power over the soul that it withdraws it to itself and separates it from the body'. In the kiss, the lover's soul moves outside itself in a contemplative motion, which Castiglione equates with 'the Burning Bush of Moses, the Cloven Tonges of Fire, the Fiery Chariot of Elias…when they leave this earthly baseness and fly toward heaven'.[46] Likewise, the kiss is part of Du Bartas's image of divine ravishment discussed above, and Quarles described the Bridegroom's kiss as a 'truer blisse, no worldly joy allowes'.[47]

The poet Francis Cockin points us to another important emphasis for understanding ravishment in divine poetry: the emphasis on place. Writing during the Interregnum, Cockin (Cockayne) published only one edition of his *Divine*

---

[45] Quarles, *Diuine poems*, 403, 408.
[46] Baldassare Castiglione, *The Book of the Courtier* (New York, 2002), 64, 69.
[47] Quarles, *Diuine poems*, 389. The language here is very similar to Francis Rous's devotional work *The mystical marriage* (see Chapter 4).

blossomes, even though they were dedicated to the popular emblem writer George Wither. Cockin's verse echoed the popular relational poetics of the Bride and Bridegroom, in which the soul (the Bride) cries out for her beloved. Cockin speaks of 'my choice', and further on, intending to 'chastily carry' on in this life, he is committed to remaining a kind of 'Virgin', in his soul, for Christ. Also, there is an expectation that he will 'ever feel the power / Of his soul-melting love', and eventually be rapt up 'in the Courts of great Jehove', when Christ finally comes for his Bride.[48] These 'Courts' are where the soul is united with Christ, where the soul 'eyes him' and is 'ravish'd' with desire.[49]

Preceding this union was the wedding feast or banquet, and Herbert's 'The Banquet', toward the end of *The Temple*, offers us one of the most popular examples of this emphasis upon place.[50] In the poem, the reader is invited into a divine banquet of the Lord's Supper. Herbert emphasizes the sense of smell, one of the most important senses at a banquet:

> Doubtlesse, neither starre nor flower
> Hath the power
> Such a sweetnesse to impart:
> Onely God, who gives perfumes,
> Flesh assumes,
> And with it perfumes my heart.

Smell is often the first scent that registers an experience. Although it was by no means thought to be the most important of the physical senses, it was thought to have unique capabilities and was very often associated with devotion.[51] While Matthew Milner points out that the 'intellective abilities' of smell were considered to be 'very limited', smell was also considered a useful gauge of good and evil, having the ability to identify virtue and vice. The predominance of the miasmatic theory of contagious odors, where foul-smelling objects were thought to indicate a foul essence, and vice versa, underpinned much of this imagery, as the scent of objects and persons could indicate moral virtue, humoral corruption, and even social class.[52] In Herbert's poem, the sweet smells of the banqueting table perfume an individual's very person, offering an olfactory metaphor of redemption. Christ's salvific aroma literally rubs off on his Bride.

Also, smell, along with taste, can create an intimacy with the external world that the other senses do not. In smelling and tasting, we take into the body substances from the outside, which are potentially enjoyable, toxic, disgusting, and/

---

[48] Cockin, *Divine blossomes*, 110.   [49] Cockin, *Divine blossomes*, 110.
[50] See also Vaughan, *Silex*, 60; Quarles, *Diuine poems*, 57.
[51] Smell is the chief sense in Quarles's series of Bridegroom Sonnets: *Diuine poems*, 395–414. Sophie Read, 'What the Nose Knew', in *Literature, Belief and Knowledge*, 175–93.
[52] See e.g., Holly Dugan, *The Ephemeral History of Perfume* (Baltimore, 2011).

or life-giving.[53] George Sandys's 'Panegyrick' to Christ, based on Psalm 45, described his 'High Raptures' being filled with the scent of Christ's garments, which smelled of 'Aloes, Myrrh, and Cassia', which seem not only to confirm Christ's identity but also indicate his saving grace, for they 'more than other Odors please'. For Crashaw, the meditation of the name of Jesus evoked the 'Flowry' aroma of Christ, which had the power to dissipate all 'Fallacy' and error in one's thinking.[54]

Another important place evoking smell was the garden, and early modern devotional poetics certainly participated in what Alec Ryrie terms 'garden spirituality'.[55] The garden is one of the more popular contexts for expressing the ravishment of the soul's senses. Hawkins distinguished the garden of heavenly delights from the two most notable biblical gardens: Eden and Gethsemane. Instead, Hawkins explained this was 'HORTVS CONCLVSVS; wherein are al things mysteriously and spiritually to be found…flowrie Beds to repose in, with heauenlie Contemplations'.[56] The Jesuit Robert Southwell's poems continued to be reproduced by legitimate printing houses in London until the civil war, even though he was executed for treason in 1595. In the final poem of *Moeoniae*, Southwell exhorts the soul to 'Seeke flowers of heauen', which 'rauisheth the minde' for 'Their leaues are stained in beauties die…Their stalks inameld with delight'.[57] In a similar political situation as Southwell, albeit a few decades later, the puritan William Prynne turned to the celestial garden for solace and inspiration, during his imprisonment on the isle of Jersey. His poem 'The Christian Paradise' suggested that terrestrial gardens heightened the possibility of ravishment, inspiring people with 'Soule-ravishing, / Sweete, heavenly Meditations which doe spring'. Like the visual memorials of divine revelation in Chapter 3, the physical plants reminded Prynne of the soul's transcendent reality, raising the imagery of the terrestrial to the celestial, where 'Groves, streames of sweetest Cordialls from Thee spring…And more than Honey sweetnesse, they would be / Rapt and inamor'd with nought else but Thee'.[58]

In a more elongated garden meditation, Henry Vaughan's 'Religion' provided a contemplation upon different passages of scripture while strolling down garden paths: 'MY God, when I walke in those groves, / And leaves thy spirit doth still fan'. Confronting the question of whether miracles have ceased, Vaughan concludes, 'Heale then these waters, Lord…Looke downe great Master of the feast; O shine, / And turn once more our water into wine!' For Vaughan, like many of

---

[53] Milner, *The Senses and the English Reformation*, 33. See also Elizabeth L. Swann, *Taste and Knowledge in Early Modern England* (Cambridge, 2020).

[54] Sandys, *A paraphrase upon the Psalms of David* (1676), 79–80; Crashaw, *Steps*, 151. Gary Kuchar's analysis of Crashaw's poem underscores the limitations of smell: *George Herbert and the Mystery of the Word* (2017), 7.

[55] Ryrie, *Being Protestant*, 166.   [56] Hawkins, *Parthenia Sacra*, 11.

[57] Robert Southwell, *Moeoniae* (1595), 32.   [58] Prynne, *Mount-Orgueil*, 117, 121.

the divine poets, the most powerful work of God was not biblical miracles but the sanctification of individual souls. The garden provided a useful context within which such sanctification could be understood, as the garden was not only a tranquil and cultivated setting but also a traditional context for both sexual advances as well as intellectual pursuits. Here, a person could be ravished by God and experience intellectual ascent. In 'Son-dayes', Vaughan returned to the language of the celestial garden to describe the Sabbath as a 'Transplanted Paradise' and 'The Cool o'the'day', a reference to God walking with Adam and Eve in Eden, giving a sense of place to the most important day of the week and connecting Sabbath activities to the tranquillity of a prelapsarian paradise.[59]

One of the key features in the relational context of divine poetry is the role of invocation, of calling upon the other, to both come and draw the speaker. Some of the most important Old Testament moments of divine revelation were immediately preceded by individuals asking God to appear to them. On Mt. Sinai, Moses implored God, 'show me thy glory' (Exodus 33.18), and King Solomon prayed to God 'arise, O Lord God, to come into thy rest' before God descended upon the newly completed Temple (2 Chronicles 6.41). Considering these biblical invocations, Donne's holy sonnet fits neatly within a larger literature of entreating God to show himself and to work within the speaker's soul.[60] Also, as in Donne, the delight and joy that often accompanied such invocations could be mixed with requests for physical pain. Thus, Vaughan's 'The Match' invited, 'Lord Jesu! Thou didst bow thy blessed head / Upon a tree, / O do as much, now unto me!'[61] The popular Catholic devotional writer Lorenzo Scupoli seems to echo Donne's 'Batter my heart' with the prayer: 'O my dear Jesu, show me thy divine Father…drown me, wound me, burn me, and consume me in thy divine flames of affection.'[62] Likewise, the Jacobean poet Nathanael Richards implored God to crucify him: 'My Armes are spread, come sempeternall Essence, / Rauish my soule; come blessed penitence, / Giue me a thousand stabs;…then let it bleed.'[63]

Such verses bring to mind the image of the burning or crucified heart that was popular in the seventeenth century. Among many examples of those images, the title page of Vaughan's *Silex* depicted a burning heart rising toward a hand from heaven that holds a lightning bolt.[64] In the second half of the century, one of the most popular images of this kind was an engraving of Peter and Mary Magdalene raising a crucified heart toward heaven (Figure 17). Initially appearing as a

---

[59] Vaughan, *Silex*, 15–16, 68.   [60] See also Davies, *The muses sacrifice*, 80.
[61] Vaughan, *Silex*, 53–4. See also George Herbert's 'Longing' in *The temple*, 142–3.
[62] Scupoli, *The Christian pilgrime*, II.81–2.
[63] Nathanael Richards, *The celestiall publican* (1630), sig. B6r.
[64] Lewalski, *Protestant Poetics* (Princeton, NJ, 1979), 206–8. The flaming heart also appeared in illustrations like that in Scupoli (cited in Chapter 4) and prints in the Low Countries available to English Catholics, like Michel de Lochom's portrait of Ana de Jesus (1622–1647), as well as Protestant works like John Saltmarsh, *Holy discoveries and flames* (1640), title page. BPI 9550.

132 EXPERIENCING GOD IN LATE MEDIEVAL & EARLY MODERN ENGLAND

Figure 17. 'Peter and Mary Magdalene with Crucified Heart' in *The Preaching Bible* (Cambridge: John Field, 1668). By permission of the Dunham Bible Museum, Houston Baptist University.

foldout in works by Jeremy Taylor in the 1650s, copies of the image circulated in several different works, including the Restoration prayer books to illustrate the first days of Lent. In the Authorised Bible (1683), the image sits opposite Psalm 51.10–19 with the invocation to God to 'Create in me a clean heart'.[65]

For Catholics, another example of this kind of suffering were the stories of Teresa of Avila, whose visions of being pierced by an arrow were memorialized most famously in a statue by Gian Lorenzo Bernini. The 1611 English translation of Teresa's life was funded by the prosperous printer Henry Jaye, and at least five subsequent editions were printed in Antwerp, Rouen, and London. Teresa described the general experience of the contemplative soul as one that is suffering a kind of crucifixion since the soul receives 'no comfort, either from Heauen, because she is not there; nor carries she anie affection at all, to the Earth'. Torn

---

[65] BPI1700 7250; *Holy Bible* (1683), sigs. 2H4–5.

between heaven and earth, the contemplative soul must suffer detachment from both before it can ascend to God.[66]

As in the devotional literature that stressed unification (Chapter 4), there is a shared movement in poetry: the sanctifying pain ravishes the soul into the wounds of Christ and this pain brings about a kind of soul-rest. Southwell described Christ's side wound as 'O place of rest, / ...O happie soule that flies so hie, / As to attain this sacred caue: / Lord send me wings that I may flie'.[67] Similarly, Prynne's poems compared Christ's body to the mountains in which Moses and Elijah hid themselves from God: 'Our Soules to ravish, we must stand, and hide / Within the Clifts of our Rock, Christ's pierced side...Where God his Face and presence doth display'.[68] Nor is there a distinct sense that such imagery should be read as metaphorical. Descriptions of gardens, banquets, bridegrooms, and Christ's wounds were not mere figures of speech; there was a literal, transcendent reality to which this language of accommodation directly referred, even if it did so incompletely. Christ was the Bridegroom of the true Church, as much as heaven was both a feast and a garden. In his sermons on the Canticles, Theodore Beza made this abundantly clear, explaining that ravishment not only revealed divine understanding, but also provided 'another kind of incomprehensible dilection and loue' for the Bridegroom. In this union, the Bridegroom will 'drawe her vp on high' to the heavenly wedding, where 'one pleasure' is followed closely by 'an other'.[69]

One important way in which this language of accommodation was imperfect was in the order of events. After all, one goes to a garden to be romanced by a lover or rapt up by the natural beauty. The bride and bridegroom attend the feast, and then, at least in the terrestrial sphere, physical consummation should follow. In other words, the imagery that poetry often evoked of the physical world did not reflect perfectly the spiritual reality. At least in this life, as Donne suggested, one must first be ravished to attend the heavenly gardens, feasts, and bridal chambers. According to Joseph Hall, the devout soul needs to be 'heavenized in thy thoughts, and affections...to contemplate that infinite Deity, who dwels in the light inaccessible', and divine poetry served as an aid in the heavenizing process.[70] Poetry, according to Du Bartas, was one of the ways that 'God, of himself...reueales him t'our intelligence'. It could help harmonize the soul to the divine, but even the harmonizing power of poetry could articulate perfectly the heavenly reality.[71]

---

[66] Teresa of Avila, *The flaming hart* (Antwerp, 1642), 258. Crashaw wrote commemorative poems to Teresa in *Steps*, 194–8.

[67] Southwell, *Moeoniae*, 23. See also Henry Garnet, *The Societie of the Rosary* (1596), 113, 121.

[68] Prynne, *Mount-Orgueil*, 13.   [69] Beza, *Master Bezaes sermons*, 31, 241.

[70] Joseph Hall, *Susurrium cum Deo soliloquies* (1651), 300–1.

[71] Du Bartas, *Deuine Weekes*, 5.

The Poetics of Ascent

The idea of the soul's ascent entered Renaissance England in a variety of ways: it was part of the medieval contemplative tradition, and the neoplatonic and humanist trends coming out of Italy carried with them their own versions of ascent. Divine poetry drew from all of these traditions in different respects. Because of his influence on later poets, it is helpful here to consider Edmund Spenser's 'An Hymne of Heavenly Beavtie', which combines Spenser's reading of Plato's *Phaedrus* with the Christian theology of *raptus*.

Like later poets, Spenser expresses frustration that the soul is not capable, on its own, of this movement toward heaven:

> But we fraile wights, whose sight cannot sustaine
> The Suns bright beames when he on vs doth shyne
> ...how can we see with feeble eyne,
> The glory of that Maiestie diuine,
> In sight of whom both Sun and Moone are darke.[72]

Divine light is a crucial element in Spenser's understanding of the soul's movement toward heaven. Light represents divine understanding, the kind of knowledge that is untainted by sin or the corruption of the physical world. Light, for Spenser, also signified the unapproachable, transcendent nature of God, because it is 'not bounded', and so, divine light provided a means to be 'Transported with celestiall desyre', as it 'carries them into an ecstasy' beyond the boundaries of the physical world.[73]

Echoing the images of divine light in Chapter 3 that comforted the godly and condemned the ungodly, light in divine poetry seemed to serve both as a sign of God's presence as well as an invitation (at least for the godly) to ascend. Light also played a role in many contemporary accounts of divine ravishment. The well-known story of the minister John Holland's deathbed revelation began after he finished a meditation on Romans 8. By all accounts, Holland said that he saw a 'Brightness...my Saviour's Shine', and then he was ravished from his body, where he witnessed 'Things that are unutterable'. Similar stories were recycled among Protestants to encourage readers that, as Isaac Ambrose reminded them, 'sometimes the spirit is pleased to shine with its bright, and glorious, and heavenly beams into our souls'.[74]

---

[72] Edmund Spenser, *Fovvre hymnes* (1596), 39.

[73] Spenser, *Fovvre hymnes*, 35, 44. See also Hugo, *Pia Desideria*, 229.

[74] Samuel Clarke, *A mirror or looking glasse* (1654), 9–12; Isaac Ambrose, *Looking unto Jesus* (1680), 502. See also the accounts in William Troughton, *Of the causes and cure* (1677), 50–9.

However, one important difference between Spenser's ascent of the soul and the platonic movement of the soul is the means by which an individual moves or is moved. Spenser's soul is 'hungry', but its motion toward heaven cannot be sated by philosophy. References to human thought in the poem speak of its insufficiency either to understand or fully communicate the 'goodly sights…[the] glorious images'. Spenser's emphasis upon the soul's inability to ascend by its own power was prominent in divine poetry, as it was in sermons and devotional literature.[75] For Crashaw, in 'To the Name Above Every Name', the soul should, 'Awake and sing, / And be all wing', but then, unable to ascend on its own, it must, 'Go and request' the key to ascend. In 'East Wings', Herbert's soul requests that God allow it to ascend, 'O let me rise / As larks, harmoniously'. Likewise, Vaughan wrote, 'Give me, my God! thy grace, / The beams, and brightness of thy face'.[76]

This reliance upon God also can be seen in the Laudian poet Robert Aylett's works. In 'Urania, or the Heavenly Muse', Aylett developed a conversation between the muse and a human soul, in which Urania explained that since the 'Soule…is Celestial fire' it must 'like the Saints be rapt up in a trance' if it is to find peace. As platonic as this seems, Aylett did not suggest that the soul was capable of such a movement on its own. Like an instrument in the hands of a musician, the soul must 'be tun'd by spheare-like ravishing', which is done by the Holy Spirit.[77] Aylett's soul pines for a 'holy fit of Heau'nly fire, / Raising my Muse to zealous contemplation', desiring it even more than a holy kiss; however, the soul can do nothing more than offer up 'Prayers that to Heau'n seeke to ascend', hoping that the prayers do not 'Fall downe like smoakie vapours'.[78] Even more explicitly, Barnabe Barnes asked the 'Lyon of Judah' to 'Illuminate my thoughts, with beames bright / Kindle my spirite with that sacred heate'. Then later, he affirmed his reliance upon God to 'illuminate my wits: / Rauish my sences with celestial fits'.[79]

The language of 'fits' in both Aylett and Barnes is interesting. Both poets seem to be referring to the senses of the soul—the imagination, memory, etc.—and the inability of the soul to control them during divine ravishment. This loss of control can be found elsewhere in the mystical poetry of the sixteenth-century Carmelite Juan de Yepes y Álvarez (John of the Cross), where the imagery of darkness

---

[75] See for example John Lightfoot, *The works* (1684), 1092. The Cambridge master preached at the Hertford assizes in 1665: 'Here we are groping after him, and much ado we have to discern a little of him;…Oh! what rapture of Soul will it be, to see all clouds dispelled, and to look with open full eye upon the Sun.'

[76] Spenser, *Fovvre hymnes*, 35; Crashaw, *Steps*, 146; Herbert, *The temple*, 34; Vaughan, *Silex*, 79.

[77] Robert Aylett, *The brides ornaments* (1625), 113. Somewhat grotesquely, Aylett used the martyrs' singing while being burned as an example of this tuning.

[78] Aylett, *The brides ornaments*, 11–12. We also find the imagery of fire alongside divine rapture in manuscript poetry of the period: 'by Divine raptus we aspire / and are inflamed with noble fire / O gracious savior Prince of Peace…save thy flock / Thy Gospell truth maintain': Cambridge University Library MS Add 8460, fols. 17–18.

[79] Barnes, *A divine centurie*, sigs. B2r, C3r. See also the madrigal writer Thomas Tomkins's 'Above the stars my savior dwells' in D. K. McColley, *Poetry and Music in Seventeenth-Century England* (Cambridge, 1997), 155.

predominates the move toward divine revelation. In 'Coplas hechas sobre un éxtasis de harta contemplación', the poet repeats the line 'Transcended knowledge with my thought', slowly ascending the mountain of contemplation, until he is 'rapt...away' (absorto y ajenado). While the speaker is more active here than in some Protestant poetry, nevertheless 'The farther I climbed...The less I seemd to understand', to the point where 'No human faculties or powers / Can ever to the top come nigh'. Here, at the precipice of all human understanding, neither the puritan divine nor the Catholic contemplative thought that they could move themselves heavenward.[80]

Where John of the Cross ascended into darkness, in Vaughan's 'The World', the individual moves toward a blinding light, which seemingly creates the same effect:

> I saw Eternity the other night,
> Like a great ring of pure and endless light,
> ...The way, which from this dead and dark abode
> Leads up to God,
> A way you might tread the sun, and be
> More bright than he.
> But as I did their madness so discuss
> One whisper'd thus,
> 'This ring the Bridegroom did for none provide,
> But for his bride'.[81]

Although Lewalski insists that this is not a 'poem of mystical vision', considering it instead to be 'a meditation' on 1 John 2, I do not think that such distinctions get us very far. After all, meditation was one of the antecedents of divine ravishment for Protestants and Catholics. The poem is certainly an admonition to eschew the things of the world (1 John 2.16), but it also engages with several aspects of raptus: the desire of the Bride for the Bridegroom, the sense of moving into an infinite 'endless light', and the notion that only 'some' ascend but not under their own power. Nevertheless, the desire to move heavenward was not simply a passive plea for God to act. Even though the soul could not ascend itself, there is a sense of reciprocity within such requests. Thus, the anonymous female author of Eliza's babes almost demands that she will not be like 'Most people' who 'hover here below'. Instead, she is confident that, 'Ile arise, and to Heaven goe', hoping never to lose sight of the beatific vision once she has experienced it, 'Still in this Rapture let me bide', clearly indicating that this is an experience occurring before death.[82] In 'On Earthly Love', the poet calls out, 'My Lord! My soule is ravisht with the contemplation of thy heavenly love; and I cannot chuse but infinitely admire thy

---

[80] St. John of the Cross, The Poems, trans. Roy Campbell (1951), 49–51.
[81] Vaughan, Silex, 91–2.   [82] Anon., Elizas babes (1652), 10.

mercies'.[83] Looking forward to when the Lord answers her call, the poet turned to music to characterize the heavenly scene, 'Angels…Oh hear, how rare, and sweet they sing! / My senses now are ravisht quite, / My Soule is fill'd with such delight'.[84] Similarly, in her manuscript collection of prayers and poems, Alathea Bethell insists that she will 'grovel Then no longer here on Earth' but will instead 'soar above ye Skys,' even though under her own soul's power she 'canst not reach at least Aspire / Ascend it not Indeed yet in desire'.[85]

While accommodating language of gardens, feasts, and bedchambers provided important images for the soul to begin the movement toward the divine, ultimately even these figures must be left behind. One of Quarles's emblems helps demonstrate the importance of this transition, depicting the figures of the Flesh and the Spirit as two women, both holding a looking glass (Figure 18). The Flesh holds out a prism, through which we can see 'The world in colours', offering no end of pleasure and enjoyment, even allowing us to 'turn upside down' the world itself. The Spirit, however, condemns this 'painted reason' for a spyglass that shows her a 'perfect view' of the end of humanity, which is depicted in the background with Christ at the Last Judgment (Heaven above and Hell below).[86]

We can see this effort to shuffle off the coloured figures of divine poetry, to focus the reader's attention upon the clear sight of the soul's ascent, in two final examples. First, Thomas Traherne, an Anglican cleric and chaplain to Charles II's Keeper of the Great Seal, published no poetry in his short lifetime, but his surviving manuscripts provide a rich *oeuvre* of religious and philosophical thought. Since Traherne believed that 'By Thoughts alone the Soul is made Divine', the pursuit of divine revelation for him was inherently intellectual. Biographical work on Traherne stresses his voracious reading of philosophy, science, and theology, as well as his almost Franciscan love of the natural world. Nevertheless, in his poem 'The Fulnesse', Traherne turned away from the intellect, and the figures it can conjure, because it was insufficient to reach the heavenly vision: 'I had not yet the Eye / The Apprehension, or Intelligence / Of Things so very Great Divine and High'.[87] And, even Traherne in 'The Improvment', cannot help but fall back on the exclamatory language that was reminiscent of biblical prophets when they encountered God: 'O Rapture! Wonder! Extasie! Delight! / How Great must then his Glory be', lacking the ability to put a more developed description together.[88] Other Traherne poems chart a contemplative path for the soul that desires divine illumination. Poems like 'The Instruction', 'The Anticipation', 'The Vision', and 'The Rapture', all wrestle with different aspects of divine ravishment. Interestingly, Traherne does not eschew the body quite as easily as other writers seem to do.

---

[83] Anon., *Elizas babes*, 65.   [84] Anon., *Elizas babes*, 18.

[85] Lambeth MS 2240, fol. 13v.   [86] Quarles, *Emblemes*, 171–2.

[87] Thomas Traherne, *The Poetical Works* (Cooper Square, 1965), 73–5, 33.

[88] Traherne, *The Poetical Works*, 20.

Figure 18. Francis Quarles, *Emblems* (London: M. G. and W, 1696), 180. The Huntington Library, San Marino, California.

The body is the container for the soul, 'An Univers enclosd in Skin', and Traherne clearly has an affinity for both, as he does not feel the need to speak pejoratively of the body. Instead, there is in Traherne's process of illumination a cleansing of the body ('Spue out thy filth') as well as an important recognition that the body cannot experience these soul-centred sensations, 'My Contemplation Dazles...Of all I comprehend. / And sours abov all Heights'.[89] For Traherne, as for most people before 1700, the material world was enclosed in the eternal, and as Lewalski points out, his poetry expresses an effort to 'win through to...spiritual vision'. Divine poetics, as Traherne writes in 'The Vision', is like 'Flight...but the Preparative', before one is given 'The Sight', which he cannot describe beyond a list of words typically associated with divine revelation, 'Deep and Infinit; / Ah me! Tis all the Glory, Love, Light, Space, / Joy, Beauty, and Varietie'.[90] Whether the 'Light' was that of Vaughan's ring or Spenser's heavenly beauty, it was attained through an ascent of the soul, which in part could be expressed through poetry. However, in Traherne, we can see a much more visceral side to divine revelation, one that easily and often pushed language to the very edge of its ability to capture what the individual experienced. Divine poetry as a preparative had its limits, which is evident every time Traherne descended into a list of words to capture what he otherwise could not describe.

A second example comes from the much less well-known work by Edward Benlowes, *Theophila*. Unlike Traherne, whose popularity slowly has grown, scholarship has not been kind to Benlowes. Born into the English gentry, Benlowes inherited Brent Hall (Essex) and, like Donne, converted from Catholicism, subsequently writing some anti-papist polemic to demonstrate his allegiances. *Theophila*, however, is noted mostly for its borrowing from greater voices. In fact, the illustrations done by Francis Barlow, which accompanied Benlowes's poems, have been treated with greater attention.[91] Nevertheless, the book was not without praise in its day, and it offers us an interesting portrait of what a non-clerical writer found to be inspiring in devotional poetry.[92] Unlike most devotional poems written in the first person, *Theophila* speaks of the lover of God as another. This second-hand approach certainly created a more romanticized poem, the sort that Margaret Cavendish feared would corrupt divine poetry. At the same time, it aligned with a tried-and-tested method of poetically exploring transcendent reality through an intermediary. Theophila appeared as Lady Philosophy appeared to Boethius and as Beatrice appeared to Dante, in 'A Form Angelick...divinely

---

[89] Traherne, *Poetical Works*, 33, 14, 56. See Jane Partner, 'Seeing and Believing', in *Literature, Belief and Knowledge*, eds Subha Mukherji and Tim Stuart-Battle, 85–107.

[90] Lewalski, *Protestant Poetics*, 379; Traherne, *Poetical Works*, 14.

[91] H. J. L. Robbie, 'Benlowes', *Modern Language Review*, 23 (1928), 342–4; Edward Hodnett described *Theophila* as 'a confused religious work', in *Francis Barlow* (Ilkley, 1978), 112.

[92] James Howell, *Poems* (1663), 123.

140 EXPERIENCING GOD IN LATE MEDIEVAL & EARLY MODERN ENGLAND

bright!...I was awake, I did not dream...my rapt Soul, ascending the Eye'.[93] Then, Theophila explains to him that 'Natural Philosophy hath not any thing in it which may satisfie the Soul'. Instead, she points to the traditional model of divine *raptus* which she organizes into threes, 'By *Humilitie*, by *Zeal*, by *Contemplation*'.[94] Part of this process is meditation upon the passion of Christ, and *Theophila* offers the reader illustrations of the Passion, including an anagram of 'Passio Christi' at the end of the work, as aids in meditation.[95] Comparing the 'high-flown Trance' of the soul to Stephen's vision of heaven, Benlowes explained, 'He's the bright *Sun*; 'twixt WHOM, and thy *Souls* Bliss, / Thy earthie Body interposed is;...Spiritual *Light* Spirituals clear: In Heav'n / Thou'lt view that *full*, what now by Glimps, like Stephen / Thou canst but *spy*'.[96] Ravishment was only a preview of the permanent state of the soul, when the 'Robe of Clay' is discarded, and yet, the effect of this preliminary rapture is overwhelming. Benlowes's *Theophila* speaks of the 'Wine of Extasie' which can 'raise the Souls to HEAV'N!', where they will be confronted with an infinite deity, who Benlowes referred to in different places as the 'LIVING FLOOD', the 'ABYSSE', and, more philosophically, the 'ARCHESSENCE'.[97]

Poetry provided a powerful means to put one's soul in the right, preparative state. Poetry's ravishing power could provide individuals an entrance into an emotional and affectionate space, which many people believed to be concomitant with the affections of divine *raptus*. Poetry's accommodating language captured this prelude of pleasures with a sense of festivity and/or tranquillity, relying upon the imageries and geographies of temples, courts, gardens, and feasts. Also, poetry expressed a relationship with God, which most often was composed of longing, invoking, thanking, imploring, and remembering. At the same time, divine poems highlighted the limitations involved in any human imaginings of divine ravishment. The pursuit of the mystical Bridegroom ultimately transcended language, even the language that expressed the ravishing power of God. As Traherne concluded in his poem 'Love':

> he comes down to me, or takes me up
>
> ...
>
> And fill, and taste, and give, and Drink the Cup.
> But these (tho great) are all
> Too short and small,
> Too Weak and feeble Pictures to Express
> The true Mysterious Depths of Blessedness.
> I am his Image, and his Friend.
> His Son, Bride, Glory, Temple, End.[98]

---

[93] Edward Benlowes, *Theophila* (1652), 72.   [94] Benlowes, *Theophila*, 15.
[95] Benlowes, *Theophila*, 269.   [96] Benlowes, *Theophila*, 53–4.
[97] Benlowes, *Theophila*, 106–8, 110.   [98] Traherne, *Poetical Works*, 66.

PART III
CHALLENGES TO THE CULTURE OF DIVINE REVELATION

6

'So unsatisfying…is Rapture'

The Word and the Spirit in the Seventeenth Century

Then the entire expression of their faces vacillates repeatedly: now happy, now sad; now crying, now laughing, now sighing—in short, they are completely beside themselves. Soon after, when they come to themselves, they say they do not know where they have been, whether in the body or out of it.

> Desiderius Erasmus, *The Praise of Folly*

Dieu d'Abraham, Dieu d'Isaac, Dieu de Jacob, non des philosophes et des savants.

> Blaise Pascal, Le Mémorial

In the early 1590s, Job Throkmorton was in hot water with London's religious authorities. He had been arrested for suspected involvement in the seditious Marprelate Tracts and was linked to the traitorous prophets William Hacket and Edmund Coppinger. Hacket was executed in 1591, Coppinger died in prison, and men like Throkmorton quickly moved to disentangle their reputations from the prophets. In an apologetic pamphlet, Throkmorton denied accusations made by Bishop Matthew Sutcliffe that he was the Marprelate author, and he did his best to explain his links to the prophets in such a way that would acknowledge the known facts and keep him out of prison. Throkmorton's testimony to his questionable associates included an account of a prayer meeting he had with Coppinger, wherein Coppinger seemed to be receiving divine revelation.[1] Despite Coppinger's claims to being ravished in the spirit, Throkmorton told his readers that he remained unconvinced by what he had witnessed. Explaining that Coppinger 'vsed many of these ohes, loude sighes and groninges', Throkmorton concluded that 'I saw no warrant' to believe Coppinger's experience was something 'out of the worde'.[2] In fact, Coppinger's revelations did not seem 'squared after the rule of knowledge, neither in method, matter nor manner', because Coppinger's behavior

---

[1] Alexandra Walsham, '"Frantick Hacket"', *The Historical Journal*, 41 (1998), 27–66.
[2] Job Throkmorton, *The Defence of Job Throkmorton* (1594), sigs, A3r, A4v.

Experiencing God in Late Medieval and Early Modern England. David J. Davis, Oxford University Press.
© David J. Davis 2022. DOI: 10.1093/oso/9780198834137.003.0007

144   EXPERIENCING GOD IN LATE MEDIEVAL & EARLY MODERN ENGLAND

was too emotional.[3] In other words, Coppinger did not live up to what Throkmorton considered to be certain basic expectations of how ravishment was experienced.

On the one hand, we should keep in mind that Throkmorton is doing damage control, and the description of his relationship with Coppinger should be taken with more than a pinch of salt. Whether he was sincere or not in his characterization of Coppinger is an important question; however, more important for our consideration is how Throkmorton attempted to distance himself from the prophets. Throkmorton deployed the discourse of divine revelation in an attempt to discredit someone claiming to be ravished in the spirit, highlighting key legitimizing elements in making his case. Coppinger's experience was irrational ('the rule of knowledge'), unbiblical ('the worde'), and lacking any soul-ravishing, because he produced several 'loude sighes and groninges'.

As we have seen in previous chapters, many claims to experiences of divine rapture were not accepted without legitimation. In England, distinguishing between true and false revelation reached a fever pitch in the 1640s and 1650s, as a variety of new sectarian religious groups appeared, many claiming some degree of prophetic authority.[4] While Protestant sectarianism was nothing new to the period, the sheer volume of such groups was overwhelming, particularly in London. In 1646 Thomas Edwards complained to the members of Parliament that the 'swarmes...of Sectaries' had overrun many of London's parishes.[5] Over the next decade, the growth of groups like the Quakers, Ranters, and Fifth monarchists only compounded what Edwards saw as a plague on England.

This chapter focuses on how an extended effort to distinguish what religious authorities considered to be experiences with God from illegitimate experiences impacted the larger culture of divine revelation. We will see how the traditional discourse of *raptus* was recontextualized, serving both as a means of legitimating and delegitimating the experiences of particular groups and individuals.[6] Rather than treating these sectarian groups as something in opposition to more widely accepted Protestant confessions, this chapter positions them as an expression of the larger culture of divine revelation. Sectarian (or radical) prophets used much of the same language to describe their experiences, as well as the biblical models

---

[3] T. H. L. Parker, *Calvin's Old Testament Commentaries* (Edinburgh, 1986), 210; Throkmorton, *The Defence*, sig. A3r.

[4] The impact that these sectarian groups had on English history and politics cannot be explored sufficiently in this chapter. Formative works include Hill, *The World Turned Upside Down*; David R. Como, *Blown by the Spirit* (Cambridge, 2004); Glenn Burgess and Matthew Festenstein eds, *English Radicalism, 1550–1850* (Cambridge, 2007); Ariel Hessayon and David Finnegan, eds, *Varieties of Seventeenth and Early Eighteenth Century English Radicalism in Context* (Aldershot, 2011).

[5] Thomas Edwards, 'The Epistle Dedicatory', *Gangraena* (1646), sig. B1r.

[6] My thinking on discursive legitimizing has been helped along by the work of van Leeuwen, *Discourse and Practice*, pp. 105–24.

of divine revelation, that we have seen in previous chapters.[7] That is to say, these prophets, and the groups they represent, were as much a part of, and products of, the religious culture as people like Edwards who roundly denounced what the prophets claimed to experience.

First, the chapter looks at how the prophets, and those who documented their lives, placed them within the larger culture of divine revelation by echoing many of the typical tropes of the culture. Second, the chapter examines two key features of the English Protestant critique of sectarian prophets, the theology of cessation and the animosity vented at what was called *enthusiasm*. This critique highlights an influential recontextualization of how divine revelation was represented and understood in the larger culture. Finally, the chapter examines how the polemical attacks upon sectarianism was a correlative of an attempt by different religious leaders to downplay the importance of divine ravishment in the lives of early modern people.

Radicalizing Revelation

According to the early modern antiquarian John Strype, a man known as 'Elizeus Hall' arrived in London in 1562, claiming to be the Old Testament prophet Elijah. Hall's proclamations included a particularly dangerous warning to the English government not to stray from Roman Catholic doctrine, just as Queen Elizabeth and her bishops were beginning to reform the church. After he was arrested, Hall explained to officials that:

> one Night in a Vision he saw a Fire in his Chamber, and heard a Voice saying unto him, Ely, Arise, Watch and Pray, for the Day draweth nigh. And that this Voice was heard thrice that Night…Further he said, That he was rapt out of the Bed, and saw Heaven and Hell, and was absent from the 9th of April, 1562, till the 11th next following.[8]

Not only was Hall supposed to be Elijah reborn, but his experience of a voice heard three times sounds suspiciously like the Old Testament prophet Samuel's first encounter with God (1 Samuel 3). Like other people claiming an experience of divine revelation, Hall (or Strype describing Hall) deployed the standard discourse of divine revelation, emphasizing the soul's dissociation from the body. Nevertheless, Hall was punished—pilloried and imprisoned in Bridewell

---

[7] Particularly in the context of millenarian beliefs, see Bryan Ball, *A Great Expectation* (Leiden, 1975). The recent re-evaluation of the term 'radical' bears witness to the blurry lines that separated the experiences of sectarian prophets: Ariel Hessayon and David Finnegan, 'Introduction', in *Varieties*, eds Hessayon and Finnegan, 1–30.

[8] John Strype, *Annals of the Reformation* (1725), 290.

146   EXPERIENCING GOD IN LATE MEDIEVAL & EARLY MODERN ENGLAND

(where he died)—for his popish beliefs, and Strype dismissed Hall's claims as 'pretended...Revelations and Voices speaking to him from Heaven'.[9]

Hall's traditional description of *raptus* raises some important questions about how far this discourse could go in establishing a person's legitimacy. How was it clear to the London officials, and Strype apparently, that Hall was a pretender? Did the content of his beliefs override any consideration for the divine experiences he described? Also, what separated Hall from people like the martyr Thomas Tomkins (Chapter 4) or the preacher John Holland (Chapter 5) who experienced similar ravishments? Approaching such questions not only helps better situate the prophets within the larger culture of revelation, but also sheds light upon the historical trajectory of the discourse of divine revelation in the seventeenth century.

Despite the fact that prophets like Hall were generally denounced, their experiences were often framed in the same language of divine revelation. For example, in the 1650s, Lodowick Muggleton and his cousin John Reeve claimed to be the two witnesses from Revelation 11, gaining a popular following in London. Muggleton described his own divine visions, which began in April 1651, as 'Elevasions in my Mind and Raptures of Joy'. Not only did Muggleton experience a five-day course of such rapture on one occasion, but also the experience was so intense that he did not move his body the entire time.[10] When it was over, Muggleton and Reeve set out on what they called the 'Third Commission', a divinely ordained mission to prepare England for the Apocalypse. Part of this preparation included condemning the many false prophets, including several of Muggleton's early influences, like the Ranter prophet John Robins (who claimed to be 'God Almighty').[11] Nevertheless, like Hall a century earlier, Reeve and Muggleton were found guilty, this time of blasphemy, and sent to prison.

Of course, the likes of Hall and Muggleton were extremes, even among radicals and sectarians. Most prophets satisfied themselves with simply drawing direct parallels with biblical exemplars, rather than claiming to be a biblical character (or God himself). The Quaker apologist George Keith held up biblical exemplars like Amos, Isaiah, Paul, and John to help people consider the ways in which God could work upon 'the Souls and Minds' of all men and women.[12] Others like the Bristol-born prophetess Grace Cary described her experiences with the phrase 'whether in the body, or out of the body' echoing Paul's vision of the third heaven (2 Cor. 12.3).[13] Likewise, Sarah Wight was said to be a devout young woman,

---

[9] Strype, *Annals*, 290.

[10] Lodowick Muggleton, *The acts of the witnesses* (1699), 15. For other examples of claims to being reincarnated biblical figures see Keith Thomas, *Religion and the Decline of Magic* (1991), 157; Walsham, *Providence in Early Modern England*, 204, 211.

[11] Muggleton, *The acts of the witnesses*, 22.

[12] George Keith, *Divine immediate revelation* (1685), 39–40.

[13] Theophilus Toxander, *Vox coeli to England* (1646), 3.

whose visions seemed to follow closely those of biblical prophets. In the account of her first 'Trance' beginning on April 10, 1647, her biographer Henry Jessey compared Wight with Saul, following his conversion on the Damascus road, as Wight and Saul both experienced 'three dayes without sight, and neither did eat, nor drinke'.[14] The millenarian visions of Anna Trapnel, who had her first vision at the age of nine, was one of the many people inspired by Wight's story.[15] Trapnel's explanation of her own visions was as orthodox as any, writing that the 'spirit takes us up' and that during her 'Raptures', like the biblical prophets, she was 'not sensible of a body'.[16] Trapnel's narrative structure echoed many aspects of the discourse of divine revelation: identifying important days of revelation, employing the language of ravishment, and coding her experiences in terms of joys, affections, and a general love for Christ.[17] In another example from later in the century, the Philadelphian Society prophet Jane Lead stated bluntly that her revelations were 'not unlike' the 'sort of Vision the Beloved John was in, when being wholly caught up *in the Spirit*'. Interestingly, Lead, like Julian of Norwich, employed the language of ravishment only on rare occasions, even though she had no qualms about writing in extensive detail about what she witnessed.[18]

What these prophets claimed to receive from God put them at odds with the authorities, but the way in which they received the revelations conformed to the well-trodden discourse. One Royalist example of this is the prophet Arise Evans, who, despite continual rejection, pressed his predictive visions into the public sphere. As early as the 1630s, the journeyman tailor Evans made his way to London to warn the king about an impending doom. In his autobiographical *An echo to the Book* (1653), Evans explained that after moving to Blackfriars around 1633, he found himself 'in high Meditations' on the Sabbath, from whence he 'did ascend in thoughts to Godward'.[19]

While Evans saw into the heavens, his efforts to see King Charles only made it as far as the Earl of Essex's chambers, who summarily dismissed the prophet. Stubborn and confident in his divine calling, Evans refused to accept rejection, becoming one of the most prolific prophets in London and publishing two dozen or so pamphlets in the 1650s.[20] When the prophet John Farly came on the London

---

[14] Henry Jessey, *The exceeding riches of grace* (1647), 15; Barbara Ritter Dailey, 'The Visitation of Sarah Wight', *Church History*, 55 (1986), 438–55.

[15] The trend of female of prophets has been carefully studied by Phyllis Mack, *Visionary Women* (Berkeley, CA, 1992).

[16] Anna Trapnel, *A legacy for saints* (1654), 11, 26.

[17] Also, like Catherine of Siena, Trapnel reported that at one point in her life she was continually experiencing divine raptures that rendered her body immobile: Trapnel, *A legacy for saints*, 25–6.

[18] Jane Lead, *A fountain of gardens* (1696), 12. A very helpful study of Lead's life and influence is the collection of essays *Jane Lead and Her Transnational Legacy*, ed. Ariel Hessayon (2016).

[19] Arise Evans, *An echo to the voice of heaven* (1652), 9–10.

[20] Christopher Hill, *Change and Continuity in 17th Century England* (New Haven, CT, 1974), 76.

148 EXPERIENCING GOD IN LATE MEDIEVAL & EARLY MODERN ENGLAND

scene, Evans seems to have taken the young prophet under his wing, promising Farly that he could interpret divine visions. In *The bloudy vision of John Farly*, Evans stressed the veracity of Farly's experiences, pointing out five criteria of his trustworthiness: 'he was not factious', Farly was not proud, Farly found a peace in his soul when he heard the interpretation, he prayed regularly, and he gave God the glory for the visions.[21]

Elsewhere, few seventeenth-century prophets crafted as detailed a persona as the Seventh-Day Baptist minister Francis Bampfield, who modelled himself after the apostle Paul. Following an Oxford education, Bampfield became the minister at St. Mary's (Sherborne) and a prebend of Exeter Cathedral, before he drifted into more radical and sectarian groups in the 1650s.[22] Then, in 1661, Bampfield underwent a spiritual transformation following an illness, going so far as to adopt a new name 'Shem Acher'. Also, like Paul (who had been Saul), Bampfield made a career as a travelling preacher, spending a good deal of time in prison for his illegal ministry. However, where the biblical apostle hesitated in describing what he experienced in the third heaven, Bampfield offered readers a description of each member of the Trinity among other wondrous sights. Nor did Bampfield shy away from overtly political messages. In 1665, he claimed to have received a vision that opposed the 'unclean Constitution' of Charles II's Act of Uniformity, telling his readers that he knew God was communicating directly with him, because he 'was on a sudden taken up in his Spirit as if he had been actually in Heaven'.[23]

That Bampfield's defense for denouncing the Act of Uniformity was a description of divine *raptus* is not insignificant. For most of these prophets, their terminology, examples, models, and essential understanding of the process were in many respects carbon copies of what they had been given by devotional and theological literature. However, their experiences were roundly denounced by religious authorities, from puritan divines to Anglican bishops. The legitimacy of the prophets was undermined by many of the same writers who celebrated divine ravishment in other contexts.

In the remainder of this chapter, we will attempt to parse out what distinguished these prophets from other accounts that we have seen as well as describe the impact that this effort to isolate true from false revelation had upon the traditional discourse of *raptus*.

---

[21] Arise Evans, *The bloudy vision of John Farly* (1653), 14.

[22] Bampfield was the kind of radical discussed by Nicholas McDowell, an educated man who turned away from a traditional clerical career. Although Bampfield denounced learning, his text is framed by Greek and Hebrew scripture: *Shem 'achar* (1681), 8.

[23] Bampfield, *Shem 'achar*, 4.

Prophecy Has Ceased

One of the important contexts for understanding the animosity toward radical prophets was the growing Protestant distrust of contemporary claims to prophetic revelation. Although prophecy and revelation were not synonymous, the former was certainly a subset of the latter, and in early modern England, whether or not God continued to communicate in a prophetic manner became hotly contested. While many Protestants by 1600 insisted that miracles had ceased at the end of the biblical era (or thereabouts), there was less certainty about the cessation of prophecy.[24]

This is interesting for a few reasons. First, it suggests experiences of divine revelation were not exactly miraculous. Certainly, the two (miracle and revelation) were associated with one another, but the relationship of a miracle to the laws of nature was not the same as that of revelation. Traditionally, the miraculous was understood not as a violation of natural laws but as a transcending of them. Divine *raptus*, however, neither violated nor transcended the natural.[25] The capacity of the soul to enjoy experiences absent from the body was a perfectly natural one, in the generally-accepted understanding of the body/soul relationship. Second, it would make sense that revelation was not necessarily considered to be miraculous, since challenges to miracles in the seventeenth century by freethinkers like Baruch (Benedict de) Spinoza did not necessarily include revelation.[26] We even can see this distinction in the middle of the eighteenth century in responses to David Hume's famous critique of miracles and prophecy. Critics of Hume from Anglican divines to the popular essayist Samuel Johnson maintained this distinction between prophecy (revelation) and miracles, asserting that a denial of the continuation of the one (i.e. miracles) did not *ipso facto* constitute a denial of the continuation, or possibility, of the other (i.e. revelation).[27]

If revelation and miracles were not the same kind of thing, when did the cessation of prophecy become a popular view? The doctrine of cessationism was foreign to most medieval understandings of God's activities in the world, and any clear position affirming cessation during the Reformation was a slow development.

---

[24] Walsham, *Providence in Early Modern England*, 226–8; D. P. Walker, 'The Cessation of Miracles', in *Hermeticism and the Renaissance* (Washington DC, 1988), 111–24. At the same time, devout and well-educated Protestants like the physician Sir Thomas Browne (who was attacked for his scepticism) were hesitant to affirm the cessation of miracles: *Religio Medici* (New York, 2012), 32–3.

[25] Charles Taliaferro, *Evidence and Faith* (Cambridge, 2005), 195. The medieval concept is summarized in Aquinas, *The Summa*, I.105.6–7. Also, see Protestant examples like John Gaule, *A collection of the best approved authors* (1657), 206.

[26] See for example Thomas Browne, *Miracles work's* (1683), 2, 8. (NB: this is not the physician and author of *Religio Medici*).

[27] Peter Harrison, 'Prophecy, Early Modern Apologetics, and Hume's Argument against Miracles', *Journal of the History of Ideas*, 60 (1999), 250–5.

150 EXPERIENCING GOD IN LATE MEDIEVAL & EARLY MODERN ENGLAND

Luther and Calvin did not insist upon a hard line when it came to prophecy, though they were generally suspicious, and other influential reformers like Peter Vermigli remained cautiously open to the possibility. In fact, the close relationship of the Holy Spirit and the Word of God in Calvin's theology almost insists upon a space for the continuance of divine revelation so long as it was grounded in biblical precedent.[28] In his *Loci communes*, Vermigli stated: 'perhaps there be some now a daies in the church, yet I thinke there be not manie'.[29] In general, Tudor and early Stuart Protestants seem to follow suit, expressing scepticism without being definitively opposed to the possibility. Works on devotion, theology, and the supernatural tended to condemn prophetic claims as nonsense or demonic.[30] Likewise, many divines described prophetic claims as a corrupt remnant of the Catholic contemplative tradition, but most were wary of drawing a hard line in the sand.[31]

The first formal statement categorically asserting the cessation of prophecy of which I am aware, appeared in the 1580s, among the many Protestant-Catholic disputes of that decade. The Cambridge theologian William Whitaker sparred with the Jesuit theologian Robert Bellarmine over the nature of scripture and its interpretation. In *A Disputation on Scripture*, Whitaker concluded, 'God does not teach us now by visions, dreams, revelation, oracles, as of old, but by the scriptures alone'.[32] Although it is always dangerous to put too strict parameters around what an infinite, omnipotent God might do, cessationism offered two major benefits for other Protestant notions. First, cessationism firmly established the primary importance of *sola scriptura*, as it made the Bible the only available source of prophetic revelation. Reading, meditating, and teaching scripture was more important now than ever.[33] Second, it provided a pre-packaged means of dismissing medieval mystics along with contemporary prophets and visionaries as superstitious, or worse.

However, few Protestant theologians before 1640 followed Whitaker's lead. They, instead, tended to take a more moderate position, by dissuading people from contemporary prophecy without ever firmly slamming the door shut. Thus, William Perkins, a colleague of Whitaker's at Cambridge, offered a qualified

---

[28] Zachman, *Image and Word*, 80, 258–9. See also G. H. Milne, *The Westminster Confession of Faith* (Milton Keyes, 2007), 45–50. While Calvin argued that predictive prophecy had ceased, he did not formally denounce the continuation of all immediate revelation (pp. 47–8).

[29] Vermigli, *The common places*, 18.

[30] George Abbot, *An exposition vpon the prophet Ionah* (1600), 10, 12; Richard Greenham, *The works* (1612), I.41; Reginald Scot, *The discoverie of witchcraft* (1665), VIII.ii, 88–9; Richard Bernard, *A guide to grand-iury men* (1627), 63.

[31] See e.g., William Perkins, *Of the calling* (1605), 56–60; Richard Bancroft, *A suruay of pretended holy discipline* (1593); Edwards, *Gangraena*, 28, 147; Edward Stillingfleet, *A discourse* (1671), 254, 258, 266, 272, 296, 340.

[32] William Whitaker, *A Disputation on Holy Scripture*, trans. Rev. William Fitzgerald (Cambridge, 1849), 521. An important analysis of the debate is Tadhg Ó hAnnracháin, 'Early Modern Catholic Perspectives on the Biblical Text', in *The English Bible in the Early Modern World* (Leiden, 2018), 104–30.

[33] G. Sujin Park, *The Reformation of Prophecy* (Oxford, 2018), 101.

warning: 'Wee must not now looke for traunces and visions, as they had, but wee must vse continuall studie in the word, which is the ordinarie means to come vnto this knowledge'.[34] Perkins was not one to mince words, and the difference between Whitaker's use of 'alone' and Perkins's 'ordinarie' is not insignificant. The latter suggested that there continued to be the potential for extraordinary means of learning directly from God, whether that means was through ravishment or otherwise. While I do not think that Perkins was making a space for contemporary prophecies, or even a robust space for divine *raptus*, he does seem to have in mind the kind of revelation more commonly called inspiration (or illumination), which he is not willing to eliminate as a means by which people might gain understanding about God.[35]

The fact that few English divines developed any elaborate argument in favor of cessationism is also telling. They relied upon pragmatic considerations, questions surrounding the uncertainty of the source, the trustworthiness of the individual, and other qualifiers to push the burden of proof upon the prophet rhetorically. Thus, Archbishop George Abbot exhorted ministers-in-training that 'although a motion euen from the Spirit of God, and an inward calling be needfull for vs', one cannot wait for the Holy Spirit to move. Since 'the word of God may not properly be said to come to vs', we must go to it by proactively turning 'to the word of God…to the Scripture'.[36] In other words, it was lazy to rely upon immediate revelation. A person should be more industrious in their devotion, by seizing upon the revelation God provided in scripture. However, this practice was not as straightforward as Abbot seems to present it. If, as many Calvinists believed, human beings were totally depraved in their desires, then a person would be 'needfull' of the Spirit's 'calling' first, in order for them to move to the Word. Also, how could the Spirit's calling, if or when the Spirit called, not be considered a kind of immediate revelation?[37]

Nevertheless, it was not until the 1640s that an English Protestant confession, the Westminster Confession, officially denied the continuation of prophetic revelation. As one of the most important achievements of the Westminster Assembly, the Confession was instrumental in reforming the Church of England between 1648 and 1660. In the first chapter of the Confession, the Assembly declared that while God had revealed himself in various ways in scripture, that 'those former ways of God's revealing His will unto His people being now ceased'.[38] God's will and any knowledge of him that can be known should be found only in the

---

[34] Perkins, *A godly and learned exposition*, 42.
[35] Milne, *The Westminster Confession*, 50–1. See for example his comments in Perkins, *The whole treatise of the cases of conscience* (1606), 75.
[36] Abbot, *An exposition*, 348.
[37] A recent study on English reformed views of free will provides some much needed nuance to the topic: Richard Muller, *Grace and Freedom* (Oxford, 2020).
[38] *The Confession of Faith*, ed. S. W. Carruthers (1946), Ch. 1.

152 EXPERIENCING GOD IN LATE MEDIEVAL & EARLY MODERN ENGLAND

canonical books of the Bible, which the Confession listed immediately below this statement.[39]

Unfortunately for those that celebrated the Westminster Confession, its limiting of what was and was not the Word of God created unforeseen problems. For example, Richard Baxter struggled to remain both within the Westminster Confession's box and internally coherent. In *The saints everlasting rest*, Baxter's argument for cessationism could be read as undermining the very doctrine he affirmed. Baxter explained that 'The more immediate the Revelation…the more sure: and the more succession of hands it passeth through, the more uncertain, especially in matter of Doctrine'. However, Baxter's 'succession of hands' was precisely the concern that contemporary critics like Spinoza and Samuel Fisher raised about the biblical text. The surviving manuscripts had passed through too many scribes and translators for the current versions to be considered as direct a revelation as the Spirit moving upon an individual's soul.[40] Downplaying the manuscripts' shortcomings as 'innocent imperfection', Baxter claimed that recorded revelation was a surer footing for faith and practice. He insisted that there was 'less danger of corruption' in the received text than sectarian prophecy 'when they deliver us that Doctrine in their own words…Therefore hath God been pleased…to leave his Will written in a form of words'.[41]

Even more important for our study of how people were understood to experience God, clerics like Baxter who embraced cessationism also encouraged readers to hope for divine *raptus*. Baxter's insistence upon God's 'Will' being delivered to people *only* in 'words' written down long ago is a jarring one, particularly in the same book in which Baxter encouraged people to advance their relationship with God in experiences of divine ravishment (see Introduction). In another example, toward the end of his career in 1677, John Owen wrote *The reason for faith*, one of his most sustained arguments for biblical authority (and cessationism). Fundamental was Owen's belief that the Bible is the place where 'God hath gathered up into the Scripture all divine Revelations given out by himself…all that shall ever be so to the end'. While this kind of statement is typical cessationism, Owen included an important caveat about the 'all', qualifying it with the phrase, 'which are of general use unto the Church'.[42] Although Owen moved on without further elaborating this point, it is evident from the context that the specific restrictions he placed upon divine revelation concern those revelations intended for the corporate, ecclesiastical body. It does not seem that divine ravishment in the life of the individual was part of the 'general use', which creates an important division in how the individual's relationship with God related to the larger body

---

[39] A thorough account of the theology of the Confession can be found in Milne, *The Westminster Confession*. See also Nicholas McDowell, *The English Radical Imagination* (Oxford, 2003), 38–40.
[40] See McDowell, *The English Radical Imagination*, 138–9.
[41] Baxter, *The saints everlasting rest*, 188, 185.   [42] John Owen, *The reason of faith* (1677), 8.

of Christ. The Holy Spirit could inspire and rapture a soul into heaven; however, this experience had little, direct 'use' for the larger religious community. It was a private affair between one's soul and God.

This leaves us with important questions that I do not think we can answer with certainty, at least not at the larger cultural level. Do such caveats from Perkins, Owens, and others demonstrate an understood loophole in English Protestantism that allowed for individual experiences with God, even within a cessationist theology? Should attacks on contemporary prophecy be understood as targeting only those claims to extra-biblical knowledge, which were intended to be shared with everyone? Without some space for the individual's direct experience of God, it would be difficult to so sequester God's communication with human beings entirely to the text of scripture without slipping into a sort of deism, and yet the Confession does not qualify or make any such space for personal revelation.

Either way, while Protestant divines wrestled with the practicalities of cessationism, groups like the early Quakers proffered much more confident arguments for what they often termed immediate revelation. In the last half of the seventeenth century, Quakers repeatedly took cessationism to task, focusing upon what they perceived to be an effort on the part of religious authorities to limit the Holy Spirit. Comparing puritan divines to the legalistic Pharisees and Sadducees of the New Testament gospels, Quakers condemned the spiritual impoverishment of cessationist dogma. The Society's founder George Fox explained that in affirming cessation, the divines simultaneously denied Christ, because they elevated human learning above the power of God. Since, Fox argued, 'none knows the Father but the Son, and he to whom the Son reveals him', then in order for people to 'know any thing' of God, they must receive it from Christ by some form of revelation, either directly or indirectly through someone 'sent of Christ'.[43] In *Rusticus ad academicos*, Quaker Samuel Fisher argued that every person possessed a supernatural 'Light' that comes 'from God and Christ into the mind and Conscience'. Fisher did not think of the Light as an extension of the human soul. Rather, the Light was a supernatural addition to the standard human faculties, an extension of the Word of God, allowing anyone to communicate with God directly. The Light was the vehicle for any divine experience. To deny its existence was tantamount, in Fisher's logic, to denying the possibility of salvation, because a person's understanding of the need for salvation came from God via the Light.[44]

For Quakers like Fox, this divine Light allowed people to open up the 'Scripture within you', which could illuminate the text of the Bible more clearly.[45] Other Quakers were less philosophical. George Keith pointed out that the same Holy

---

[43] George Fox, *To all who would know the vvay to the kingdome* (1654), 12. Earlier in the century, the Familist minister John Everarde made similarly withering attacks on the ecclesiastical authorities in England: Como, *Blown by the Spirit*, 247–9.

[44] Samuel Fisher, *Rusticus ad academicos* (1660), IV.ii.69, I.iii.89.

[45] Fox, *To all who would know*, 8.

154   EXPERIENCING GOD IN LATE MEDIEVAL & EARLY MODERN ENGLAND

Spirit that gave prophecy to biblical figures was also responsible for inspiration in contemporary devotion. How could people claim that the Spirit performed the latter but not the former? Keith exclaimed, 'Surely it was not Gods design to give us the Scriptures, that he might take away his spirit from us', leaving Christianity anchored to the text, unable to ascend in the spirit.[46] The preacher Edward Burrough, who was converted by Fox's sermons, condemned the 'stubble' of 'trad-itions...you have gathered together by imitation from the letter' as a kind of idolatry that characterized established Protestant religion. Those divines that say 'revelation...is ceased' neglect the eternal nature of the Word, 'that which was before the Scripture', relying solely upon 'the letter' rather than 'that which shall endure forever'.[47] Continuing in this vein, the bombastic shipowner, William Bayly wrote, 'O People! Awake...How can you see, who closed your Eye?' Pointing to scriptures like Proverbs 29.18 ('where there is no vision, the people decay'), he fashioned a simple paradigm of light and dark, contending that cessa-tionism abandoned people in darkness. Without immediate revelation, Bayly warned, 'Sight and Knowledge is ceased', which Bayly feared was exactly what the religious authorities wanted: 'You love Darkness...because your Deeds are evil'.[48]

Unfortunately, as with many of the Quakers' teachings that diverged from the norm in seventeenth century England, this debate inspired more rancour than it did reflection on all sides, which left many questions underexplored and many more completely unasked. For example, what was included in the notion of the Word of God? How much (if any) of human experience could be understood as divinely revealed? Was divine inspiration qualitatively different from prophecy or contemplative visions? Few clear answers were forthcoming from any side. Also, as is typical of polemic, criticism was followed by reproach. On the one side, to be critical of prophets was to despise the Holy Spirit. On the other, to enjoy a more robust understanding of how the Spirit communicates with people was to be a wild-eyed enthusiast.

Enthusiasm and All That Jazz

On February 28, 1660, John Gauden, who was soon to become Bishop of Exeter, preached a sermon to commemorate the restoration of the 'secluded members' of Parliament, who had been excluded in 1648 because of their opposition to the trial of Charles I. Gauden condemned the 'spiritual maladies' of the past two dec-ades, which had led people to trusting 'Enthusiasm, any glow-worm of fanatic

---

[46]   Keith, *Divine immediate*, 117.

[47]   Edward Burrough, *Truth defended* (1654), 4. See also the Baptist minister Daniel King's *A way to sion sought* (1650), 180–1.

[48]   William Bayly, *A call and visitations* (1673), 29–31. Also see Evans, *An eccho*, sig. A3v.

'SO UNSATISFYING...IS RAPTURE' 155

fancy and fury...instead of Gods candles and lamps of pure Religion in well-ordered Churches.[49] For Royalists like Gauden, the civil wars, the abolition of the monarchy, and the Cromwellian dictatorship were perpetrated not only by political radicals but also by religious sectarians consumed by 'enthusiasm', which Gauden understood to be a false sense of divine revelation, based on nothing more than an individual's feelings and internal reasoning. As a pejorative term attacking sectarian groups, Protestants introduced *enthusiasm* as early as the Lutheran conflicts with Anabaptists in the 1520s. The term described a frame of mind that relied upon internal inspiration with little or no regard for any confirmation from reason or authority (divine or otherwise). In subsequent decades, enthusiasm became a handy word to distinguish true and false prophecy, as sects began to break away from larger reform movements. Depending upon who one spoke with, enthusiasm soon included a panoply of ideas and beliefs, including: Paracelsian alchemy, Cartesian rationalism, Quakers, Ranters, and Libertines.[50]

Scholars usually locate enthusiasm in English religion as a characteristic of the middle of the seventeenth century; however, concern over enthusiasm was evident long before. For example, around the same time that Job Throkmorton distanced himself from the enthusiasm of Edmund Coppinger, Richard Bancroft was attacking Elizabethan puritans, because he considered them to be too 'addicted vnto their own opinions'. In the puritan impulse to remove the episcopal hierarchy, Bancroft thought that puritans 'thirsteth to drinke the waters, which they haue drawn out of their own cisternes', rather than rely upon reason and/or scripture. Similar accusations cut a wide swathe in the late sixteenth and early seventeenth centuries, from sectarian prophets to the Gunpowder Plot conspirators.[51] In fact, by the time that Thomas Edwards was cataloguing different religous sects in the 1640s, enthusiasm was believed to be running rampant across England. Among the kinds of 'Errours' Edwards warned against, readers should look out for anyone who believed, 'Tis ordinary for Christians now in these days, with Paul to be rapt up to the third Heavens, and to hear words unutterable'. Such experiences were central to their dogma, providing them 'assurance of being Christians'.[52]

Other signs of religious enthusiasm, as opposed to true revelation, were the physical gestures and uncontrollable bodily motions made by some prophets. The

---

[49] John Gauden, *A sermon in St. Paul's Church* (1660), 33.

[50] John Calvin explained that the biblical prophets 'had never fallen into an ecstasy, had never been *enthousiasmos*', (Parker, *Calvin's Old Testament Commentaries*, 210). See also Frederick Beiser, *The Sovereignty of Reason* (Princeton, 2016), 188–9; Michael Heyd, *'Be Sober and Reasonable'* (Leiden, 2000).

[51] Bancroft, *A suruay*, sig. **r, p. 5. See also Patrick Collinson, *Richard Bancroft and Elizabethan Anti-Puritanism* (Cambridge, 2013), 130–1; Walsham, '"Frantick Hacket"', 48. For the Gunpowder Plot conspirators, see the accusations of enthusiasm made against them in their trial: Thomas Howell, *State Trials* (1809), II.253–4.

[52] Edwards, *Gangraena*, 28.

156   EXPERIENCING GOD IN LATE MEDIEVAL & EARLY MODERN ENGLAND

Anglican controversialist Peter Heylyn explained that enthusiastic prophets were irrational and 'frantick'. He contrasted them with 'the Prophets inspired by God', who 'very well understood what they said and did, and did not only prophesie what should come to pass, but did it in a constant and coherent way of expression, and with a grave and reverent deportment of themselves in the act thereof'. Whereas the biblical prophets were governed by 'a grace and reverent' manner, which reflected the gravity and sacrality of the experience, enthusiasts generated uncontrollable sensations and motions.[53] For Heylyn, the physical signs of enthusiasm were as tell-tale as those of other infirmities. Similarly, in 1634, Archbishop William Laud encountered a frantic prophet, Robert Seal from Croydon, who had found his way to Lambeth Palace to tell the archbishop that God was not at all pleased with Laud's reforms to Anglicanism. Seal claimed that on the previous Shrovetide God spoke to him about Anglican priests 'not Preaching the Word sincerely'. Unfortunately for Seal's credibility, Laud found the man to speak and act 'somewhat wildly', indicating to the archbishop that 'the poor Man was overgrown with Phansie'.[54]

Much less sympathetically, pamphlets against the Quakers attacked them for their 'sudden agonies, trances, quakings, shakings, raptures', which were thought to cozen the ignorant and vulnerable. In *The Quakers wilde questions*, the priest Richard Sherlock warned of the 'wilde, exotique, and uncivil gestures', including 'frothing at the mouth, throwing themselves upon the ground'. Quakers 'confusedly talk much of holy things', Sherlock continued, and were often to be heard 'heap[ing] Scripture phrases' upon one another but 'without order, and right application'.[55] Even when these enthusiasts made a pretence of referring to an external authority, it was done only to confirm what they already believed to be true.

Sober religion became contrasted with the enthusiasts, who were characterized as excessive, discomposed, fanciful, distempered, melancholic, drunkards, and satanic. The puritan minister Thomas Parker, from his parish in Newbury (Massachusetts), warned his sister, the Berkshire prophet Elizabeth Avery, that she had 'gone by fancy and not by Reason, by an ungrounded apprehension and not by Scripture, by a Conscience without a Rule, made by Conceit, and not by the Word of God'. Although Parker made allowances for the weakness of his sister's gender, he believed the most alarming aspect of her abandonment of presbyterian theology was that her reasoning was based entirely upon enthusiastic revelations.[56]

[53] Peter Heylyn, *Theologia veterum* (1654), 91.
[54] William Laud, *The history of the troubles* (1695), 50.
[55] Anon., *The Quakers fiery beacon* (1655), 7; Richard Sherlock, *The Quakers wilde questions* (1655), 87.
[56] Thomas Parker, *The copy of a letter written by Mr. Thomas Parker* (1649), 18. Avery was the only female prophet among a large cadre of enthusiasts and sectarians. See T. C., *A glasse for the times* (1648).

It was common to question the intellectual capacity and educational background of the radicals, suggesting that their willingness to fall into such traps was the sign of a weak mind.[57] Thus, Thomas Comber's *Christianity, no enthusiasm* (1678) claimed that enthusiasts have 'Reason...extinguished', snuffed out by their 'Revelations', which do not conform to reason or authority. The physical excesses of the radical prophets were evidence of an imbalanced soul; enthusiasm quashed reason and, by extension, godly religion. The popular Cambridge minister Matthew Scrivener seems well acquainted with the Quaker community in Cambridgeshire, which was already boasting 600 members by 1655. Scrivener complained that their prophets speak of having 'transported minds', though according to his own observations, he could find nothing more in them than 'ridiculous actions inconsistent with the gravitie, and the puritie of the divine Presence'. Expanding upon his assessment, Scrivener noted at least six different causes of ecstatic behaviour. While vanity and demonic possession were popular culprits, he was convinced that as often as not the source of enthusiasm was more benign and natural.[58]

Interestingly, this kind of naturalising explanation was not uncommon. In one influential example, Henry More's *Enthusiasmus Triumphatus* approached enthusiasm as an intellectual or emotional ailment.[59] More believed enthusiasm was a malformation of an individual's understanding, where 'the inward sense is so vigorously affected...so that the opinion of the truth of what is represented to us...is far stronger then any motion or agitation from without'.[60] This malformation could be induced by a variety of things, from drugs and insect bites to melancholy, or another humoral imbalance. Similarly, the most popular authority on melancholic maladies, Robert Burton, noted that 'Philautia', or self-love, could induce women and men to 'ravisheth our senses' into '*amabilis insania*, a delectable phrensy'. Burton compared people who suffer from this sort of melancholy to the Greek hunter Narcissus who fell in love with his own reflection, because they are enamored by that which 'proceeds inwardly from our selues...from an overweening conceit' of the self.[61] These were people predisposed to this sort of behavior; they did not need music or poetry to lose themselves. Furthermore, as More reminded his readers, enthusiastic experiences were accompanied by the kind of charismatic 'fopperies' that Heylyn described as contradicting the biblical

---

[57] Thomas Comber, *Christianity, no enthusiasm* (1678), 67.

[58] Scrivener, *The method and means*, 316. For the Quaker community see Margaret Spufford, *Contrasting Communities* (Cambridge, 1979), 228–9.

[59] Henry More was a leading proponent of what Beiser terms the 'Naturalistic Argument' in *The Sovereignty of Reason*, 206. Robert Burton chalked up such enthusiasms to 'much fasting, and bad diet': *The anatomy*, 267.

[60] Henry More, *Enthusiasmus triumphatus* (Cambridge, 1656), 4.

[61] Burton, *The anatomy*, 162. Not unimportantly, Richard Rolle made a similar distinction between those suffering from melancholy and those that experienced divine revelation, who were capable of achieving a divine melody because they were not so self-interested (Chapter 1).

158   EXPERIENCING GOD IN LATE MEDIEVAL & EARLY MODERN ENGLAND

models of divine revelation. Interestingly, for More, these fopperies included not only uncontrolled gesticulations and frantic gestures but also 'an unfounded kind of popular Eloquence, a Rapsodie of slight and soft words', which are seductive enough to fool 'the heedless and pusillanimous'. More was not one to discourage delightful rhetoric, but sweet-sounding words were not indicative of good ideas, and the 'popular Eloquence' was not university-trained rhetoric but rather the kind of eloquence of street preachers, ballads, and low-brow poetry.[62]

Certainly, not everyone was as convinced as More that disordered emotions and imbalanced humors were the most likely causes of enthusiasm. The nonconformist minister and physician Richard Gilpin warned that 'Extasies, Trances, and quakings…their Prophesying' were brought about not only by human frailty but also, and perhaps more powerfully, by the Devil who 'soars a loft, and pretends the highest divine warrant for his falsehoods'.[63] What made matters worse in Gilpin's opinion was the fact that human beings want to believe these lies. We are endowed with a '*hasty* credulity', which overrides our rational faculties, because of a proclivity to believe that God is speaking.[64] One of the reasons for this credulity is that God had employed prophecy to communicate in the past, and human beings naturally expected this to continue. Interestingly, however, Gilpin believed that a 'kind of Revelation' could still be experienced through the teaching and leading of the Holy Spirit, echoing other nonconformists like Baxter and Owen. This inspiration was nothing like the extravagancies of enthusiasm, and, like Owen, Gilpin did not believe that such divine encounters were intended for the corporate body of the church.[65]

One final characteristic of the criticism levelled at enthusiasts was the tendency to conflate all sorts of religious enthusiasm. Following the model set out by Edwards's *Gangraena*, critics tended to lump all enthusiasts together. The Anglican theologian Edward Stillingfleet suggested that sectarians and papists shared the same 'Fanaticism', an 'Enthusiastick way of Religion', which he described as a general sentiment of resistance to authority 'under a pretence of Religion'. For Stillingfleet, the Roman Catholic doctrine of papal infallibility was as enthusiastic as the 'Fanatical Revelations…[and] fopperies' of Anna Trapnel and Muggleton. One critic of the Quakers lumped them together with evocative imagery, describing George Fox as having licked 'up the Froth from the mouth of Mother Julianna in one of her Enthusiastick raving Fits'.[66] Likewise, Comber explained that, 'The Church of Rome hath Plowed much with this Heifer' of

---

[62]   More, *Enthusiasmus*, 23. For further analysis see Temple, *Mysticism*, 101–6.
[63]   Richard Gilpin, *Demonolgia sacra* (1677), 105, 222.   [64] Gilpin, *Demonologia*, 224.
[65]   Gilpin, *Demonologia*, 224.
[66]   Edward Beckham, *The principles of the Quakers* (1700), 9. This kind of conflation even appeared on the London stage in the anonymous comedy *Mr. Turbulent* (1682), 60.

'SO UNSATISFYING ... IS RAPTURE' 159

enthusiastic prophecy, and the sectarians followed the papist furrow.[67] Gilpin fished with an even broader net, scooping together ancient Greek oracles, the prophet Muhammad, medieval saints, and recent prophets like Edmund Coppinger into the same enthusiastic catch.[68] That these groups believed distinctly different theologies was beside the point; their beliefs followed the same epistemically-flawed path, whether the cause was an imbalance of their humours or the fruit of demonic possession.

Not surprisingly, English Catholics saw the matter quite differently, pointing out that enthusiasm was particular to Protestantism. Catholic writers like the Jesuit James Sharpe argued that enthusiasm was the logical result of the Protestant 'private spirit', which was both the source and judge of enthusiasm.[69] Sharpe denounced enthusiastic displays as things contrary to both the contemplative tradition and the established hierarchy of ecclesiastical superiors. Contrastingly, Protestantism nurtured enthusiastic disorder by trusting too much in individual intuition and understanding. The Holy Spirit, Sharpe explained, worked on the 'superior parts of the soule', and the Spirit encouraged people to 'ways ordinary, plaine...not aspiring to works and effects extraordinary high, prodigious, miraculous, beyond reach of our reason'.[70] Similarly, Augustine Baker's *Sancta Sophia* distanced Catholic contemplatives from enthusiasts, the former being filled with 'that Spirit of Charity and Peace' while the latter suffered from the 'spirit of Disorder, Revenge, Wrath, and Rebellion'.[71] Unlike the Protestant enthusiasts who made claims to new doctrine and anti-ecclesiastical authority, the Catholic contemplative, according to Baker, was humble, reasonable, and submissive to the Roman Catholic Church.

Sadly, as is often the case in such over-generalizations, there were innocent victims of this tendency to regard all enthusiasts as the same species. One unfortunate example was the execution of the preacher John James, following the quashed rebellion known as Venner's Rising, a violent insurrection in London led by the Fifth-monarchist Thomas Venner. After days of street fighting in January 1661, most of the rebels were arrested and prosecuted by London's authorities; however, months later the city remained watchful. Even though James, a Seventh-Day Baptist preacher, had no connection to the rebellion, his sectarian sermons were well known, making him an easy target. At his trial, the prosecutors punctuated

---

[67] Edward Stillingfleet, *A discourse concerning the idolatry practised in the Church of Rome* (1671), 209, 224; Comber, *Christianity, no enthusiasm*, 69–79, quote on p. 79. See also Temple, *Mysticism*, 52–64.

[68] Gilpin, *Demonologia*, 188, 222–3.

[69] The private spirit was personified as a musician of discord and cacophony, in the anti-Protestant title-page engraving for William Malone's *A reply unto Mr. Iames Vssher* (See Figure 8).

[70] James Sharpe, *The trial of the Protestant private spirit* (St. Omer, 1630), sig. L3v. See also Malone, *An answer*, sig. *1v–2r; David Abercromby, *Scolding no scholarship* (Douai, 1669), 69–71.

[71] Augustine Baker, *Sancta Sophia* (1657), p. xxv. Despite Baker's condemnation of sectarian enthusiasts, groups like the Philadelphians were inspired by his book: Temple, *Mysticism*, Ch. 5. See also Luis de la Puente, *Meditations* (Douai, 1610), 56–7.

160 EXPERIENCING GOD IN LATE MEDIEVAL & EARLY MODERN ENGLAND

their accusations against James with comments about his holding to the Fifth-monarchists' 'sort of enthusiasm' and that James's sermons rested upon 'pretended revelations'. Whatever the reasoning behind the charges and despite James's wife pleading before the king, James met his fate at Tyburn in November 1661.[72]

James certainly was not the only innocent victim of the attack on religious enthusiasm. In fact, divine revelation itself was beginning to suffer from the polemical assault that had begun to conflate a wide body of religious experience. Raptures, ravishings, revelations, prophecies—these terms were thrown about, often with little care for distinction or definition. The discourse of divine revelation was deployed to condemn radical enthusiasts in such a way that threatened to undermine the veracity of all experiences of divine revelation. This threat was compounded, as we will see in the final section of this chapter, by a direct undermining of divine ravishment on the part of several Protestant writers, who, while not denying the possibility of ravishment, began to question its role in people's lives.

Letting the Discourse Fall

William Strong was one of the many independent ministers whose life was uprooted by the civil war. Driven from his Dorset parish by Royalist forces in 1643, he found a new home (and parish) in London, eventually joining the Westminster Assembly. During his time in London, he wrote one of the more developed, reformed statements on the beatific vision, providing us with an altogether puritan understanding of divine revelation. Although Strong believed that in this life, humans can only look upon God *via negativa*, 'by Resemblance and Metaphors', he contended that this sight is nevertheless real and substantial, because we can 'look upon the fulness of Christ here with delight', beholding 'the glory of God with satisfaction'. Drawing on a breadth of scholarship from Thomas Aquinas to John Calvin, Strong argued that it was possible to experience an 'intellectual Vision of God...*visio mystica*', which can be had 'by discoveries made unto the eye of their faith'.[73] Strong likened the beatific vision in this life to a wife looking upon her husband's 'glory and excellencies'. In the same way, Strong explained, God is seen in the material world, 'Discursively...from these similitudes'. While the ungodly ('a stranger') also experiences the discourse of God's glory in this world, she or he ultimately 'lets the discourse fall again', forgetting what the husband looks like. Only the godly person maintained the discourse (of her husband) in the mind's eye, allowing it to germinate to the 'fulness of satisfaction', through prayerful meditation and discipline.[74]

---

[72] Howell, *State Trials*, VI.106–7.
[73] William Strong, *Discourse of the two covenants* (1678), 286–7, 290.
[74] Strong, *Discourse*, 287, 286.

'SO UNSATISFYING...IS RAPTURE' 161

Even at the end of the seventeenth century, there was no shortage of examples of people, even among Protestants, who enjoyed such an experience of discursive clarity with God. Not only did many of the texts that we have explored in previous chapters remain in circulation, but new accounts also appeared. The popular writer and champion of Protestant nonconformity Samuel Clarke celebrated individuals' revelatory experiences in multiple biographical works of divines and 'eminent persons'. Here, people could read of men like the Yorkshire minister Samuel Winter who experienced several divine ravishments following a sickness in 1666, where he was shown 'the great Mystery of heavenly Glory'. Winter's 'Understanding and Memory', Clarke stressed, were not 'overcome', as the enthusiasts' minds seem to have been. Instead, like the apostle Paul, Winter found himself for several hours unaware of whether he 'were in the Body or not'.[75] The Oxford-trained, nonconformist minister Joseph Allein even noted that when he was wracked with sickness and convulsions, he 'had not those Ravishing Joys...which some did pertake of' and of which Allein 'expected' to enjoy. Nevertheless, a few years later, Clarke assures us, at the end of his life Allein 'was much ravisht', which were like 'Tokens' from Christ.[76]

At the same time, we can detect an increasing anxiety in the way that many Protestants spoke about such experiences with God. Like the stranger in Strong's analogy, there is evidence of letting the traditional discourse of divine revelation fall away. While the discourse is not forgotten immediately, or consciously, the discursive representations of divine revelation were undermined in different ways, particularly as leading Protestants wrestled with the blight of enthusiasm. Part of this drift, as I have already alluded to, had to do with the messiness by which different terms were being deployed to consider, describe, extol, and/or condemn claims to divine revelation. Until the mid-seventeenth century divine *raptus* in England was largely reserved for experiences that were believed to be sincere, legitimate experiences of God's self-disclosure. This was no longer the case following the efforts to silence enthusiastic religion.

Richard Sherlock's attack on the Quakers illustrates the confusion quite well. Even though earlier Protestants stated emphatically that the biblical prophets were not ecstatic in their revelations, Sherlock insisted that prophets had been ecstatic. He distinguished between divine and diabolic extasy: 'one of the Reasonable soul...without the instrumental mediation of the senses', and the other through the 'Sensitive soul...by sensible objects'.[77] Since his description corresponds fairly well with the traditional discourse of *raptus*, it raises the question of why he used the term *extasy* for divine revelation. Then, Sherlock offered a second distinction

[75] Clarke, *The lives*, 99–100. Elsewhere ministers could be found extolling such experiences in their own personal devotions: John Owen, *Pneumatologia* (1676), 187; Thomas Wadsworth, *Wadsworth's remains* (1680), 29; Trench, *Some remarkable passages*, 15–18.

[76] Clarke, *The lives*, 152, 156.

[77] Sherlock, *The Quakers wilde*, 81–5, quote on p. 85.

162 EXPERIENCING GOD IN LATE MEDIEVAL & EARLY MODERN ENGLAND

between kinds of ecstasies of the reasonable soul: natural and supernatural. The supernatural extasy, Sherlock argued, was the experience of the biblical prophets, which he specifically distinguished from 'those holy, divine, and ravishing contemplations', which 'all truly and fervently pious, and heavenly minded men are ordinarily extasied, and transported'. The latter seem to fall into neither natural nor supernatural extasy, even though Sherlock identified them as holy transportations of the soul. Finally, throughout the text, Sherlock tended to use 'contemplation' to describe pagan or papist practices, both of which he considered to be ungodly. When the contemplative is in fact godly, they seem to be a rare breed, according to Sherlock, which he treated with caution rather than encouragement:

> although it be true, that some few divine celestial souls, by their private fervent prayers, holy desires, heavenly contemplations,…have a nearer and more close familiarity with him, then in, and by the use of external ordinances is attainable: yet so to be above ordinances, as to live without them, is to live besides the rules of the Gospel.[78]

Nor was Sherlock the only one struggling to parse out enthusiasm from divine revelation. One of Sherlock's sources, the Swiss classicist Meric Casaubon wrote that 'Ecstasies taken for a total suspension of all sensitive powers, the effect sometimes Contemplation, and earnest intuition of the mind', but other times, they were 'Enthusiastick Delusions'.[79] Likewise, the Huguenot theologian David Blondel reminded readers of the difficulties that even church fathers like Ambrose had in explaining the difference between biblical prophets and pagan seers. Whereas one is a 'servile transportation' that 'darkens the light of their minds', the other is a 'holy Ravishment' which 'refined the understanding'.[80] Others, like Obadiah Walker, the master of University College (Oxford), expressed uncertainty about the details surrounding divine ravishment. Unlike earlier writers we have seen, Walker did not insist upon a dissociation of body and soul: 'we may conceive a mans spirit remaining in the Body to receive such visions'. Walker is intentionally ambiguous ('may conceive'), and he included all biblical visions in this assessment: 'and thus, St. Pauls Rapture will be most agreeable with other Scripture-rapts. Where also are the same expressions of the transportation of the Spirit, or Body…[and] Whether the Spirit remaining in the body…I cannot tell'.[81] Although it was not entirely unusual to suggest that some divine inspirations may

---

[78] Sherlock, *The Quakers wilde*, 240.

[79] Meric Casaubon, *A treatise concerning enthusiasme* (1656), sig. A3v. Casaubon's works were influential in the conflict between traditional religion and enthusiasm. See also Heyd, *'Be Sober and Reasonable'*, Ch. 3.

[80] David Blondel, *A treatise of the sibyls* (1661), 63. Peter Heylyn pointed to Tertullian as another example of a church father cozened by enthusiasts: Heylyn, *Theologia veterum*, 91.

[81] Obadiah Walker, *Paraphrases and Annotations* (Oxford, 1684), 161.

be experienced in the body, the idea that Paul's vision of the third heaven, the template for divine *raptus* in much of the commentary literature, occurred in the body, flew in the face of a long tradition and discourse.

When it came to applying divine revelation to the lives of contemporary Christians, Jeremy Taylor defended the true revelations of the prophets and the apostles in scripture, which were not 'excesses of Religion', but he warned against those people who keep their own 'Fancy...continually warm and in a disposition and aptitude to take fire, and to flame out in great ascents'. Taylor did not reject the possibility of divine rapture, but he was cautious of what he called the 'suburbs of beatifical apprehensions', which he thought of as a dangerous place where the soul could become lost in its own fantasies and delusions (i.e. enthusiasm). Far from encouraging readers to pursue divine revelation, he questioned whether the uncertainty of the source of the ravishment outweighed the potential benefit to the individual, since 'they that think best of it cannot give a certainty' of how to detect whether the ravishing is from God.[82] Taylor encouraged people toward a more mundane existence:

> to dig the earth, and to eat of her fruits than to stare upon the greatest glories of the Heavens...so unsatisfying a thing is Rapture and transportation to the Soul; it often distracts the Faculties, but seldom does advantage..., and is full of danger in the greatest of its lustre.[83]

Likewise, Matthew Scrivener noted that in recent times, 'Extasies and Raptures' were 'too muched famed by some', stressing the divisiveness that they had brought to English religion. Since, as he argued, an individual's faith is 'not proved' nor sustained by 'such excesses', it is better to avoid them because they too easily 'blinde the eyes of Reason'. John Owen also questioned the ultimate efficacy of ravishment, rejecting the idea that a person's regeneration in Christ could come through 'Enthusiastical Raptures'. Similarly, Comber attacked what he saw as an essential tenet of sectarian religion: the belief that 'Inward Experience' could serve as a 'bottem' for Christian faith and practice. Even Moses, according to Comber, 'was not hasty in believing' when he saw the burning bush, restraining the credulity that seemed so natural to the human condition.[84]

Although these concerns seem entirely sincere, they represent a distinct unsettling of the culture of divine revelation. The fact that such sharp criticisms were levelled neither by freethinking sceptics nor materialists but rather by leading members of different Protestant confessions (nonconforming puritans

---

[82] Taylor, *Antiquitates*, 60–1. [83] Taylor, *Antiquitates*, 61.

[84] Scrivener, *The method and means*, 309, 315, 229; Owen, *Pneumatologia*, 186; Comber, *Christianity*, 158. Similar questions were raised about ravishment while participating in the sacrament: Jean d'Espagne, *The eating of the body of Christ* (1652), 132.

164   EXPERIENCING GOD IN LATE MEDIEVAL & EARLY MODERN ENGLAND

and Anglicans) is most significant in understanding the shifting attitudes toward divine revelation in the period.

What place did Strong's theology of the beatific vision in this life have if it was not only uncertain but potentially dangerous for one's soul? Should the everyday Christian pray for a vision like John Donne's or was it better to avoid the apparently murky waters of the soul's beatific ascent? Increasingly, and in the face of the tide of enthusiastic prophets, many English Protestants were promoting a religion that was nearer to the ground. Taylor exhorted people to 'dig the earth', rather than, with George Herbert, ask God to 'shew thy self to me'.[85] Would it not be safer for the average person simply to let the discourse fall, to focus upon the domestic practice of religion than risk being lost in a sea of rapture?

The early eighteenth-century philosopher Lord Shaftesbury exemplifies the epistemic uncertainty surrounding divine revelation that was only beginning to emerge in the middle of the seventeenth century. In *A Letter Concerning Enthusiasm*, Shaftesbury concluded that human beings are incapable of distinguishing between the 'outward marks' of such authentic divine encounters and those that are enthusiastic excesses, because 'the passion they raise is much alike'. In this regard, Shaftesbury departed from his old tutor John Locke who described revelation as 'the highest reason', and enthusiasm as 'extravagancy...and all the error of wrong principles'.[86] Nor was Shaftesbury willing to allow his assessment to apply only to contemporary experiences. We cannot even 'resolve', he continued, 'what spirit that was which prov'd so catching among the antient prophets', whether it was 'the evil' or 'the good spirit of prophecy'. Both spirits, for Shaftesbury, moved a person in an enthusiastic manner: 'eyes glow with the passion, and heaving breasts are laboring...the very breath and exhalations of men are infectious, and the inspiring disease imparts it-self by insensible transpiration'.[87] Shaftesbury's almost bacchanalian description was exactly the sort of thing that leading divines condemned as ungodly, sectarian enthusiasm. Like the different claims to immediate revelation that saturated the air in the middle of the seventeenth century, the traditional language of *raptus* was being lumped in with enthusiasm. Not only were ecclesiastical authorities struggling with arguments over cessationism, but there was also a seemingly genuine concern about the value of pursuing such experiences with God. Although many divines insisted that divine revelation was an enlightening of the rational faculties, it was an experience that was becoming increasingly difficult to separate from the stench of enthusiasm and, by extension, to celebrate as something that should be desired and pursued.

---

[85] Herbert, *The temple*, 99.

[86] Anthony Ashley Cooper, Earl of Shaftesbury, *A letter concerning enthusiasm* (1708), 81; John Locke, *An Essay Concerning Human Understanding* (Indianapolis, 1996), IV.xvi.14.

[87] Shaftesbury, *Letter*, 69–70.

7

'The foundation of all Knowledge'

The Rationale of Divine Revelation

What comes from heaven onely can there ascend.
...The souls still working, patiently to bend
Our minds to sifting reason, and clear light.

Henry More, *Philosophical Poems*

the soule beginning to be freed from the ligaments of the body, begins
to reason like her selfe.

Thomas Browne, *Religio Medici*

At the height of Isaac Newton's career, somewhere between his ground-breaking lectures on optics (1670–1672) and the publication of his *Philosophiae Naturalis Principia Mathematica* (1687), the mathematician wrote thousands of pages on prophecy and revelation.[1] In the early pages of an untitled treatise on revelation, Newton exhorted his reader:

Let me therefore beg of thee not to trust to the opinion of any man concerning these things...Much less oughtest thou to rely upon the judgment of the multitude, for so thou shalt certainly be deceived...search the scriptures thy self & that by frequent reading & constant meditation...& earnest prayer to God to enlighten thine understanding if thou desirest to find the truth.[2]

Newton was one of the last in a long line of seventeenth-century English thinkers—including Francis Bacon, Joseph Mede, and Robert Napier—seeking a definitive method for interpreting biblical prophecy. Although as Christopher Hill noted long ago, 'no science of prophecy...emerged' during the period, this was not for a lack of trying.[3] In this passage, Newton pointed his readers to the surest methodology he knew for understanding divine revelation: by careful

---

[1] There is a great deal of recent scholarship on Newton's religious beliefs, most notably Rob Iliffe, *Priest of Nature* (Oxford, 2017).

[2] 'Untitled Treatise on Revelation', section 1.1. Yahuda MS. 1, fols. 1v–2r. *The Newton Project* http://www.newtonproject.ox.ac.uk/view/texts/normalized/THEM00135

[3] Hill, *The World Turned Upside Down*, 231 (see also pp. 73–8).

Experiencing God in Late Medieval and Early Modern England. David J. Davis, Oxford University Press.
© David J. Davis 2022. DOI: 10.1093/oso/9780198834137.003.0008

study and meditation through the inspiration of the Holy Spirit. Ultimately, understanding biblical revelation came through another kind of revelation.

We ended the last chapter with Lord Shaftesbury's critique of enthusiasm, and his struggle to identify any empirical basis by which he might distinguish enthusiasm from divine *raptus*. Shaftesbury and Newton are some of the most original English thinkers of their period, their births separated by only thirty years, and yet the gulf between their views on revelation is immense. Shaftesbury's scepticism exemplifies the much larger challenge to revelation (and religion) in the spheres of philosophy and science that would come full-bloom in the eighteenth century. The fact that the revival of classical philosophies and the creation of new ones during the Renaissance and early Enlightenment challenged many traditional norms needs little elaboration.[4] Equally important, however, is the fact that many (if not most) philosophical and scientific minds in England like Newton maintained a confident belief that a traditional understanding of divine revelation was compatible, or at least not incompatible, with many of the new philosophies and mechanical sciences.[5]

This chapter looks at the philosophical challenges to divine revelation that became apparent in early modern England and the rationales that were developed in response to those challenges.[6] Rather than framing these challenges as a conflict between religion and philosophy, I think it more appropriate to approach these challenges as issues largely within the same intellectual and religious culture, a culture that assumed God had communicated with human beings through direct encounter and still could do so. This approach provides a more accurate picture of the seventeenth century, at least for most of the people involved who assumed an accurate philosophical description of reality would correspond to their religious beliefs.[7] In order to frame the challenges in this way, I want to examine some of the important fracture lines opening up beneath revelation as a source of human knowledge, which will provide important insight into the shifting cultural perspective on how divine experiences were understood. The chapter examines three key areas where new philosophies challenged the traditional understanding of divine revelation: first, the means by which divine revelation

---

[4] See for example Jonathan I. Israel, *Enlightenment Contested* (Oxford, 2006), Ch. 26; Richard Popkin, *The History of Scepticism* (1979).

[5] The classic work is Richard S. Westfall, *Science and Religion in Seventeenth-Century England* (New Haven, CT, 1958). More recently see *Philosophy, Science, and Religion in England, 1640–1700*, eds Richard Kroll, Richard Ashcraft, and Perez Zagorin (Cambridge, 1992); *Rethinking the Scientific Revolution*, ed. Margaret J. Osler (Cambridge, 2000); Michael Hunter, *Boyle: Between God and Science* (New Haven, CT, 2010). In philosophy, see Charles Taliaferro, *Evidence and Faith* (Cambridge, 2005); Nathan Guy, *Finding Locke's God* (New York, 2020).

[6] Unlike previous chapters, references to revelation in this chapter usually refer to biblical revelation. However, as we have seen, biblical revelation was the most authoritative, that is epistemically trustworthy, form of the broader understanding of revelation, as a communicative act initiated by God.

[7] This framework is by no means original to me. See e.g., Michael Hunter, *Science and the Shape of Orthodoxy* (1995); Ann Thomson, *Bodies of Thought* (Oxford, 2008).

was communicated, particularly whether or not a person's rational faculties were involved; second, the relationship between human reason and divine revelation; and third, whether or not the human soul was immortal (and immaterial), making it, at least in many people's minds, more capable of experiencing God. Here, we want to understand both the significance of these philosophical challenges as well as how different thinkers responded to them. As robust as the challenges were, they were met with a variety of arguments, which were often influenced by the new philosophies and sciences, defending the traditional understanding of divine revelation as epistemically valid.

Spinoza's Imagination

One of the most significant challenges to the traditional understanding of divine revelation was the question of what human faculty (or faculties) most commonly participated in the experience. From at least Augustine forward, there was in Western thought a broadly-held belief that God raptured the soul from the body as a means of communicating with a person's rational faculties. Traditionally, the Augustinian *visio intellectualis*, a kind of mind-to-mind communication free of any mediating images or representations, was thought to be the highest form of divine rapture.[8] If divine revelation was communicated to other parts of the human being (e.g. physical senses, imagination, base passions), that would go a long way in challenging the epistemic validity of revelation.

One of the most significant challenges to divine revelation along these lines was the controversial and incendiary philosophy of Baruch Spinoza. In November 1675, Henry Oldenburg, secretary of the Royal Society, wrote to Spinoza concerned that Spinoza's *Tractatus Theologico-Politicus* (1670) had raised many apprehensive eyebrows in Oldenburg's circles of influence. Of course, Spinoza's impact on philosophy writ large is well known; however, Spinoza's influence on late seventeenth-century England is less clear. His *Tractatus* only appeared once in English before 1700, though it is evident from Oldenburg's letters and others' critiques of the Dutch philosopher that Spinoza was well known. Certainly, few Englishmen would declare themselves a Spinozan disciple, but his sweeping textual analysis of scripture, his condemnation of things he deemed superstitious, and his assessment of religion's role in early modern politics were all hot topics in the second half of the seventeenth century.

Thus, Oldenburg warned the young sceptic that the *Tractatus* 'tormented its readers' with a heterodox assessment of some of the most fundamental Christian doctrines, including the relationship between God and Nature as well as the fact

---

[8] See 'Kenney, *The Mysticism of Saint Augustine*, 130–3.

that Spinoza 'appear[ed] to many to take away the authority and value of miracles...[and] the certainty of Divine Revelation'. Spinoza's response was diplomatic but blunt. As to the first point, he admitted that his own 'opinion' about the relationship of God to Nature was 'very different from that which Modern Christians are wont to defend'. Spinoza was effectively a pantheist, so it is not shocking that concerning miracles, he was emphatic that 'divine revelation can be based only on the wisdom of the doctrine', for miracles were nothing more than superstitious 'ignorance'.[9] Although Spinoza did not support the blind acceptance of textual revelation as true, he did not dismiss prophecy and revelation in the same way he did miracles. Claims to divine revelation were not strictly superstitious, but neither were they authoritative.

That is not to say that Spinoza had much intellectual respect for revelation. In fact, I struggle to read Spinoza's comment about what he calls the 'wisdom of the doctrine' as anything other than tongue-in-cheek. One of the first things that Spinoza does in the *Tractatus* is assert that divine revelation is completely separate from reason. When a person encountered God, according to Spinoza, it was their imaginative faculty, not their reason or understanding, that was doing the heavy lifting.[10] In Chapter 1, Spinoza explained, 'It was by images, unreal and dependent only on the prophet's imagination, that God revealed' things to the biblical prophets, in both Old and New Testaments. Spinoza placed revelation squarely in the imaginative camp, which is why, he contended, biblical prophecies took different forms and occurred in such varying degrees of coherency. Some prophets' imaginations were more stable, even though all imaginations were far less trustworthy than was human reason, which dealt in matters best left to philosophy. Spinoza was convinced that the prophets' biological humours could sway the general direction of a prophecy: gloomy prophets had visions of wars and joyful prophets predicted prosperity.[11] While Spinoza drew heavily from Jewish scholars like Moses Maimonides who put stock in prophecy, he challenged many of the long-standing ideas about divine revelation as a source of knowledge. Placing the prophetic experience solely in the confines of the imagination, Spinoza intentionally destabilized divine revelation as a form of knowledge, for the imagination was 'fleeting and inconstant', leaving the prophet (and the reader of prophecy) without any certain and 'assured principles' to undergird what was experienced. As Richard Popkin quipped, Spinoza reduced prophecy to

---

[9] Baruch Spinoza, *The Correspondence of Spinoza* (1966), 340, 343.

[10] Steven Nadler, *A Book Forged in Hell* (Princeton, NJ, 2011), 74; Nancy K. Levene, *Spinoza's Revelation* (Cambridge, 2004), 113–15. Michael Jaeger Smith connects Spinoza's thinking on the imagination and revelation to earlier thinkers, arguing that Spinoza remained convinced that revelation continued to serve as a moral guide: 'Imagination, Authority, and Community in Spinoza's Theological-Political Treatise', (PhD thesis, 2014).

[11] Spinoza, *Theological-Political*, 23. It remains unclear to me how Spinoza was able to determine the personality types, or emotional states, of long-dead prophets.

'THE FOUNDATION OF ALL KNOWLEDGE'   169

'uninteresting opinions of some people who lived long ago', making any question
of whether or not revelation occurred almost inconsequential.[12]

On this point, we may be able to detect Thomas Hobbes's influence on Spinoza.
While it is not always clear what Spinoza took from Hobbes, Spinoza, like Hobbes,
built an epistemological wall separating philosophy and theology, largely based
upon a distrust of divine revelation.[13] Thus, in *Leviathan*, Hobbes sounded as
dubious as Spinoza, if not more so, dismissing the significance of any divine
'Visions' or 'Inspiration', that can be found in the Bible or anywhere else.
Regardless of who claims they have experienced such a 'dream', Hobbes argued, it
'obliges no man to believe he hath so done'.[14] Although Spinoza certainly agreed
with Hobbes that prophecy offered no firm epistemological foundation, the
Dutchman spent much more time wrestling with the details of why that was
the case.

By the time Oldenburg wrote to Spinoza, critics were already attaching the
Dutch philosopher's name to Hobbes as the two greatest threats to religion.
Several book-length English critiques challenged different points of Spinoza's
philosophy.[15] For example, the rector of Selsey (Sussex) William Nicholls saw
Spinoza's notion of divine revelation as a direct attack on religion. In his dialogue
A conference with a theist, Nicholls pitted the Spinoza-reading character
Philologus against the Christian character Credentius. After Philologus parroted
Spinoza's understanding of divine revelation as a product of the imagination,
Credentius cried out, 'you endeavor to make Religion stand upon as loose a bottom
as you can'.[16] Elsewhere, the schoolmaster Matthias Earbery offered a more
measured response, granting that the imagination was a valuable 'Repository of
Knowledge', housing the mind's sensory information. In this regard, he suggested
that the 'Certainty of the Imagination differs not from the Certainty of the Senses',
highlighting the potential hazard of questioning the epistemological power of the
imagination. If a person could not trust the imagination, then she or he could not
trust their perceptions of the physical world (which are kept in the imagination).
Second, Earbery did not understand Spinoza's insistence that revelation must be

---

[12] Spinoza, *Theological-Political*, 20; Popkin, *The History of Scepticism*, 231.

[13] Noel Malcolm, *Aspects of Hobbes* (Oxford, 2002), Ch. 2; Popkin, *The History of Scepticism*, 235.
For Hobbes, see his *Elements of philosophy* (1656), 8.

[14] Thomas Hobbes, *Leviathan* (1651), XXXII.6, p. 196.

[15] See for example Browne, *Miracles work's*; Matthias Earbery, *An answer to...Tractatus theologico
politicus* (1697); Matthias Earbery, *Deism examin'd* (1697); William Nicholls, *A conference with a theist*
(1699). See Richard Baxter, *Catholick theologie plain* (1675) and his *The nonconformist plea* (1680).
Spinoza's ideas were often misunderstood or mischaracterized by English writers: Thomson, *Bodies of
Thought*, 42–55.

[16] Nicholls, *A conference*, 144. For false prophecy and the imagination, see for example John
Spencer, *A discourse concerning vulgar prophecies* (1665), 14, 18, 75–7. Nicholls's accusation is only
slightly unfair. As Nancy Levene explains, Spinoza considered revelation as 'continuous with natural
knowledge', such that it was an experiential knowledge derived from the individual's interaction with
the natural world (*Spinoza's Revelation*, 114).

restricted entirely to the imagination, even if the 'Mind may indeed be impos'd upon by help of the Imagination'.[17] Indeed, in the *Tractatus*, Spinoza demonstrated that the imagination must be involved in revelation (particularly divine visions), but he offered no definitive statement as to why revelation must be segregated from reason. Finally, pointing to the manner in which the prophecies of the Jewish messiah were written in the Old Testament, Earbery cannot imagine human reason uninvolved in the process. The details of the messiah's life 'Out of thousands of possible Circumstances', Earbery protested, are evidence of a rational faculty overseeing the organization of what the prophet was experiencing, regardless of whether the content of the revelation passed through the person's imagination.[18]

Part of the protest against Spinoza on this point had to do with seventeenth-century biases toward the imaginative faculties, since imagination often was considered to be an ignoble faculty. It was the lesser faculty of the soul, which was not unimportant though it was certainly disorderly and chaotic if left unattended. Thinkers rarely stressed the aesthetic power of the imagination, which became a more common position in the eighteenth century.[19] According to John Owen, God often communicated by 'Impressions' to the imagination, through which his will could be understood by the rational soul, which Owen deemed subordinate forms of revelation to the 'pure Acts of the Understanding' that individuals like the apostle Paul received.[20] The imagination played a subservient role to a person's understanding in experiences like the *visio spiritualis*. Edward Reynolds described the imagination as an 'assistant to the Vnderstanding and the Will', allowing the mind to be lifted up with objects and words to what 'Philosophers called Extasie'. While the 'Act of Apprehending be the proper worke of the Vnderstanding', the 'restlessnesse of the Imagination' provided the 'forme and qualitie of that Act'.[21] Human reason was insufficient to understand God, but the rational faculties of the will and understanding were nevertheless the object of divine *raptus*.

The master of Christ's College (Cambridge) Ralph Cudworth provides one of the more thorough rebuttals of Spinoza's imagination thesis. Although his reputation is usually overshadowed by some of his colleagues like Henry More, Cudworth's *The true intellectual system of the universe* (1678) is significant as the first English work of philosophy that systematically assessed René Descartes's mechanical philosophy and its relationship to the soul.[22] In his chapter

---

[17] Earbery, *An answer*, 30–34, quote on p. 33.   [18] Earbery, *An answer*, 34.

[19] See for example Jean le Rond d'Alembert's comment, 'We take imagination in the more noble and precise sense, as the talent of creating by imitating' in 'Preliminary Discourse', *Encyclopedia* (Chicago, 1995): https://quod.lib.umich.edu/d/did/

[20] Owen, *Pneumatologia*, 106.   [21] Reynolds, *A treatise...of the soule*, 23–4.

[22] See e.g., J. A. Passmore, *Ralph Cudworth* (Cambridge, 1951), 90–106; Benjamin Carter, 'Ralph Cudworth', in *Early Modern Philosophy of Religion* (Abingdon, 2014), 113–26.

'THE FOUNDATION OF ALL KNOWLEDGE' 171

'A Confutation of Atheism', Cudworth defined the imagination as that faculty that 'can frame Compounded Ideas of things, which no where Exist', as well as compose ideas from sense-derived information that do exist. Cudworth nevertheless remained critical of the imagination. For example, he explained that the imagination could not positively conceive 'of that which is *Absolutely Nothing*'.[23] Nor was the imagination powerful enough to construct the prophecies about the messiah—particularly those in Daniel and Isaiah—at least not without the assistance of reason.[24] Finally, Cudworth found human imagination too constrained in its abilities to construct accurate images of certain material realities, like the size of the Sun, because 'we never had a Sense or Sight of any Vast Bigness'. The projection of such an image upon the imagination without recourse to the rational faculties would be meaningless. These limits for Cudworth were the most obvious rebuttals to Spinoza's thesis. It is the reason and the understanding that undergird the imagination, and it follows for Cudworth that if the imagination is so limited 'as to *Sensible* things themselves', it would be ridiculous for God not to employ the higher faculties of the soul to allow the prophets to see '*Things Insensible*'.[25]

Not all English women and men were so antithetical to Spinoza. For example, clergyman and Royal Society member Joseph Glanvill found some important overlappings between his own thought and Spinoza's. Glanvill was something of an intellectual hermit crab, making his home for a time in the shells of Cartesian rationalism, Pyrrhonic scepticism, Neoplatonism, and the experimental philosophy of his beloved Royal Society. Popkin describes Glanvill as being aligned with a brand of 'mitigated skepticism' that was popular among many English philosophers, who, having rejected dogmatism, refused to plunge into the fideism of the French sceptics.[26] In *Plus ultra*, Glanvill expressed an affinity for Spinoza's view of revelation, without mentioning Spinoza. When God communicated with the prophets, Glanvill argued, God generally was wont to 'apply himself much to the Imagination' with condescending images and representations. Glanvill divided instances of biblical prophecy into categories of imaginative and intellectual, the latter being so rare that he pointed to Moses and Paul as the only examples (to whom he communicated 'without…mediation'). However, unlike Spinoza, Glanvill did not see why imaginative revelation should be considered epistemologically invalid simply because it relied upon human imagination. He dismissed criticism that his division depicted God as working through disorder and chaos by stating that it is 'presumptuous to bring down *Infinite* Wisedom to our *Rules*'.[27] A few pages later, Glanvill doubled-down, insisting that most revelation occurred on 'the *Stage* of *Imagination*', even describing such experiences as

---

[23] Ralph Cudworth, *The true intellectual system of the universe* (1678), 694.
[24] Cudworth, *The true intellectual system*, 714.
[25] Cudworth, *The true intellectual system*, 780.   [26] Popkin, *The History of Scepticism*, 213.
[27] Joseph Glanvill, *Plus ultra* (1668), 130–3.

'the *Enthusiasms* of the...*Prophets*' because of the reliance the prophets had upon their imaginations.[28] Could the veracity of biblical prophecy be ensured if it was little more than a divine masquerade within the soul? Unfortunately, Glanvill did not address the potential problems seemingly inherent in his description. Nor does he completely isolate revelation to the imagination, which provided at least some distance between his ideas and those of Spinoza. While most biblical prophecy may have played out on the imagination's stage, it remained for Glanvill a performance intended for an audience of the rational faculties.

Elsewhere, even scholars interested in Spinoza's hermeneutic of scripture, like Genevan theologian Jean le Clerc, rarely divorced revelation from the rational soul.[29] As an Arminian and a proponent of religious tolerance, le Clerc was popular among many Anglican clergy toward the end of the seventeenth century. In *Five letters concerning the Inspiration of Holy Scripture*, le Clerc grouped the Bible's books into prophecies, histories, and doctrine, based upon what he understood to be their reliance upon divine revelation.[30] Although Le Clerc affirmed that divine inspiration was supra-rational (a person's understanding of it 'could not be increas'd by the Application of the Mind'), he stopped short of isolating the process of revelation entirely in the imagination.[31] Similarly, the Catholic scholar Richard Simon, a member of the French Oratory and an early proponent of the historical-critical method, followed many of Spinoza's hermeneutic principles. Turning to the question of divine inspiration, Simon considered Spinoza's notion ridiculous, that 'the Spirit of God' would 'deprive...[the prophets] of their Reason and Memory'. The Holy Spirit, which led people into all truth (John 16.13), would not strip the prophets of the one faculty they needed to understand that truth. Simon continued by saying that what Spinoza had done in restricting revelation in this way was to fashion all prophets into 'Enthusiasts, who are more like Men push'd on by a Spirit of Fury'.[32] Although Simon rejected Spinoza's imagination thesis, his assessment of the results is not insignificant. Simon insisted that reason be involved in the process of revelation to avoid the kind of conflation that plagued thinkers like Lord Shaftesbury, who were unable to discern any empirical difference between revelation and enthusiasm.

---

[28] Glanvill, *Plus ultra*, 130–4.

[29] Between 1690 and 1700, editions of le Clerc's writings went through more than twenty editions in English, rivalling the output of many English divines. For example, John Owen's writings had sixteen editions during the same period, and Edward Stillingfleet's had twenty-six. At the same time, Richard Baxter logged a whopping forty-five editions (RSTC).

[30] Jean le Clerc, *Five letters* (1690), 70, 75. William Lane Craig, "'Men Moved by the Holy Spirit Spoke from God'", in *Oxford Readings in Philosophical Theology* (Oxford, 2009), 167–9. It is important to note that while figures like Locke were friends of le Clerc, they were also hesitant about the strict limits he placed upon divine inspiration: Kim Ian Parker, 'Spinoza, Locke, and Biblical Interpretation', in *Locke and Biblical Hermeneutics* (Cham, 2019), 169–70.

[31] Le Clerc, *Five letters*, 75.

[32] Richard Simon, *A critical history...of the New Testament* (1689), 61, 82. Between 1682 and 1700, his critical histories of the Bible went through several London editions.

'THE FOUNDATION OF ALL KNOWLEDGE' 173

Interestingly, an early sympathizer of Spinoza's approach to scripture was a member of an enthusiastic sect. The Quaker Samuel Fisher developed a method of biblical criticism that demonstrated a common ground with Spinoza's insistence that biblical prophecy was experienced apart from the rational faculties.[33] Although Fisher did not live to see Spinoza's *Tractatus*, he certainly knew of Spinoza. Fisher's book *Rusticus ad academicos* was a formative work in Quaker theology that echoed many of Spinoza's basic ideas in this regard. Where Spinoza sought to unhinge theology from reason by attaching revelation to the imagination, Fisher challenged the presumption that clergy were more authoritative than the raucous, uncouth prophets of contemporary, sectarian groups. Fisher's divine Light was 'distinct' from reason:

> The Light...comes from God and Christ into the mind and Conscience, not as the Soul, and its essential faculties of understanding, will, &c. do...as a thing distinct and separable from the man in whom it is, and a witness against him, when he runs from the Will of God revealed to him in it.[34]

As a gift to all women and men, the Light was something separate from the human soul, and Fisher did not seem to think that the Light relied upon the soul in its communion with God. Fisher's Light elevated prophecy whereas Spinoza's imagination diminished it, but both removed divine revelation from the context of human understanding.[35]

Although Fisher's description of Light seems to echo many of the texts from earlier chapters, it is different in at least two important respects. First, Fisher's Light is entirely distinct from the rational faculties of the soul. Second, where Fisher's Light emanated from within the individual, the traditional discourse usually described divine light as either shining in a person's soul to reveal their sin or providing an external guide by which a person can be moved toward God.[36]

My point here is not that Spinoza's attempt to isolate divine revelation to the realm of the imagination was immediately popular in England. Instead, I think Spinoza's ideas were a lightning rod, a flashpoint, around which an important contest about divine revelation began to unfold in the latter half of the seventeenth century. Spinoza's notion about the imagination and revelation was widely attacked, but it was not without intellectual affiliates. It stirred polemical pens, as

---

[33] McDowell, *The English Radical Imagination*, 174–5; Stefano Villani, 'Fisher, Samuel (bap. 1604, d. 1665), Quaker preacher and writer', *ODNB*.

[34] Fisher, *Rusticus*, IV.ii.69–70.

[35] Fisher, *Rusticus*, IV.ii.70. Although the two views may seem quite disparate, it is worth noting that Pieter Galling, one of Spinoza's close associates, sounded more like Fisher than Spinoza in his work: *The light upon the candlestick* (s.n., 1663), 6. See Alec Ryrie, *Unbelievers* (Cambridge, MA, 2019), 180–1.

[36] A late seventeenth-century example of this understanding of revelation comes from the Lucasian professor of mathematics Isaac Barrow in his work *Of the love of God* (1680), 32–3.

174 EXPERIENCING GOD IN LATE MEDIEVAL & EARLY MODERN ENGLAND

well as more pensive responses, which included addressing questions that had not been widely considered before. Finally, it is important to recognize that Spinoza's imagination, Hobbes's dreams, and Fisher's Light all provided a path for divine revelation to persist in English religion beyond the reach of reason and philosophy. Although many at the time saw this separation of revelation and reason to be abhorrent, it certainly could create a proverbial safe space for many people who were disillusioned by the more mainline confessions. If revelation was a-rational, rather than suprarational, then the only authority for the experience of divine revelation was an individual's own internal senses. Disconnected from the rational faculties, divine revelation would not be hampered by cumbersome epistemological and ontological questions which might otherwise undermine the individual's enjoyment of God.

Revelation and Reasonable Religion

Shortly before he assumed the bishopric of Chichester, Simon Patrick examined the evidence for the newly established feast of the Virgin's immaculate conception, instituted by Pope Alexander VII in 1661. Patrick noted that one piece of evidence used to substantiate the claims of the Virgin's immaculate nature was the late-medieval Tuscan saint Oringa's vision of a feast being 'celebrated in Heaven', after she 'was rapt up in an Ecstasy into Heaven'. Patrick repeated Oringa's account, concluding that he believed the story to be especially specious. Citing Bernard of Clairvaux in support of his position, Patrick contended that such tales should be given 'slender Credit', because they are 'neither back'd with Reason nor favoured by certain Authority'.[37]

As a member of a small but influential group of Anglican clerics known as the Latitudinarians, Patrick was committed to what often was termed 'reasonable religion'. Other prominent Latitudinarians included bishops like Thomas Tenison, John Tillotson, and Edward Stillingfleet. Their reasonable religion was not a form of deism but instead rested upon the notion that 'reason was a gift from God, and ought to be employed in his service'.[38] Reasonable religion assented to the weight of evidence presented by testimony, self-evident axioms, deductions, experience, and the senses, which included claims to divine revelation. The Latitudinarians believed that approaching religion in this manner set it apart from the excitable

---

[37] Simon Patrick, *The Virgin Mary misrepresented* (1688), 99–100. For a Catholic source on the establishment of the feast see George Leyburn, *Holy characters* (Douai, 1662), 22.

[38] Martin I. J. Griffin, Jr., *Latitudinarianism in the Seventeenth Century* (Leiden, 1992), 59–62, quote on p. 59. Theological and historical scholarship often has been unkind to Latitudinarianism, framing their theology in terms of a kind of deism or a rationalizing moralism. For a more robust assessment of this scholarship see Jacob M. Blosser, 'John Tillotson's Latitudinarian Legacy', *Anglican and Episcopal History* 80 (2011), 142–73.

'THE FOUNDATION OF ALL KNOWLEDGE' 175

claims of enthusiasts and other spurious traditions, exemplified for them in Roman Catholicism.[39] However, what the Latitudinarians meant by reason, and reasonable, is less straightforward. I think it is certain that clerics like Patrick would not define reason as 'a spirit of free enquiry: the exercise of human intelligence upon some form of truth or supposed truth', which is how a recent study of the topic has described it.[40] While this definition enjoys a Cartesian kind of simplicity, which was attractive to some thinkers, the limits of reason were much more evident to the Latitudinarians than reason's freedom. Even Spinoza, who possessed a relatively high view of reason, considered it to be a limited faculty, 'a grasping of things not all at once but fragmentarily.'[41] For Calvinists, the human mind was too corrupted by sin for reason to function properly (without divine sanctification). Even when we take into account the Latitudinarian emphasis upon God's grace, clerics like Patrick would not have considered human intelligence entirely 'free' from sin.

We can see the same sort of uncertainty when we consider what different people believed to be the relationship between revelation and reason. Certainly, many devout people refused to acknowledge any empirical or rational evidence that might threaten their faith. Some people embraced a kind of acquiescent uncertainty about what was believed to have been divinely revealed. The popular writer and Norwich physician Sir Thomas Browne explained that 'If therefore there rise any doubts in my way' about doctrines like the Incarnation or the Trinity, 'I doe forget them, or at least defer them, till my better settled judgement, and more manly reason be able to resolve them'. Browne's *Religio medici*, an autobiographical, spiritual wrestling with the practical parts of religion went through more than ten editions before 1700. The book exhibited an intellectual flexibility (unusual even for our day) that allowed Browne to wink at such doubts, which he considered to be 'a solitary recreation'. Further on, he admitted that his faith was not of the sort that led him to take any action that would contradict reason. For instance, he would 'not have been one of the Israelites that passed the Red Sea', suggesting at least some intellectual distinction between a person's assent and their action.[42] Perhaps this is why Browne settled on a more modern understanding of the relationship between faith and reason, in which he determined that 'Reason', 'Faith', and 'Passion' 'bee all Kings, and yet make but one Monarchy, every one exercising his Sovereignty and Prerogative in a due time and place'.[43]

In certain respects, Browne's approach to religion echoed the French sceptic Michel de Montaigne's *Essais*, which went through at least ten editions in English before 1700. Montaigne saw reason as an impediment to belief, because it could

---

[39] See e.g., Edward Stillingfleet, *Origines sacrae* (1663), 112, 148.
[40] Christopher Walker, *Reason and Religion in Late Seventeenth-Century England* (2013), 3.
[41] Michael LeBuffe, *Spinoza on Reason* (Oxford, 2018), 62–3, quote p. 63.
[42] Thomas Browne, *Religio Medici* (New York, 2012), 9, 12.
[43] Browne, *Religio Medici*, 24.

176 EXPERIENCING GOD IN LATE MEDIEVAL & EARLY MODERN ENGLAND

not grasp things like revelation. 'Belief', he explained was like 'the Impression of a Seal stamp'd upon the Soul', but reason hardened the soul through a destructive reliance upon, what Montaigne scornfully called, 'fine Understanding'.[44]

Other English thinkers were not nearly so melancholy as Browne. Reason was considered to be an imperfect and incomplete form of divine revelation, and relying too much upon human understanding was just as dangerous as being overly credulous.[45] In his commencement sermon in 1696, the master of Trinity College (Cambridge) Richard Bentley described the problem to the university's undergraduates as a struggle between 'the extravagancies of Fanaticism...[and] the indifferency of Libertinism'.[46] Reason, Bentley assured the audience, provided a 'sure ground to believe', allowing people to comprehend, to some degree, what was made evident by divine revelation. Divine revelation's epistemic value, however, was not entirely contingent upon human reason. Bentley admittedly agreed with rationalists about the importance of reason in matters of religion, but he refused to grant a *carte blanche* 'jurisdiction' to reason. He celebrated reason's role in understanding revelation, but he disagreed with rationalists over 'the exercise of it' over and above revelation.[47]

At a more popular level, the English essayist Owen Felltham's *Resolves* explained that 'Reason' was the right arm of human understanding, '[it] gives us the anatomy of things, and illustrates with a great deal of plainness all the way that she goes'. Felltham's popular collection of essays have been underappreciated in modern scholarship, as they provide a helpful counterpart to Montaigne's fideism. Clarity and comprehension are reason's virtues, Felltham argued. While they could not reach so high as divine revelation, he refused to separate the two: 'yet is there a reason to be given of our faith. He is a fool that believes he knows neither what nor why' he believes what he believes.[48] This relationship between reason and revelation went beyond the latter picking up where the former left off. Reason protected human credulity, serving as an important tool in distinguishing true and false revelation. Conversely, revelation aided reason. Echoing Felltham in the latter part of the century, John Locke argued that revelation provided essential insights that could improve 'our Rational Faculties...enabling us to look more judiciously into the Frame and Laws of Nature'. Without revelation, Locke

---

[44] Michel de Montaigne, *Essays* (1700), 276, 282. For more on Montaigne's seemingly sincere, but certainly odd, sort of Catholicism, see Ryrie, *Unbelievers*, 61–5.

[45] For example, Anthony Nixon, *The dignitie of man* (1612), 35–6. Nixon reminded his readers that reason operated in much the same way as revelation, 'without the helpe of bodily instruments.' See also Christopher Hill, '"Reason" and "reasonableness" in Seventeenth-Century England', *The British Journal of Sociology* 20 (1969), 235–52.

[46] Richard Bentley, *Of revelation* (1696), 7.

[47] Bentley, *Of revelation*, 9–11. See also Earbery, *An answere*, 175.

[48] Owen Felltham, *Resolves* (1696), 24.

'THE FOUNDATION OF ALL KNOWLEDGE' 177

explained, humans could know nothing of God's nature nor of the most important aspects of true religion.[49]

One important context where this relationship was being explored can be found in the experiments and speculations of the Royal Society. From its inception, the Society's adoption of mechanical philosophy had raised alarms with several puritan divines who feared Europe's philosophical and scientific leaders would be led into atheism. As a response, Glanvill assured these critics that the 'experimental philosophy' of the Society upheld as a prime 'Maxim of Reason...[that] whatsoever God saith is to be believed though we cannot comprehend the manner of it'. Philosophy, Glanvill continued, provided a powerful 'defence of the greatest sublimities of Faith; and common Reason doth the best, by shewing the certainty, and divine Original of Testimony'.[50] Following Glanvill, one of the Society's most respected members, Robert Boyle, eventually waded into the debate in the 1670s. Son of the Earl of Cork and suffering from poor health most of his life, Boyle generally avoided controversy, which might give us some indication of how important he believed the debate to be.[51] Boyle argued that reason should 'judge of' prophecy and revelation 'before she judges *by* them'. Reason was responsible for determining what was, and was not, true revelation before it allowed revelation to take an authoritative position, over and above reason. Nevertheless, true revelation was greater than 'fallible Reason' in Boyle's view, because it demonstrated things about God that are impossible for reason to grasp on its own.[52] While Boyle sympathized with the puritan concerns, he assured them that there was no atomistic or materialist view that opposed Christianity, which was not 'also repugnant to Reason'. In fact, 'assenting' to Revelation is not to 'reject the Authority of Reason, but only appeal from Reason to it self, i.e. from Reason, as it is more *slightly*, to its Dictates, as 'tis more *fully* informed'.[53]

If members of the Royal Society and the Latitudinarians stressed the close relationship between revelation and reason, other people emphasized the dangers when one or the other ran amok. For example, Thomas Manningham, a fellow of New College (Oxford), echoed the concerns puritans had about the new philosophies. Manningham lambasted anyone associated with either Descartes or Spinoza, because he believed their philosophies championed reason against revelation. In his *Two discourses* (1681), Manningham joined the mounting polemic

[49] John Locke, *Reason and religion* (1694), 132. See also Locke's *The reasonableness of Christianity* (1695). Nathan Guy contends that Locke 'builds a [political] theory consonant with revelation': *Finding Locke's God*, 132.

[50] Joseph Glanvill, *Philosophia pia* (1671), 209–10, 81–4. Interestingly, Glanvill notes the same tell-tale sign for both enthusiasm and vain philosophy. They are 'bold, and sawcy' (p. 85).

[51] See e.g., David Sytsma, *Richard Baxter and the Mechanical Philosophers* (Oxford, 2017), 54–6; Jan W. Wojcik, 'The theological context of Boyle's *Things above Reason*', in *Robert Boyle Reconsidered* (Cambridge, 2003), 139–56; Hunter, *Boyle: Between God and Science*, 200.

[52] Robert Boyle, *Some considerations* (1675), xv, 11.   [53] Boyle, *Some considerations*, 88–9.

178 EXPERIENCING GOD IN LATE MEDIEVAL & EARLY MODERN ENGLAND

against Spinoza, who he considered 'has opened another Gate in Hell'. Descartes was not much better, since he 'uncatechizes himself' in order to present his readers 'a more splendid method of his Errors', even if Descartes's conclusions were not as heretical as Spinoza's.[54] According to Manningham, revelation was the 'true...foundation of all Knowledge', and to begin with any other presuppositions was folly.[55] Surveying a broad swathe of philosophy, from the ancient Greeks and Babylonians to modern natural philosophers, Manningham explained, all human learning about the world began with some initial divine revelation. The 'dry evidence of Apprehension, and Perspicuity' of the human mind, Manningham contended, would never achieve the kind of certainty the philosophers sought. Human reason was a faculty of 'Assent' to something that was revealed, and without something higher to which reason can assent, people are left in a 'Faire-Land' of doubt and error.[56]

Certainly, a prime example of where such doubt and error could lead was the deism found in John Toland's book *Christianity not mysterious* (1696). Educated in Glasgow, Edinburgh, Leiden, and Oxford, Toland advanced an understanding of divine revelation that limited it to only those things that were not 'inconceivable'. In other words, Toland refused to submit reason to revelation, even biblical revelation, voicing a similar level of consternation as Manningham, but in the opposite direction. Revelation was 'not a necessitating Motive of Assent', for rationalists like Toland, instead it was merely 'a Mean of Information'. One should not attempt to cross the Red Sea simply on the authority of revelation, because above all revelation needed to conform to reason in order for it to be acceptable.[57] To hold revelation in any higher regard (as an authority), would be 'no real Faith...but a rash Presumption, and an obstinate Prejudice' that would lead people into enthusiasm. How else could human beings be expected to trust divine revelation 'if what he [God] said did not agree with...common notions'?[58]

Toland and Manningham represent two poles at the end of the seventeenth century. Some thinkers advocated revelation's supremacy in its relationship with reason, while others demanded that reason be the ultimate standard by which we understand existence. A reasonable religion did not only make a place for reason; it conferred upon reason a certain degree of authority in the practice and belief of that religion, even if that authority ultimately surrendered to the supremacy of divine revelation. Natural philosophers like Boyle and empiricists like Locke believed there were some paths that human reason could not tread; there were

---

[54] Thomas Manningham, *Two discourses* (1681), 13, 71.

[55] Manningham, *Two discourses*, 51, 67–8.   [56] Manningham, *Two discourses*, 81.

[57] John Toland, *Christianity not mysterious* (1696), 38. See Paul Helm, *The Divine Revelation* (Vancouver, 2004), 20–1.

[58] Toland, *Christianity*, 127–8. There are parallels between Socinian rationalism and Toland's thought; however, I have intentionally not explored Socinianism in this chapter, because, as Sarah Mortimer has demonstrated, it was mostly a polemical punching bag in England until the end of the century: *Reason and Religion in the English Revolution* (Cambridge, 2010).

'THE FOUNDATION OF ALL KNOWLEDGE'   179

certain questions and lines of inquiry for which only revelation could provide sufficient answers.

The Soul of the Matter

A final issue that challenged divine revelation as a form of knowledge was the long-standing debate over the immortality of the soul.[59] While all three of the issues discussed in this chapter are significant in their own ways, I think this issue represents the most substantive challenge to the traditional understanding of divine revelation. Not only does it go to the basic, ontological connection between human beings and the divine (i.e. both are, at least in part, an immortal spirit), but the immortality of the soul was also a necessary precursor to the process of ravishment. That is to say, if the soul is not like God in its substance (i.e. a non-corporeal or immaterial substance which lacks mass and is indivisible), then that raises the question of whether or not it is even capable of experiencing *raptus*.[60] Furthermore, many theologians and philosophers believed the soul, in part or in whole, to be, or contain, the *imago Dei*, the image of God imprinted on humanity.[61] If one were to assume the mortality of the human soul, then either one must deny the spiritual connection between humanity and God via the nature of the soul or diminish the divine essence to something mortal (perhaps even corporeal or material).[62]

In 1692, Richard Bentley was chosen as the first Boyle lecturer, a position endowed by Robert Boyle and intended to serve as an apologetic vanguard against atheism. The opportunity was certainly a boon for the thirty-year old classicist Bentley, and he took to the task with gusto. In 'Matter and Motion cannot Think', the second of eight addresses Bentley delivered that year, he objected to the notion that the human soul was a material substance. Speaking at St. Martin's-in-the-Fields Church (London) on April 2, Bentley asked, 'For what can be said more to such persons, that are either so disingenuous or so stupid, as to profes to believe…all these admirable Endowments and Capacities of Human Nature…can proceed from the blind shuffling and casual clashing of Atoms'.

---

[59] The debate over the soul is much larger than I am able to explore here. For more complete accounts see Thomson, *Bodies of Thought*, chs. 2–4; David Garber, 'Soul and Mind', *Cambridge History of Seventeenth Century Philosophy*, vol. I (Cambridge, 1998), 759–95.

[60] While we might be able to imagine an immaterial substance that is not also immortal, most early modern thinkers tended to understand that a substance's immateriality implied its immortality: Margaret J. Osler, 'Early Modern Uses of Hellenistic Philosophy', in *Hellenistic and Early Modern Philosophy* (Cambridge, 2003), 30–44, esp. 39–40.

[61] This notion of the human soul, or at least part of the soul, as the *imago Dei* goes at least as far back in Christian theology as Augustine: Zwollo, *Augustine and Plotinus*, 151–5.

[62] See the philosopher John Smith's comments about this inherent problem with mortalism in *Select discourses* (1660), 384.

180   EXPERIENCING GOD IN LATE MEDIEVAL & EARLY MODERN ENGLAND

These endowments included a 'penetrating Understanding…Memory and readiness of Wit…a rich Vein of Poetry…lofty Flights of Thought…exalted Discoveries of Mathematical Theorems', reaching an intellectual apex with 'Divine Contemplations'.[63] Like many other thinkers at the end of the seventeenth century, Bentley was convinced that the new mechanical sciences only confirmed a known truth of human nature: humans were composed of more than atomic matter.[64]

The question of the soul's immortality had been battered about for over a century and scepticism around the notion had philosophical roots in Hellenistic Greece. As early as the Fifth Lateran Council (1512–1517), the Roman Catholic Church was concerned about the re-emergence of such scepticism. Pope Leo X called upon theologians to defend the soul's immortality (and the existence of God), particularly against the revival of Epicurean philosophy.[65] The pope's commission stirred many more attacks on mortalism (including the doctrine known as 'soul-sleeping') from across western Europe, than there were treatises insisting upon the soul's mortality.[66]

In the 1640s, one of the only English books to provide a sustained argument in favor of mortalism was written by the Leveller Richard Overton. *Mans mortalitie* (1643) went through five editions before the end of the century, and the popularity of such a scandalous book suggests a significant interest in Overton's ideas, beyond the confines of English sectarianism.[67] Possibly one reason for Overton's popularity was his attack on the 'heathenish' roots of the immortality of the soul. He contended that it was a 'ridiculous invention', which early Christians blindly adopted from philosophers like Plato. Overton found it functionally untenable for two completely different substances to persist, let alone interact, in the same person, concluding that the soul must be much nearer the body ontologically.[68] Presenting a kind of monistic understanding of human nature, Overton intermingled the soul (the 'Forme') and body (the 'Matter') to such a degree that he

---

[63] Richard Bentley, *Matter and motion* (1693), 25. It would seem that Bentley's ordering of the soul's 'endowments' is a structured hierarchy, with divine contemplation as the highest endowment the human soul is capable of.

[64] So convinced was Bentley that he requested feedback from Isaac Newton, whose *Principia Mathematica* (1687) shaped Bentley's thinking on physical matter, and Bentley would help steer a new edition of the *Principia* through to publication in 1709: James Henry Monk, *The Life of Richard Bentley* (1833), 228. Interestingly, Newton's own mortalistic views of the soul demonstrate how messy the lines being drawn were: James Force, 'The Nature of Newton's "Holy Alliance"', in *Rethinking the Scientific Revolution*, ed. Margaret Osler (Cambridge, 2000), 261–2. See also Thomson, *Bodies of Thought*, 58–61.

[65] The papal bull *Apostolici regiminis* was issued in 1513, and the leading Italian Epicurean thinker Pietro Pomponazzi published his critique of the Christian view of the soul in *Tractatus de immortalitate animae* (Bologna, 1516).

[66] Norman T. Burns, *Christian Mortalism from Tyndale to Milton* (Cambridge, MA, 1972); Thomson, *Bodies of Thought*, 42–55.

[67] RSTC. For example, John Milton certainly knew of and was sympathetic to Overton's ideas: McDowell, *The English Radical Imagination*, 189–90.

[68] Richard Overton, *Mans mortalitie* (Amsterdam, 1644), 9; Burns, *Christian Mortalism*, 157.

'THE FOUNDATION OF ALL KNOWLEDGE' 181

could see no functional difference between the two. Overton argued, 'The Forme is so in the Matter, and the Matter so in the forme…So that, take away Forme, and Matter ceaseth; take away Matter and Forme ceaseth'.[69] Much of his argument hinged upon the inseparability of the body and the soul. Even to discuss the one without the other was essentially meaningless.[70] Such direct and intimate interaction between body and soul necessitated a similarity of substance. For Overton, even more interesting than the philosophical issues were the theological implications of the soul's immortality. For instance, since humans had been condemned to death by Adam's sin in the Garden of Eden, the entire human person (form and matter, soul and body) should suffer condemnation, according to Overton. Otherwise, as he writes, 'this Death threatned was a meer Scar-crow, even nothing at all; for He, that is, his constitutive part (his Soul) continued immortall, and unchanged'.[71] Since the body cannot act without the soul (nor the soul act in the material world without the body), to condemn the one without the other would be unjust. Later on, concerning the doctrine of original sin (the belief that all human souls were marred by Adam's corruption), Overton demanded that immortalists must choose either that God infuses a tainted soul into a foetus at conception, making God the 'Author of all sinne', or God does it later in the pregnancy. The latter, Overton mockingly suggested, would make God a 'nigromancer', who goes about 'putting a spirit into a dead body'.[72] It goes without saying that neither option was appealing to the majority of early modern Christians.

Another important work that raised the question of immortality was John Evelyn's translation of Lucretius's *De rerum natura*. Unlike Overton, Evelyn was by no means a sectarian or a radical. As a member of the Sussex gentry and the Royal Society, Evelyn's interest lay more in discovery than controversy, who preferred writing works on plant cultivation to engaging in polemic. Nevertheless, Evelyn became interested in classical atomism at an early age, particularly through the writings of the French philosopher Pierre Gassendi, and he hoped his translation might demonstrate a possible synthesis between Christian theology and Lucretian atomism.[73] One of the greatest hurdles to overcome was Lucretius's view on the soul. The classical Epicurean philosopher had asserted that 'the substance of the mind must therefore be material', and this material is not 'a single

---

[69] Overton, *Mans mortalitie*, 12.
[70] It is worth noting that Overton did not adopt Hobbes's materialism. For one thing, Overton does not insist that all existing things are corpulent substances, and second, he is clear that the soul's substance is unlike that of the angels and God. For Hobbes's position, see Garber, 'Soul and Mind', 774–5. Overton, *Mans mortalitie*, 11.
[71] Overton, *Mans mortalitie*, 3.   [72] Overton, *Mans motalitie*, 35.
[73] Gillian Darley, *John Evelyn* (New Haven, CT, 2006), 141–6.

182   EXPERIENCING GOD IN LATE MEDIEVAL & EARLY MODERN ENGLAND

element'. Minds were made of four atomistic components, according to Lucretius, and they were neither indivisible nor immortal.[74]

Recognizing the storm that such an opinion might cause, Evelyn attempted to create more context for understanding Lucretius's materialism. Following his translation, Evelyn wrote an 'Animadversions', in which he pointed out that there was no agreement either among the ancient Greeks or early Christian thinkers about the soul's substance. While Evelyn was definitive in his own assent to the orthodox 'certainty of the Souls immortality', the host of examples he provided to illustrate these various opinions in late antiquity suggests that Evelyn knew the matter was much more complicated.[75] Then, Evelyn offered a means by which one might fit Lucretius's square peg in the round hole of Christianity. If we consider what Lucretius described as the soul, Evelyn suggested, the 'substance...actuating and furnishing it [the body] with all its passions, motions, and faculties', then we could understand this as what some call the 'material soul', rather than the immortal, 'Intellectual' soul.[76]

While distinguishing between different souls or parts of the soul, some material and some immaterial, was not foreign to seventeenth-century philosophy, Evelyn's efforts to rescue Lucretius were not entirely convincing. Even many of Evelyn's friends found his interest in Lucretius more than a little disturbing. In a series of letters, one of these friends, the cleric Jeremy Taylor pressed Evelyn about his own ideas concerning the soul.[77] While Taylor was willing to dispute the exact substance(s) and composition of the soul, he refused to even broach the question of whether or not the soul was immortal. Not only, wrote Taylor, had the most respected, ancient philosophers 'confessed' the soul's immortality, but the apostle Paul's 'rapture into heaven' confirmed the soul's ability to persist and move outside the body and into a realm that Taylor believed to be immaterial.[78] Other English divines, like Richard Baxter, marvelled why anyone would have any interest whatsoever in either Epicurus or Lucretius. 'Even the moderate latitudinarian Cicero', Baxter mocked, 'hath spit so oft in the face of Epicurus', that Gassendi has spent a great deal of time 'in wiping it'.[79] Baxter seemed sincerely confused about

---

[74] Lucretius, On the Nature of the Universe (1951), 101–3. The recovery of Lucretius's work by the fifteenth-century, Tuscan scholar Poggio Bracciolini, and the subsequent dissemination of Epicurean materialism into European thought, was one of the more formative contributions of classical philosophy to the early Enlightenment: Clark, Vanities of the Eye, 212–13.

[75] John Evelyn, An essay on...De rerum nature (1656), 114–18, quote p. 116. Evelyn refers to quite a few philosophers and theologians including: Hippocrates, Aristotle, Plato, Apollonius, Origen, Jerome, Averroes, Thomas Aquinas, and William of Occam.

[76] Evelyn, An essay, 114–18, quote on p. 117.

[77] Both men were associated with the scholarly community known as the Great Tew Circle: Sarah Mortimer, 'Great Tew Circle', ODNB.

[78] John Evelyn, Diary and Correspondence (1887), 99–101.

[79] Baxter, The reasons of the Christian religion (1667), 496. Among Anglicans, see the critical voice of Charles I's chaplain Alexander Ross who never met a philosophical or scientific innovation of which he approved: The philosophicall touch-stone (1645), 114.

'THE FOUNDATION OF ALL KNOWLEDGE' 183

why anyone would hope to find value in thinkers he considered to have been debunked long ago.

Despite Baxter's bluster here, it is evident in his concerns about the Royal Society (discussed earlier) that the impact of materialist philosophies, or the perceived impact, was already evident. For example, the Catholic natural philosopher Kenelm Digby was a member of Charles I's privy council and an active fellow of Gresham College (a forerunner of the Royal Society). Fascinated by Epicureanism, Digby's *Of Bodies, and of Mans Soul* (1644) sounded dangerously like Lucretius, when he wrote, 'Shew me a Soul and I will tell you how it works'.[80] The substance of his book exemplified how someone might adopt an atomistic approach to the natural world without abandoning a relatively orthodox view of the soul. Digby's purpose in *Of Bodies* was to first highlight the limits of physical (atomical) science and then to study the soul by passing, what he called, 'the Rubicon of experimental knowledge', relying only upon the 'evidence of Reason'.[81] Convinced that the soul was both indivisible and immortal, Digby set out arguments about the soul's intellective and active capacities. First, following Descartes, Digby insisted that the soul cannot be located in any particular part of the body. If one removed any part (or multiple parts) of the body, 'a Substance, a Thinker' remained who 'is no whit diminished' by the loss. Also, while the soul may suffer, because of its relationship to the body's sensory faculties, the soul is itself undiminished by the damage done to the body.[82] Second, and equally important for Digby, the soul transcended ('out of the reach of') time. The soul was believed not only to comprehend time and measure it ('set it limits') but also, through the memory and imagination, the soul 'can think of things beyond it'.[83] Past, present, and future are open to the soul's perception, as well as the possibility of realms unencumbered by the passage of time (e.g. Heaven and Hell). For Augustine, this ability was a key marker in recognizing the divine nature of human souls, and for Digby, it was one of the more profound pieces of evidence that the soul was immortal. It also marked a threshold for Digby, beyond which even reason could not tread. To go beyond the soul's ability to transcend time, Digby believed that one must turn away from science and toward contemplative authorities like Julian of Norwich and Pseudo-Dionysus. It is through these contemplatives that the soul 'must be, first, irrigated' in preparation for life after the body.[84]

---

[80] Kenelm Digby, *Of Bodies* (1669), 51.

[81] Digby, *Of Bodies*, 79. See also Garber, 'Soul and Mind', 770–1.

[82] Digby, *Of Bodies*, 81, 85. Interestingly, many of Digby's arguments (which are rooted in Descartes) are seeing something of a renaissance in analytic philosophy. See, for example, Alvin Plantinga, 'Against Materialism', *Faith and Philosophy*, 23 (2006), 3–32.

[83] Digby, *Of Bodies*, 86. Since Augustine, the power of the memory to transcend time played a crucial role in understanding the soul's independence from the body: Augustine, *Saint Augustines confessions*, 589–98.

[84] Digby, *Of Bodies*, 142.

184 EXPERIENCING GOD IN LATE MEDIEVAL & EARLY MODERN ENGLAND

Similarly, despite his attraction to Gassendi's atomism, the London physician Walter (William) Charleton affirmed the immortality of the soul. A member of both the Royal Society and the Royal College of Physicians, Charleton remains an unappreciated figure in the scientific revolution, perhaps because his thought is difficult to categorize. In 1654, Charleton published *Physiologia Epicuro-Gassendo-Charletoniana*, which incorporated aspects of Gassendi's philosophy. Three years later, in response to accusations of mortalism (and materialism) in his *Physiologia*, Charleton responded with *The immortality of the human soul*, in which he claimed that the soul's immortality was the 'grand Base of Religion' and beyond philosophical dispute.[85] What Charleton was attempting in the *Physiologia* was a 'Christianized version...of Epicurean atomism', in which the physics of atomism could be harmonized with Christian theology.[86] Similar to Galileo Galilei's *Dialogo sopra i due massimi sistemi del mondo* (1632), Charleton fashioned a dialogue between three characters: Athanasius (the Christian apologist), Lucretius (the atomistic materialist), and Isodicastes (a moderating persona).[87] Charleton's arguments tracked with Digby's reasoning for the soul's immortality, even citing his friend and fellow Gassendi-disciple alongside the likes of Descartes. Following two lengthy dialogues, the character Isodicastes determined that Athanasius successfully repelled Lucretius's attacks against immortality, even though there was insufficient, experimental evidence to assume immortality. While the case for immortality had not been 'precisely... Demonstrated', Isodicastes declared, the moral and physical 'Reasons' that Athanasius made were 'not much Inferiour to absolute Demonstrations'.[88] Where Galileo's *Dialogo* ended in a similar capitulation, Charleton's surrender to the religious party line seems to be more sincere than the Italian mathematician's assent to geocentrism.[89]

It is also worth noting that both Digby and Charleton were compelled by their own observations to move beyond the boundaries of atomism in their efforts to defend the soul's immortality. Neither offered definitive, empirical evidence for their view of the soul's immortality, and both acknowledged the potential impossibility of ever being able to do so. As such, Digby and Charleton exemplify an important problem moving forward in western intellectual and religious history. In a world increasingly understood to be governed by mechanistic laws and principles of matter, what place did an immaterial soul have? If such a 'Demonstration',

---

[85] Walter Charleton, *The immortality of the human soul* (1699), 58.

[86] Thomson, *Bodies of Thought*, 73.

[87] Even though Galileo's book was ordered burned by the Church, though many survived and several Latin editions began circulating (e.g. Augsburg, 1635; Lyons, 1640; London, 1661) . Cambridge scholars had access to copies at least as early as the 1640s: David A. Michaud, *Reason Turned into Sense* (Leuven, 2017), 57.

[88] Charleton, *The immortality of the human soul*, 188.

[89] For more on Galileo's *Dialogo* see Maurice A. Finocchiaro, *The Routledge Guidebook to Galileo's Dialogue* (2014).

'THE FOUNDATION OF ALL KNOWLEDGE' 185

of the kind Isodicastes is looking for, is ultimately impossible, then does science and philosophy need to refer to the soul at all? Would it be better, as Digby suggests, to leave such talk to the contemplatives and the divines?

For at least one group of English philosophers, such an ostracizing of the soul from philosophical inquiry was out of the question. The Cambridge Platonists, led by Benjamin Whichcote (Cambridge's vice chancellor in the 1650s), produced some of the more vigorous rebuttals of mortalism in seventeenth-century England.[90] Holding to a form of innatism, the Cambridge Platonists wrestled with both the theological and epistemological implications of mortalism. As Charles Taliaferro explains, much of their philosophy was concerned with 'whether human reasoning and value can find a place in a cosmos', which was increasingly explained in 'mechanistic terms'.[91]

One of their number, Ralph Cudworth (who we have already discussed) found that the 'Doctrine of Incorporeal Substance sprung up together' with 'Atomical Physiology', both being intellectual innovations in ancient Greece.[92] Following a lengthy excursus demonstrating this relationship from the Greek sources, Cudworth summarized the arguments for immortalism. In an uncharacteristic moment of pithiness, Cudworth wrote, 'no Body could ever move it self…[so] there must be something else in the World besides Body'. Then, he presented three arguments for immortality based upon sense perception. First, perception involves 'Phancie' (i.e. positive or negative impressions in the mind), which 'is no mode of the Body'. Second, human fancies create 'Phantastick Ideas' about sensible things, so much so that 'Sense it self is not a mere Corporal Passion…[but] some activity of the Soul'. Third, these ideas must be created by an internal judge, 'a higher Self-active Vigour of the Mind', which is unconstrained by the physical senses since the judge clearly has power over the senses.[93]

As formidable as these arguments were, the Cambridge Platonists recognized some important difficulties. Perhaps the two most significant questions were: how does a material body and an immortal soul interact? Also, how can we directly detect the soul? Since, as Henry More admitted, we cannot discover any operation of the soul except 'what it first works upon…Matter', knowing the soul directly in any empirical way was perhaps impossible.[94] More was more prolific in his writing than Cudworth, and much pithier, making More among the most popular of the Cambridge Platonists. In *The immortality of the soul*, More developed the notion of a 'plastick faculty' or principle, which 'ties the Soul and this or that Matter together'. Although not original to More, a 'plastick' principle or

---

[90] Three leading members wrote extensive defenses of the immortal soul: Henry More, *The immortality of the soul* (1659); John Smith, *Select discourses* (1660), 59–112; Cudworth, *The true intellectual system*, 20–56.

[91] Taliaferro, *Evidence and Faith*, 41. [92] Cudworth, *The true intellectual system*, 29–30.

[93] Cudworth, *The true intellectual system*, 47.

[94] More, *The immortality of the soul*, 202. See Garber, 'Soul and Mind', 776–8.

faculty allowed Platonists a workaround to the question of how the body and soul might interact. More argued that the plastic faculty was the inferior faculty of the soul, which extended throughout the material world, serving as an organizing fabric for the soul's ordering of matter.[95] Not only did this plastic principle resolve issues that the Cambridge Platonists saw within materialism, but it also created a certain amount of space between the material world and God. Cudworth argued that without some sort of intervening principle like 'Plastick Nature' then we are left with either a materialistically determined universe where 'every thing comes to pass…without the Guidance and Direction of any *Mind* or *Vnderstanding*' or else 'God himself doth all *Immediately*'. The former Cudworth found to be logically impossible, given the fine-tuned order of the universe. The latter, however, raised the questions of why a perfect God would create things with malformations, would not be able to overcome the 'Indisposition of Matter', and would not keep his creation from suffering the 'Slow and Gradual Process' of degeneration.[96]

The final Cambridge Platonist we will look at who tackled the substance of the soul was, historically, the first. John Smith was a fellow of Queens' College (Cambridge), until his death at the young age of 34 (possibly of tuberculosis). His *Select Discourses* were published posthumously (1660), and while he has never been very popular within the wider scholarship, his importance in late seventeenth- and early eighteenth-century English religious thought is difficult to overstate.[97] Dedicated to developing a rational explanation for the ascent of the soul to God through moral discipline and study, Smith provided an entire discourse on the soul's immortality, although it is clear that he struggled to believe that any reasonable person would hold to mortalism.[98]

Of more pressing importance for Smith were the questions surrounding what the immortal soul could acquire (in terms of knowledge), which he grouped into four kinds of knowledge: sensual, self-reflective, knowledge purged of sensual passion, and contemplative.[99] The first two occupy the 'terrene' (terrestrial) parts of the soul, and could be deceived. The latter two seemed to have a much greater defense against deception, demonic or otherwise:

> this Pseudo-prophetical Spirit only flutters below upon the more terrene parts of mans Soul, his Passions and Phansie. The Prince of darkness comes not within the Sphere of Light and Reason to order affairs there, but that is left to the sole Oeconomy and Soveraignty of the Father of Lights. There is a clear and bright

---

[95] More, *The immortality of the soul*, 265, see also 216–19.

[96] Cudworth, *The true intellectual system*, 147–50, quotes on pp. 147, 150. Keith Allen, 'Cudworth on Mind, Body, and Plastic Nature', *Philosophy Compass* 8 (2013), 337–47.

[97] Michaud, *Reason Turned Into Sense*, 194–9.

[98] Smith found the soul's immortality to be as self-evident a notion as one's own existence. His essential argument can be found at *Select discourses*, 63–6.

[99] Smith, *Select discourses*, 17–20.

heaven in mans Soul, in which Lucifer himself cannot subsist, but is tumbled down from thence as often as assayes to climbe up into it.[100]

The rational faculties were the foundation of a person's *summum bonum*. They were a haven from demonic interference because they were capable of receiving divine revelation. Although Smith believed that 'it was rare' for contemporary prophecy to occur, his epistemology is rooted in the necessity of soul-rapture by God.[101] Here, Smith is perhaps at his most original in the seventeenth century and nearest to the classical philosopher Plotinus. While Protestants agreed that the Devil was incapable of true prophecy, Smith asserted that the rational soul, the site of the prophetic, was unassailable by demonic forces.[102]

Smith's fourth kind of knowledge, contemplative knowledge, ultimately leads a person to a union with God that he considered to be a prelude to the beatific vision after death. Unlike Fisher's inner Light, Smith argued it was the soul's understanding, working through, and eventually beyond, reason that achieved this enlightenment: 'God only, who is the true light...can so shine out of himself upon our glassy Understandings, as to beget them a picture of himself'.[103] The enlightening of the soul deepened a person's understanding, and it transformed the soul into something godlike. What Smith described as 'an Infant-Christ' is 'formed in...[the] Soul', which for Smith is analogous to Christ's relationship to the Father.[104] In his chapter 'The Excellency and Nobleness of True Religion', Smith outlined the means by which a person cultivates such a union. Much like the contemplative tradition of the later middle ages, Smith advocated mental and meditative discipline in the pursuit of ravishment. One must persist in 'chasing away all that misty darkness of his own *Self-will* and *Passions*', by study, contemplation, and the practice of true religion. These disciplines transformed the 'inward Senses', allowing them '[to be] affected with the sweet relishes of Divine Goodness' to such a degree that the 'Mind climbs up by these Sun-beams and raises up it self to God'.[105] When these senses were aligned appropriately with 'Divine Goodness', they functioned at their most perfect capacity, while simultaneously transforming the person into a more divine being. The knowledge of revelation was essentially experiential for Smith, and like Newton, Smith considered revelation to be a necessary precursor to realizing certain aspects about God and reality.

---

[100] Smith, *Select discourses*, 203.   [101] Smith, *Select discourses*, 272.

[102] See for example the distinction made by John Gaule in *A collection*, 196–7; Smith, *Select discourses*, 193. For the parallels between Smith and both Augustine and Plotinus on this point, see Zwollo, *Augustine and Plotinus*, 188, 320.

[103] Smith, *Select discourses*, 384.

[104] Smith, *Select discourses*, 21. J. E. Saveson, 'Differing Reactions to Descartes among the Cambridge Platonists', *Journal of the History of Ideas*, 21 (1960), 564–6.

[105] Smith, *Select discourses*, 428, 434.

188 EXPERIENCING GOD IN LATE MEDIEVAL & EARLY MODERN ENGLAND

Although his *Select Discourses* was not the most popular book of philosophy, Smith's influence was significant in other respects. At his funeral, a former student, the young Simon Patrick compared Smith to the Old Testament prophet Elijah, and his students as Smith's Elishas. Patrick explained that Smith was dedicated to disciplining his mind, until he was a 'living Library' and a 'walking Study' pursuing 'the more divine accomplishments of the soul'.[106] We can see the fruit of this walking, talking library of contemplative wisdom in the eighteenth century, particularly in the lives of two influential English Protestants, Jonathan Edwards and John Wesley. Both the North American puritan and the English evangelist found Smith an inspiring fountain for both their theological and devotional approaches to religious life.[107]

Perhaps even more important for our purposes in this chapter, Smith represents one distinctive voice in an increasingly variegated field of philosophical and scientific views that explore how God had been, and might still be, experienced. Far from a clear trajectory of secularization that some scholars have posited, what we have seen here is a much more complicated situation of different, compelling (some more so than others) philosophical explanations of divine revelation that were very much alive as the Enlightenment took shape at the end of the seventeenth century.[108] Although Christopher Hill's comment about there not being a science of prophecy is technically true, the problem was not that the leading minds lacked an effective response to the challenges we have examined. If the epistemic authority of divine revelation was losing ground in the seventeenth century, it was not beating a retreat from the onslaught of secular philosophy. The likes of Glanvill, Boyle, Digby, Cudworth, Bentley, and Smith were not stumped by the likes of Spinoza and Hobbes. Nor were they entirely numb to the problems that the new philosophies and sciences raised concerning the traditional understanding of how divine revelation worked. Instead, I think it more accurate to say that there were too many sciences of prophecy in the period, but no single philosophy or theory became paradigmatic. There was no Copernicus or Newton or Darwin of divine revelation, no intellectual clarion with an organizing principle, blasted through the noise and excitement of intellectual discovery. A bounty of possible answers can be just as, if not more, difficult to overcome than no answer at all.

---

[106] Smith, *Select discourses*, 501, 506–7.   [107] Michaud, *Reason Turned into Sense*, 194–200.
[108] See e.g. C. John Sommerville, *The Secularization of Early Modern England* (Oxford 1992). See Thomson's assessment of the issues in *Bodies of Thought*, 14–16. Also relevant to this topic is Ethan Shagan's recent challenge to scholars to reframe our understandings about belief and secularization in the period, arguing that secularization 'was not about the segregation of belief from the world, but the promiscuous opening of belief to the world': *The Birth of Modern Belief*, 29.

Conclusion

A constant Mirror of Eternitie. / Let my pure Soul, transformed to
a Thought, / Attend upon thy Throne, and as it ought / Spend all its
Time in feeding on thy Love.

Thomas Traherne, 'Thoughts. IV'

My hope for this book is that it has demonstrated a way of understanding divine
revelation that was shared by most late medieval and early modern English people,
even if they parted ways with one another on certain details. This collective
representation of revelation, as a rapturous experience of the soul initiated by
God, was the dominant way of describing experiential encounters with God until
at least 1700. Built upon the Augustinian understanding of *visio* as well as a
robust, medieval contemplative tradition, both Protestants and Catholics believed
that God could, and did, intervene in the normal course of events, to communicate truth to an individual's soul. The emphasis people placed on certain details,
expectations, and requirements of divine revelation shifted over the course of our
period; however, the most basic elements of the discourse and what was understood to be happening to the individual's soul remained consistent, even if it faced
a variety of challenges.

Although I stated in the Introduction that this book would not be a narrative
of decline, it is important that we spend a few moments considering the future of
divine revelation that followed the seventeenth century.

At the end of our period, even among England's leading thinkers, divine revelation as a legitimate form of knowledge and human experience continued to
have significant currency. The notion that a transcendent deity had moved, and
still could move, upon an individual's soul with such force to effectively separate
the soul from the body in order to communicate with that person, remained an
idea that was not dismissed easily as superstitious or nonsensical. At the same
time, the culture of divine revelation faced many challenges to its philosophical
coherency and its devotional necessity. Not only were there several challenges to
the traditional understanding of divine revelation as an epistemic authority, but
the increasingly popular enthusiastic expressions of divine revelation also undermined for many people what was understood to be a largely rational experience
of the soul. Experiences of God did not disappear from English Christianity, but
the collective representation of them as an epistemically valid experience in

Experiencing God in Late Medieval and Early Modern England. David J. Davis, Oxford University Press.
© David J. Davis 2022. DOI: 10.1093/oso/9780198834137.003.0009

190 EXPERIENCING GOD IN LATE MEDIEVAL & EARLY MODERN ENGLAND

which the soul received direct understanding from God, suffered some significant deterioration.

In fact, if the Great Awakenings, the evangelical movement, and other English and American revivals are any indicator, one might argue that such experiences with God became more popular in the eighteenth and nineteenth centuries. In the early decades of the eighteenth century, while Lord Shaftesbury was complaining that it was impossible to tell the difference between true revelation and enthusiasm, there was a growing number of Englishwomen and men seeking the physically stirring style of religion embodied in the first Great Awakening. What had been dismissed as religious enthusiasm in the previous century became something to be sought after and experienced as much as possible by a growing number of the English-speaking population. At the same time, it is evident that these movements exemplified a religion that was considered by many, particularly within the Anglican hierarchy, to be as Mark Noll described it, 'too emotional and...uncultured' to represent true religion.[1] A few eighteenth-century examples of leading evangelicals wrestling with the proliferation of such experiences will offer us some important perspectives and perhaps a helpful way of bringing this book to an end.

First, during the first Great Awakening, the Scottish presbyterian minister James Robe began documenting examples of 'extraordinary works(s) of the Spirit of God', collecting them into a single volume. Turning to the Covenanter visionary Elizabeth Cairns's claims she had been raptured into heaven, Robe wrote:

I am persuaded she was a good woman, I do not look upon the visions and other things mentioned as incompatible with a good and gracious state, neither do I look upon these as any part of her goodness, or evidence of it: which are precisely my sentiments, with reference to any few of the people who have been thus affected.[2]

For Robe, experiences of divine rapture were not evidence of either virtue or vice, nor did he encourage people to draw too much significance from such accounts. Around the same time, the leading colonial theologian and minister Jonathan Edwards wrote to Robe seeming to affirm Robe's views:

Many among us have been ready to think, that all high raptures are divine; but experience plainly shows, that it is not the degree of rapture and ecstasy (although it should be to the third heavens), but the nature and kind that must

---

[1] Mark Noll, *The Rise of Evangelicalism* (Westmont, IL, 2015), 182. See also David Bebbington, *Evangelicalism in Modern Britain* (Abingdon, 2003).
[2] James Robe, *Narratives of the Extraordinary Work of the Spirit of God* (Glasgow, 1790), 235.

CONCLUSION   191

determine us in their favor...that sort of humility that is not a noisy showy humility, but rather this, which disposes to walk softly, and speak trembling.[3]

Anyone familiar with Edwards will know that he was not throwing a wet blanket on either divine rapture or religious fervor.[4] Instead, Edwards advocated discretion and discernment, for while some 'high raptures are divine', other claims and experiences clearly were not.

Similarly, within the Methodist movement, there was a tension between affectionate religious experience and the 'noisy showy' demonstrations, which Edwards had cautioned against. In 1749, Bishop George Lavington accused John Wesley of celebrating religious enthusiasm. Wesley's response to such criticism was pithy and pointed, defending his use of a story about one Peter Wright who heard heavenly voices on his deathbed. After he corrected misquotes and expanded other quotes that Lavington had taken out of context, Wesley protested that neither Lavington nor Wesley

> were...to judge of the Spirit whereby any one spoke, either by Appearances, or by common Report, or by their own inward Feelings...nor by any Dreams, Visions or Revelations, supposed to be made to their Souls, any more than by their Tears or any voluntary Effects wrought upon their Bodies.... They might be from God, and they might not, and were therefore not simply to be relied on...but to be tried by a farther Rule; to be brought to the only certain Test, the Law and the Testimony.[5]

In using Peter Wright's account, Wesley conveyed upon it a degree of legitimacy; however, he admitted that he did not know with any certainty what happened to Wright. He could only point his audience to more certain tests of such claims while refusing to pass judgment upon the particular causes. According to Wesley, the biblical text ('the Law and the Testimony') offered the only confident measure for contemporary divine experiences, and beyond that standard, Wesley could find no more certain measure. He concluded the matter with the challenging quip, 'can you shew them a better Way?'[6]

What is fascinating about these accounts is the interesting shift in description that seems to have taken place between these eighteenth-century leaders and those of a century earlier. As we have seen throughout this book, the traditional culture of revelation modelled ravishment after biblical precedents like Saul's experience on the Damascus road and Stephen's experience during his martyrdom. In the biblical accounts, no one else seems to have heard the voice of Christ

---

[3] Jonathan Edwards, *Letters and Personal Writings in Works of Jonathan Edwards*, vol. 16, 109.
[4] See e.g., Boersma, *Seeing God*, Ch. 12.
[5] John Wesley, *A Letter to the Author* (1750), 39–40.   [6] Wesley, *A Letter to the Author*, 40.

that Saul heard nor seen the heavenly vision that Stephen saw. If anything, any 'voluntary Effects wrought upon their Bodies' that Wesley described, traditionally would have been considered signs of enthusiasm, which seems to be the position taken by Lavington. Earlier accounts of divine revelation had no expectation of any outward, empirical signs of a person's experience that could be detected by others. The less the body was involved, the more trustworthy the experience seems to have been.

Interestingly, while both Wesley and Edwards read John Smith, neither of them seemed willing to hold to Smith's hard line between the 'Prophetical' and 'pseudo-Prophetical' spirits by their physical manifestations, or lack thereof. Where the former works 'upon the Reason', Smith explained, the latter works upon the 'Phansie and Imaginations'.[7] Edwards preferred people to 'walk softly', but neither Edwards nor Wesley condemned such emotional displays nor drew too clear a distinction between the kind of ravishment of the soul we have been studying and the experiences of Cairns, Wright, and others. In fact, for Wesley, passing judgment upon whether such things are 'of the Spirit' was neither his role nor within his power ('They might be from God, and they might not').

Since there was no 'Rule' by which experiences of divine revelation could be judged, they were protected from any philosophical assault because philosophy had no purview. However, this protection would come at a price: divine revelation (at least immediate revelation) cannot be epistemically authoritative and, at the same time, be immune from investigation. Here, we can detect a clear shift away from attempting to determine the epistemic significance of someone's religious experience. Although the raptures of Cairns and Wright clearly presented more empirical evidence to onlookers than did those of figures like Richard Rolle, Katherine Stubbes, Julian of Norwich, John Donne, or Isaac Ambrose, the empirical evidence was placed beyond human judgment by leading religious authorities.

It is not so surprising then that two centuries later, the philosopher Charles Taylor has detected a significant division in Christianity between what he calls 'spirituality' and religion, to a degree that the one has become a pejorative for the adherents of the other. Like the enthusiasm of the seventeenth and eighteenth centuries, modern spirituality focuses upon an 'experience', which often presents very evident, physical manifestations.[8] Unfortunately, as Taylor describes, the rifts between the more emotive spirituality and the established (or mainline) churches have never been bridged. Perhaps this is why a contemporary version of the contemplative language and practices of late medieval and early modern writers who pursued soul-ravishment is very difficult to find. Although the emotional religion of the early eighteenth century continues to bear its particular fruit

---

[7] Smith, *Select discourses*, 193. [8] Taylor, *A Secular Age*, 506–10, quote on p. 507.

CONCLUSION 193

in different groups and denominations, according to Tom Schwanda, Protestants seem to have lost the kind of spiritual engagement exemplified by the writings of people like Francis Rous and Simon Patrick.[9] Along these same lines, Hans Boersma is unable to identify many theologians (Catholic or Protestant) who have a developed conception of the beatific vision (the ultimate fulfillment of divine ravishment), leaving him with the question of why such a fundamental aspect of traditional Christian theology is so 'unfamiliar to many of us'.[10]

Today, if one is going to take such accounts of divine experience seriously, at least in the way that John Calvin, St. John of the Cross, and John Smith took them seriously, perhaps the best place to begin is with analytic philosophers of religion.[11] Working on the premise that if God communicates with human beings, then humans should be able to understand and analyze what God communicates (whether it is in sacred texts or in immediate revelation), many of these thinkers have returned to some of the issues discussed in Chapter 7.[12] Not only has this scholarship placed a renewed emphasis upon the immaterial nature of the soul (so fundamental to the traditional understanding of divine revelation), but also many of these thinkers have reinvigorated the study of testimonial claims of transcendent experiences, which earlier generations would have dismissed as superstitious.

Nor is this literature a purely academic exercise, simply exploring the rationality underpinning an archaic way of thinking about reality. According to Richard Swinburne, while 'natural reason can discover unaided the general moral truths' within religious belief, more transcendent realities like 'the truth about the universe' are too far 'removed from ordinary human experience' to be accessible through empirical or rational methods. Swinburne convincingly argues that without an epistemically authoritative notion of divine revelation, we lose some of the most significant reasons for religion to exist, because 'We need help from above, in order to understand the deepest reality'.[13] Others, like William Abraham, explore the place of divine revelation (what Abraham calls 'divine intervention') in historical explanation and other academic disciplines. 'To accept', Abraham writes, 'that one can only explain the events of the past either by natural causation or by human psychological causation is to accept at the same time that God does not intervene in the world'. Abraham does not require scholars to include a theological cause in their investigations of reality. He does point out, however, that if scholars entirely prohibit the possibility of such a cause, then we commit

---

[9] Schwanda, *Soul Recreation*, ch. 6.   [10] Boersma, *Seeing God*, 33–41, quote on p. 17.
[11] See e.g., William J. Abraham, *Divine Revelation and the Limits of Historical Criticism* (Oxford, 1982); Swinburne, *Revelation*; Wolterstorff, *Divine Discourse*.
[12] See e.g., Richard Swinburne, *The Evolution of the Soul* (Oxford, 1986).
[13] Swinburne, *Revelation*, 72–3.

194   EXPERIENCING GOD IN LATE MEDIEVAL & EARLY MODERN ENGLAND

ourselves to the bias that 'accepting that God has intervened will seem to be the mark of an uncritical and even superstitious mentality'.[14]

If nothing else, these philosophers have highlighted some important blind spots within contemporary Western thought and the intellectual arrogance that is common to every age. However, it seems to me their works accomplish much more than simply chastising our own society's inflated confidence about what we think we know. By asserting the rationality of divine revelation, particularly using different analytical and linguistic approaches, this scholarship provides a framework for accounts of divine experience, even immediate revelation, to be taken seriously in our own day. As we have seen here, it was not that long ago that many of the foremost thinkers in Christianity possessed such an understanding of divine revelation, holding to a collective representation which was rooted in biblical precedent and buttressed by their philosophy of the soul and a theology which placed the beatific vision at the center of human existence.

Perhaps it is fitting that the pupils of Lady Philosophy are the ones restoring some intellectual dignity to divine revelation. As the traditional queen of the sciences, it is her muses after all who are illumined by heavenly Truth on the ceiling of the Sheldonian Theatre.

[14] Abraham, *Divine Revelation*, 110. See also Charles Taylor's arguments about the limits of materialistic explanations in 'Interpretation and the Sciences of Man', *The Review of Metaphysics*, 25 (1971), 48–51.

Bibliography

Manuscripts

British Library, London
Cotton MS Faustina B VI, vol. II
BL Add MS 71474

Cambridge University Library, Cambridge
MS Add 8460
Yahuda MS. 1

Houghton Library, Cambridge, MA
MS Eng. 701
MS Richardson 22

Huntington Library, San Marino, CA
HM 128

John Rylands Library, Manchester
English MS 87
English MS 701

Lambeth Palace Library, London
MS 2240

Leeds University Library, Leeds
Brotherton Collection MS Lt 91

Newberry Library, Chicago, IL
Stanton A. Friedberg Collection MS 5017

New Testaments & Bibles

NB: without short title catalogue numbers for non-English Bibles, I have included publisher's information to identify the edition more easily.

Das newe Testament (Basel, 1523).

Figures des histoires de la Sainte Bible, avec des discours (Paris: Robert Pepie, 1688).

Geneva Bible: A Facsimile of the 1560 edition (Madison, WI, 1969).

La Biblia. Qve es, los sacros libros del Viejo y nuevo testament (Basel: Samuel Apiarius f. Thomas Guarin, 1569).

The New Testament in English, translated by John Wycliffe and revised by John Purvey with an introduction by Donald L. Brake (Portland, OR, 1986).

196 BIBLIOGRAPHY

The New Testament of Iesus Christ faithfully translated into English (Douai, 1633: RSTC 2946).

The Bible: that is, the Holy Scriptures contained in the Old and New Testament [Geneva edition] (London, 1616: RSTC 2244).

The history of ye Old & new Testament in cutts (London, 1671: Wing H2173B).

The Holy Bible [Authorised edition] (London, 1638: RSTC 2329.4).

The Holy Bible, containing the Old Testament and the New [Authorised edition] (London, 1630: RSTC 2292).

The Holy Bible containing the Old Testament and the New [Authorised edition] (London, 1631: RSTC 2295.4).

The Holy Bible, containing the Old Testament and the New [Authorised edition] (London, 1678: Wing B2304A).

The Holy Bible in Sculpture or The History's mentioned in the Old and New Testament lively represented in copper cutts [Authorised edition] (London, 1683: Wing B2330A).

Editions of the Book of Common Prayer

The Book of Common Prayer, 1559: The Elizabethan Prayer Book, ed. John E. Booty (University of Virginia Press, 2005).

The book of common-prayer and administration of the sacraments and other rites and ceremonies of the Church according to the use of the Church of England (London, 1664: Wing B3628).

The book of common prayer, and administration of the sacraments, and other rites and ceremonies of the Church (London, 1676: Wing B3646).

Printed Primary Sources

Abbot, George. *An exposition vpon the prophet Ionah. Contained in certaine sermons* (London, 1600).

Abbot, John. *Iesus praefigured: or A poeme of the holy name of Iesus in fiue bookes* (Antwerp?, 1623).

Abercromby, David. *Scolding no scholarship: in the abyss or, groundless of the Protestant religion* (Douai, 1669).

Adams, Thomas. *The temple. A sermon preached at Pauls Crosse the fifth of August. 1624* (London, 1624).

Adams, Thomas. *Fiue sermons preached vpon sundry especiall occasions* (London, 1626).

Ambrose, Isaac. *War with devils: ministration of, and communion with angels* (Glasgow, 1769).

Ambrose, Isaac. *Media: the middle things, in reference to the first and last things* (London, 1657).

Ambrose, Isaac. *Looking unto Jesus. A view of the everlasting gospel* (London, 1680).

Andrewes, Lancelot. *Responsio ad apologiam Cardinalis Bellarmini* (London, 1610).

Andrewes, Lancelot. *XCVI. sermons by the Right Honorable and Reverend Father in God, Lancelot Andrevves* (London, 1629).

[Andries, Judocus]. *The Perpetval crosse, or, Passion of Iesvs Christ* (Antwerp, 1649).

Annand, William. *Mysterium pietatis, or The mysterie of godlinesse* (London, 1671).

Anon. *The prouffytable boke for ma[n]nes soule, and right comfortable to the body, and specyally in aduersitee [and] trybulacyon... The chastysing of goddes chyldern* (Westminster, 1493).

BIBLIOGRAPHY   197

Anon. *Here begynneth the kalendre of the newe legende of Englande* (London, 1516).

Anon. *A bryefe summe of the whole Byble* (London, 1549).

Anon. *The praise of musicke wherein besides the antiquitie, dignitie, delectations, & vse thereof in civill matters, is also declared* (Oxenford, 1586).

Anon. *A manual of prayers newly gathered out of many famous and godly authours* (Douai, 1613).

Anon. *Eliza's babes: or, The virgins-offering. Being divine poems, and meditations* (London, 1652).

Anon. *The Quakers fiery beacon or, The shaking-ranting ghost* (London, 1655).

Anon. *Mr. Turbulent: or, The melanchollicks* (London, 1682).

Anon. *A manual of prayers and other Christian devotions* (London, 1686).

Anon. *The Chastising of God's Children and the Treatise of Perfection of the Sons of God*, eds Joyce Bazire and Eric Colledge (Oxford, 1957).

Anon. *The Vision of Edmund Leversedge: A 15th-Century Account of a Visit to the Otherworld, Edited from BL MS Additional 3,193, with an Introduction, Commentary, and Glossary*, ed. W. F. Nijenhuis (Nijmegen, 1991).

Anon. *The Cloud of Unknowing*, ed. Patrick J. Gallacher (Kalamazoo, MI, 1997).

Aquinas, Thomas. *The Summa Theologica*, trans. Fathers of the English Dominican Province (New York, 1947).

Assisi, Clare of. *The rvle of the Holy Virgin S. Clare. Together with the admirable life, of S. Catharine of Bologna, of the same Order* (St. Omer, 1621).

Augustine. *Certaine select prayers gathered out of S. Augustines meditations* (London, 1574).

Augustine. *Saint Augustines confessions translated: and with some marginall notes illustrated*, trans. William Watts (London, 1631).

Augustine. *Letters of St. Augustine*, ed. Philip Schaff (Ann Arbor, MI, 1956).

Augustine. *The Confessions of Augustine: An Electronic Edition*, ed. James J. O'Donnell (Oxford, 1992).

Austin, William. *Devotionis Augustinianae flamma, or, Certaine devout, godly, and learned meditations* (London, 1635).

Avila, Teresa of. *The flaming hart or The life of the glorious S. Teresa*, trans. Sir Tobie Matthew (Antwerp, 1642).

Aylett, Robert. *The brides ornaments, viz fiue meditations, morall and diuine* (London, 1625).

Baker, Augustine. *Sancta Sophia. Or, Directions for the prayer of contemplation &c.* (Douai, 1657).

Bale, John. *The image of both churches after reulacion of saynt Johan the euangelyst* (Antwerp, 1545?).

Bampfield, Francis. *Shem 'achar. A name, an after-one...An historical declaration of the life of Shem Acher* (London, 1681).

Bancroft, Richard. *A suruay of pretended holy discipline* (London, 1593).

Barker, Jane. *Poeticall recreations: consisting of original poems, songs, odes, &c.* (London, 1688).

Barnes, Barnabe. *A divine centurie of spirituall sonnets* (London, 1595).

Barry, James. *A reviving cordial for a sin-sick despairing soul in the time of temptation* (London, 1699).

Bates, William. *The four last things: viz. death, judgment, heaven, hell, practically considered and applyed* (London, 1691).

Baxter, Richard. *The saints everlasting rest: or, A treatise of the blessed state of the saints in their enjoyment* (London, 1650).

Baxter, Richard. *The reasons of the Christian religion* (London, 1667).

198 BIBLIOGRAPHY

Baxter, Richard. *A Christian directory: or, A sum of practical theologie, and cases of conscience* (London, 1673).

Baxter, Richard. *Richard Baxter's Catholick theologie: plain, pure, peaceable* (London, 1675).

Baxter, Richard. *The second part of The nonconformist plea for peace, or An account of the matter of their nonconformity* (London, 1680).

Bayly, Lewis. *The practise of piety directing a Christian how to walk that he may please God* (London, 1613).

Bayly, William. *A call and visitation from the Lord God of heaven and earth unto Christendom* (London, 1673).

Beckham, Edward. *The principles of the Quakers further shewn to be blasphemous and seditious* (London, 1700).

Bellarmine, Robert. *Jacob's ladder consisting of fifteene degrees or ascents to the knowledge of God* (Douai, 1638).

Bellarmine, Robert. *Christian doctrine composed by Robert Bellarmine* (s.l., 1676).

Benlowes, Edward. *Theophila, or Loves sacrifice. A divine poem* (London, 1652).

Bentley, Richard. *Matter and motion cannot think: or, A confutation of atheism from the faculties of the soul* (London, 1693: Wing B1938).

Bentley, Richard. *Of revelation and the Messias: a sermon preached at the publick commencement at Cambridge, July 5th 1696* (London, 1696).

Bentley, Thomas. *The monument of matrones conteining seuen seuerall lamps of virginitie* (London, 1582).

Bernard, Richard. *A guide to grand-iury men, diuideed into two bookes* (London, 1627).

Beza, Theodore. *Master Bezaes sermons vpon the three chapters of the canticle of canticles*, trans. John Harmar (Oxford to be sold in London, 1587).

Blondel, David. *A treatise of the sibyls, so highly celebrated, as well by the antient heathens, as the holy fathers of the church* (London, 1661).

Bolton, Robert. *Instructions for a right comforting afflicted consciences* (London, 1631).

Bonaventure. *Stimulis diuini amoris: that is, The goade of divine love...Englished by B. Lewis A.* (Douai, 1642).

Bonaventure. *The Journey of the Mind to God*, trans. Philotheus Boehner (Indianapolis, 1993).

Boyle, Robert. *Some considerations about the reconcileableness of reason and religion* (London, 1675).

Bradshaw, Henry. *Here begynneth the lyfe of saynt Radegunde* (London, 1525).

Bradshaw, William. *A meditation of mans mortalitie. Containing an exposition of the ninetieth psalme* (London, 1621).

Brightman, Thomas. *A revelation of the Apocalyps, that is, the Apocalyps of S. Iohn* (Amsterdam, 1611).

Brinsley, John. *Two treatises. I. A groan for Israel, or The Church's salvation temporall, spirituall, the desire and joy of saints...* (London, 1656).

Brough, William. *Sacred principles, services, and soliloquies, or, A manual of devotions* (London, 1659).

Browne, Thomas. *Pseudodoxia epidemica: or, Enquiries into very man received tenents* (London, 1646).

Browne, Thomas. *Miracles work's above and contrary to nature* (London, 1683).

Browne, Thomas. *Religio Medici and Hydriotaphia, Or Urne-Buriall*, eds Stephen Greenblatt and Ramie Targoff (New York, 2012).

Bullinger, Henry. *A hundred sermons vpon the Apocalipse of Iesu Christ* (London, 1573).

Bullinger, Henry. *Fiftie godlie and learned sermons diuided into fiue decades, conteyning the chiefe and principall pointes of Christian religion* (London, 1577).

BIBLIOGRAPHY   199

Bunny, Edmund. *A book of Christian exercise, appertaining to resolution, that is shewing how that wee shoulde resolue our selues to become Christians indeed* (London, 1586).

Bunyan, John. *A treatise of the fear of God* (London, 1679).

Burgess, Anthony. *CXLV expository sermons upon the whole 17th chapter of the Gospel according to St John* (London, 1656).

Burnet, Gilbert. *An exposition of the Thirty-nine articles of the Church of England written by Gilbert Bishop of Sarum* (London, 1700).

Burrough, Edward. *Truth defended. Or, Certain accusations answered, cast upon us who are called Quakers* (London, 1654).

Burton, Robert. *The anatomy of melancholy, what it is* (Oxford, 1621).

C., T. *A glasse for the times by which according to the Scriptures, you may clearly behold the true ministers of Christ, how farre differing from false teachers* (London, 1648).

Calvin, John. *A faythfull and moost godlye treatyse concerning the most sacred Sacramanet of the blessed boy and bloude of our saviour Chryst* (London, 1548).

Calvin, John. *Two epystles, one of Henry Bullinger, wyth the consent of all the learned men of the Churche of Tygury: an other of Johan Cauyne, chefe preacher of the church of Geneue* (London, 1548).

Calvin, John. *Commentaries on the Prophet Ezekiel, vol. I*, trans. and ed. Thomas Myers (Edinburgh, 1849).

Calvin, John. *Calvin's Commentary of Isaiah, vol. I*, trans. William Pringle (Grand Rapids, MI, 1948).

Calvin, John. *Institutes of the Christian Religion in 2 vols.*, ed. John T. McNeill and trans. Ford Lewis Battles (Louisville, KY, 1970).

Calvin, John. *Sermons on Acts*, trans. Rob Roy McGregor (Edinburgh, 1994).

Capilla, Andrés. *Les Meditations dévotes sur les évangiles de toutes les dimanches & festes de l'année* (Lyons, 1638).

Capua, Raymond of. *Here begynneth the orchard of Suon in whiche is conteyned the revelacyons of seynt Katheryne of Sene* (London, 1519).

Capua, Raymond of. *The life of the blessed virgin, Sainct Catharine of Siena*, trans. Iohn Fen (Douai, 1610).

Carew, Thomas. *Poems* (London, 1640).

Carruthers, S. W., ed. *The Confession of Faith of the Assembly of Divines at Westminster: From the Original Manuscript written by Cornelius Burges, in 1646* (London, 1946).

Cartwright, Thomas. *A plaine explanation of the vvhole Revelation of Saint John* (London, 1622).

Casaubon, Meric. *A treatise concerning enthusiasme, as it is an effect of nature* (London, 1656).

Castiglione, Baldassare. *The Book of the Courtier*, ed. Daniel Javitch and trans. Charles S. Singleton (New York, 2002).

Cavendish, Lady Margaret. *CCXI sociable letters* (London, 1664).

Cawdrey, Robert. *The First English Dictionary, 1604*, intro. John Simpson (Oxford, 2007).

Charleton, Walter. *The immortality of the human soul demonstrated by the light of nature* (London, 1699: Wing C3676).

Clapham, Henoch. *Theologicall axioms or conclusions publicly controuerted, discussed, and concluded by that poore English congregation, in Amsterdam* (Amsterdam, 1597).

Clarke, Samuel. *A mirror or looking glasse both for saints & sinners wherein is recorded, as Gods great goodness to the one, so his seveare iudgment against the other* (London, 1654).

Clarke, Samuel. *A generall martyrologie, containing a collection of all the greatest persecutions which have befallen the church of Christ from the creation to our present times* (London, 1660).

200 BIBLIOGRAPHY

Clarke, Samuel. *The lives of Sundry eminent persons in this later age* (London, 1683).

Clerc, Jean le. *Five letters concerning the inspiration of the Holy Scriptures* (London, 1690: Wing L815).

Cockin, Francis. *Divine blossomes. A prospect or looking-glass for youth* (London, 1657).

Comber, Thomas. *Christianity, no enthusiasm: or, The several kinds of inspirations and revelations pretended to by the Quakers* (London, 1678).

Cooper, Earl of Shaftesbury, Anthony Ashley. *A letter concerning enthusiasm* (London, 1708).

Cooper, Thomas. *A Briefe homily, wherein the most comfortable and right use of the Lords Supper is very plainly opened and delivered* (London, 1580).

Cooper, Thomas. *The cry and revenge of blood. Expressing the nature and haynousnesse of willfull murther* (London, 1620).

Cosin, John. *A collection of priuate deuotions; in the practice of the ancient church, called The houres of prayer* (London, 1627).

Cowper, William. *The triumph of a Christian, containing three excellent and heauenly treatises* (London, 1608).

Cowper, William. *The workes of Mr. William Cowper* (London, 1626).

Cranmer, Thomas. *Catechismus, that is to say, a shorte instruction into Christian religion for the singular commoditie and profyte of childre[n] and yong people* (London, 1548).

Crashaw, William. *Steps to the Temple. Sacred poems, with other delights of the muses* (London, 1670).

Cross, St. John of the. *The Poems*, trans. Roy Campbell (London, 1951).

Cudworth, Ralph. *The true intellectual system of the universe. wherein all the reason and philosophy of atheism is confuted and its impossibility demonstrated* (London, 1678).

Culmer, Richard. *A parish looking-glasse for persecutors of ministers* (London, 1657).

d'Alembert, Jean le Rond. 'Preliminary Discourse', *Encyclopedia of Diderot & d'Alembert Collaborative Translation Project*, trans. Richard N. Schwab (Chicago, 1995): https://quod.lib.umich.edu/d/did/.

Damascus, John of. *Three Treatises on the Divine Images*, trans. Andrew Louth (New York, 2003).

Davies, John. *The original, nature, and immortality of the soul. A poem* (London, 1697).

d'Espagne, Jean. *The eating of the body of Christ, considered in its principles* (London, 1652).

Dent, Arthur. *Plaine-mans pathway to heauen* (London, 1607).

Dent, Arthur. *The ruine of Rome: or, An exposition upon the whole revelation* (London, 1603).

Dolben, John. *A sermon preached before the king, Aug. 14. 1666. Being the day of thanksgiving for the late victory at sea* (London, 1666).

Donne, John. *Poems* (London, 1633).

Donne, John. *LXXX sermons preached by that learned and reverend divine, Iohn Donne, Dr. in Divinity, late deane of the cathedral church of S. Pauls London* (London, 1640).

Donne, John. *The Variorum Edition of the Poetry of John Donne, Vol. 7, part 1 The Holy Sonnets*, ed. Gary A. Stringer (Bloomington: University of Indiana Press, 2005), LX–LXVII; *DigitalDonne: The Online Variorum* http://digitaldonne.tamu.edu/index.html.

Du Bartas, Guillaume de Salluste. *La Seconde Semaine ou Enfrance du Monde* (Paris, 1584).

Du Bartas, Guillaume de Salluste. *Du Bartas. his deuine weekes and works translated…by Josuah Syluester* (London, 1611).

Du Fresnoy, Charles Alphonse. *De arte graphica. The art of painting…Translated into English, together with an original preface containing a parallel betwixt painting and poetry. By Mr. Dryden* (London, 1695).

Durham, James. *A commentarie upon the book of the Revelation* (Edinburgh, 1658).

BIBLIOGRAPHY 201

Earbery, Matthias. *An answer to a book intitled Tractatus theologico politicus* (London, 1697).

Earbery, Matthias. *Deism examin'd and confuted* (London, 1697).

Edwards, Jonathan. *Letters and Personal Writings* (Works of Jonathan Edwards Online, Vol. 16), ed. George S. Claghorn: http://edwards.yale.edu/archive/.

Edwards, Thomas. *Gangraena: or a catalogue and discovery of many of the errours, heresies, blasphemis and pernicious practices oc the sectaries of this time, vented and acted in England these four last years* (London, 1646).

Erasmus, Desiderius. *The Praise of Folly*, trans. Clarence H. Miller (New Haven, CT, 1979).

Essary, Kirk. *Erasmus and Calvin on the Foolishness of God: Reason and Emotino in the Christian Philosophy* (Toronto, 2017).

Evans, Arise. *An eccho to the voice of heaven, or, A narration of the life, and manner of the special calling, and visions of Arise Evans* (London, 1652).

Evans, Arise. *The bloudy vision of John Farly, interpreted by Arise Evans* (London, 1653).

Evelyn, John. *An essay on the first book of T. Lucretius Carus De rerum nature* (London, 1656).

Evelyn, John. *Diary and Correspondence of John Evelyn*, ed. William Bray (London, 1887).

Eynsham, Adam of. *The prologe of this reuelation* (London, 1483).

Eynsham, Adam of. *The Revelation of the Monk of Eynsham*, ed. Robert Easting (Oxford, 2002).

Falconer, John. *The admirable life of Saint VVenefride virgin, martyr, abbesse* (St. Omer, 1635).

Felltham, Owen. *Resolves: divine, moral, political* (London, 1696: Wing F658).

Fisher, Nicholas. *Symon Patrick (1626–1707) and His Contribution to the Post-1660 Restored Church of England* (Newcastle upon Tyne, 2019).

Fisher, Samuel. *Rusticus ad academicos in exercitationibus expostulatoriis, apologeticis quatuor* (London, 1660).

Foster, William. *The means to keepe sinne from reigning in our mortall body* (London, 1629).

Fox, George. *To all who would know the vvay to the kingdome, whether they be in forms, with out forms, or got above all forms* (London, 1654: Wing F194A).

Foxe, John. *The first volume of…the actes and monuments of thynges passed in euery kynges tyme in this realm* (London, 1570: RSTC 11223).

Franco, Solomon. *Truth springing out of the earth that is, the truth of Christ proved out of the earthly promises of the Law* (London, 1668).

Frere, W. H. and C. E. Douglas, eds, *Puritan Manifestoes: A Study of the Origin of the Puritan Revolt* (London, 1972).

Fulke, William. *Praelections vpon the sacred and holy Reuelation of S. Iohn,* trans. George Gyffard (London, 1573).

Furnivall, Frederick J. ed. *Political, Religious, and Love Poems* (London, 1903).

Galling, Pieter. *The light upon the candlestick*, trans. William Ames (s.n., 1663).

Garnet, Henry. *The Societie of the Rosary. Newly augmented* (London?, 1596).

Garter, Bernard. *A Newyeares gifte dedicated to the Popes Holiness* (London, 1569).

Gauden, John. *A sermon in St. Paul's Church London, before the right honourable the Lord Major, Lord General, aldermen, common counciol, and companies of the honourable city of London February 28 1659* (London, 1660).

Gaule, John. *A collection of the best approved authors containing Histories of Visions, Apparitions, Prophecies, Spirits, Divinations* (London, 1657).

Gavin, Antonio. *The frauds of Romish monks and priests set forth in eight letters* (London, 1691).

Gee, John. *The Foote out of the Snare with A Detection of Svndry Late practices and Impostures of the Priests and Iesuits in England* (London, 1624).

202 BIBLIOGRAPHY

Gerson, Jean. *Jean Gerson: Early Works,* trans. Brian Patrick McGuire (New York, 1998).

Gifford, George. *Sermons vpon the whole booke of Reuelation* (London, 1598).

Gilpin, Richard. *Demonolgia sacra: or, a treatis of Satan's temptations* (Edinburgh, 1677).

Glanvill, Joseph. *Philosophia pia; or, A discourse of the religious temper, and tendencies of the experimental philosophy* (London, 1671).

Glanvill, Joseph. *Plus ultra: or, The progress and advancement of knowledge since the days of Aristotle* (London, 1668: Wing G820).

Godden, Thomas. *Catholicks no idolaters, Or a full refutation of Doctor Stillingfleet's unjust charge of idolatry against the Church of Rome* (s.l., 1672).

Gould, Robert. *A satyrical epistle* (London, 1691).

Granada, Luis de. *Of prayer, and meditation. Wherein are conteined fovvertien deuoute meditations for the seuen daies of the weeke, bothe for the morninges, and eueninges* (Paris, 1582: RSTC 16907).

Granada, Luis de. *Granados deuotion. Exactly teaching how a man may truly dedicate and deuote himself vnto God* (London, 1598).

Greenham, Richard. *The workes of the reuerend and faithfull seruant af Iesus Christ M. Richard Greenham* (London, 1612).

Hakewill, George. *An apologie of the povver and prouidence of God in the gouerment of the world* (London, 1630: RSTC 12612).

Hall, Joseph. *The arte of diuine meditation: profitable for all Christians to knowe and practise* (London, 1606).

Hall, Joseph. *The devovt soul, or, Rules of heavenly devotion* (London, 1650).

Hall, Joseph. *Susurrium cum Deo. Soliloquies: or, Holy self-conferences of the devout soul, upon sundry choice occasions* (London, 1651: Wing H420).

Hall, Joseph. *Holy Raptures or, Pathetical Meditations of the Love of Christ* (London, 1654: Wing H386A).

Hammond, Henry. *Of Idolatry* (Oxford, 1646).

Hammond, Henry. *Sermons preached by that eminent, famous & great divine, Henry Hammond, D.D.* (London, 1664).

Harrington, James. *Horae Consecretae or, Spiritual pastime. Concerning divine meditations upon the great mysteries of our faith and salvation* (London, 1682: Wing H803E).

Hawkins, Henry. *The history of S. Elizabeth daughter of the King of Hungary According to sundry authours who haue authentically written her life, distributed into three bookes* (Rouen, 1632).

Hawkins, Henry. *Parthenia Sacra. Or The mysterious and delicious garden of the sacred Parthenes* (Rouen, 1633).

Hayter, Richard. *The Apocalyps unveyl'd; or A praraphrase on the Revelatino of the Holy Apostle and evangelist John* (London, 1676).

Herbert, George. *The temple. Sacred poems and private ejaculations* (Cambridge, 1633: RSTC 13183).

Herbert, George. *Select hymns, taken out of Mr. Herbert's Temple, and turn'd into the common metre* (London, 1697).

Peter Heylyn. *Cosmographie in four bookes* (London, 1652: Wing H1689).

Peter Heylyn. *Theologia veterum, or, The summe of Christian theologie, positive, polemical, and philological* (London, 1654: Wing H1738).

Hicks, William. *Apokalypsis apokalypseos, or, The revelation revealed. Being a practical exposition on the revelation of St. John* (London, 1659: Wing H1928).

Hilliard, John. *Fire from heauen. Burning the body of one Iohn Hittchell of Holne-hurst* (London, 1613: RSTC 13507.3).

BIBLIOGRAPHY 203

Hilton, Walter. *The Scale of Perfection*, ed. Thomas H. Bestul (Kalamazoo, MI, 2000).

Hobbes, Thomas. *Leviathan, or The matter, forme, & power of a common-wealth ecclesiastical and civill* (London, 1651: Wing H2246).

Hobbes, Thomas. *Elements of philosophy, the first section, concerning body* (London, 1656: Wing H2232).

Holbein, Hans. *The images of the Old Testament, lately expressed, set forth in Ynglishe and Frenche vuith a playn and brief exposition*, trans. Gilles Corrozet (Lyons, 1549).

Hooker, Richard. *The Folger Library Edition of the Works of Richard Hooker, 2 vols.*, eds Georges Edelen and W. Speed Hill (Cambridge, MA, 1977).

Howell, James. *Poems on several choice and various subjects* (London, 1663).

Howell, Thomas. *Cobbett's Complete Collection of State Trials and Proceedings of High Treason* (London, 1809–1826).

Hugo, Herman. *Pia Desideria: or, divine addresses, in three books*, trans. Edm. Arwaker (London, 1690: Wing H3351).

Jeffray, William. *Hodos tethlimmēnē. The narrow way to glory. Delivered in a sermon by the Archdeacon of Shrewsbury* (London, 1634).

Jessey, Henry. *The exceeding riches of grace advanced by the spirit of grace, in an empty nothing creature, viz. Mris Sarah Wight* (London, 1647: Wing J687).

Junius, Franciscus. *Apocalypsis. A briefe and learned commentarie vpon the reuelation of Saint John the apostle and evangelist* (London, 1592: RSTC 2988).

Junius, Franciscus. *The Apocalyps, or Reuelation of S. Iohn the apostle and euangelist of our Lord Iesus Christ* (Cambridge, 1596).

Keith, George. *Divine immediate revelation and inspiration, continued in the true church second part* (London, 1685: Wing K158).

Kempe, Margery. *Here begynneth a shorte treatyse of contemplacyon taught by her lorde Jhesu cryste, or taken out of the boke of Margerie kempe of lyn[n]* (London, 1501).

Kempe, Margery. *The Book of Margery Kempe*, ed. Lynn Staley (Kalamazoo, MI, 1996).

Kempis, Thomas. *A boke newely translated out of Laten in to Englysshe, called The folowynge of Cryste* (London, 1504: RSTC 23961).

Kempis, Thomas. *Of the Imitation of Christ, three, both for wisedome, and godliness, most excellent bookes*, trans. Thomas Rogers (London, 1580: RSTC 23973).

King, Daniel. *A way to sion sought out, and found, for believers to walke in* (London, 1650: Wing K490).

Lambert, François. *Exegeseos Franciscus Lamberti Avenionensis in sanctam Divi Joannis Apocalypsim* (Marburg, 1528).

Laud, William. *The history of the troubles and tryal of the most reverend father in God, and blessed martyr, William Laud, Lord Arch-Bishop of Canterbury* (London, 1695).

Lightfoot, John. *The works of the Reverend and learned John Lightfoot D.D.* (London, 1684).

Lisboa, Marcos de, Bishop of Porto. *The life of the glorious virgin S. Clare Togeather with the conuersion, and life of S. Agnes her sister* (St. Omer, 1622).

Loarte, Gaspar. *The exercise of a christian life* (London, 1579: RSTC 16641.5).

Loarte, Gaspar. *Instructions and aduertisements, how to meditate the mysteries of the Rosarie* (London, 1597: RSTC 16646).

Locke, John. *Reason and religion: in some useful reflections on the most eminent hypotheses concerning the first principles, and nature of things* (London, 1694).

Locke, John. *An Essay Concerning Human Understanding*, ed. Kenneth P. Winkler (Indianapolis, 1996).

Losa, Francisco de. *The life of Gregorie Lopes that great servant of God, natiue of Madrid*, trans. N.N. [i.e. Thomas White] (Paris, 1638).

204 BIBLIOGRAPHY

Lucretius, *On the Nature of the Universe,* trans. R. E. Latham (London, 1951).

MacMath, James. *The expert mid-wife: a treatise of the diseases of women with child, and in child-bed* (Edinburgh, 1694).

Maffei, Giovanni Pietro. *Fuga saeculi. Or The holy hatred of the world,* trans. H.H. (St. Omer, 1632).

Maie, Edward. *A sermon of the communion of saints* (London, 1621).

Mall, Thomas. *A cloud of witnesses; or, the sufferers mirror, made up of the swanlike-songs, and other choice passages of several martyrs and confessors to the sixteenth century* (London, 1665).

Malone, William. *A reply to Mr. Iames Vssher his ansvvere wherein it is discouered hovv ansvverlesse the said Mr. Vssher returneth* (Douai, 1627).

Manningham, Thomas. *Two discourses: the first, shewing how the chief criterions of philosophical truth* (London, 1681: Wing M510).

Marcos, Lisboa de. *The life of the glorious virgin S. Clare Togeather with the conuersion, and life of S. Agnes her sister* (St. Omer, 1622).

Marlorat, Augustin. *A catholike exposition vpon the Reuelation of Sainct Iohn* (London, 1574: RSTC 17408).

Mayer, John. *Ecclesiastica interpretatio: or The expositions vpon the difficult and doubtful passages of...the Reuelation* (London, 1627).

Milton, John. *A Treatise on Christian Doctrine,* trans. Charles R. Sumner (Cambridge, 1825).

Montaigne, Michel de. *Essays of Michael, seigneur de Montaigne,* trans. Charles Cotton (London, 1700: Wing M2481).

More, Henry. *Enthusiasmus triumphatus, or, A discourse of the nature, causes, kinds, and cure, of enthusiasme* (Cambridge, 1656).

More, Henry. *The immortality of the soul, so farre forth as it is demonstrable from the knowledge of nature and the light of reason* (London, 1659).

More, Henry. *An appendix to the late antidote against idolatry* (London, 1673).

Muggleton, Lodowick. *The acts of the witnesses of the spirit in five parts* (London, 1699).

Napier, John. *A plaine discouery of the whole Reuelation* (London, 1593: RSTC 18354).

Ness, Christopher. *A Christians walk and work on earth* (London, 1678: Wing N443).

Nicholls, William. *A conference with a theist. Part II. Shewing the defects of natural religion* (London, 1699).

Nixon, Anthony. *The dignitie of man both in the perfections of his soule and bodie* (London, 1612).

Norwich, Julian of. *XVI Revelations of Divine Love, Shewed to a Devout Servant of our Lord, called Mother Juliana, an Anchorete of Norwich* (London?, 1670).

Norwich, Julian of. *The Shewings of Julian of Norwich,* ed. Georgia Ronan Crampton (Kalamazoo, MI, 1994).

Nowell, Alexander. *A Catechism written in Latin by Alexander Nowell, Dean of St Paul's,* ed. G. E. Corrie (Cambridge, 1853).

Oates, Titus. *The discovery of the Popish Plot being the several examinations of Titus Oates* (London, 1679).

Overton, Richard. *Mans mortalitie: or, A treatise wherein 'tis proved, both theologically and philosophically, that whole man (as a rationall creature) is a compound wholly mortall* (Amsterdam, 1644: Wing O629E).

Owen, John. *Of communion with God the Father, Sonne, and Holy Ghost, each person distinctly* ([London] Oxford, 1657: Wing O777).

Owen, John. *Pneumatologia: or, A discourse concerning the Holy Spirit* (London, 1676: Wing O793).

BIBLIOGRAPHY   205

Owen, John. *The reason of faith, or An answer unto that enquiry, wherefore we believe the scripture to be the word of God* (London, 1677: Wing O801).

Owen, John. *Christologia, or, A declaration of the glorious mystery of the person of Christ, God and man* (London, 1679: Wing O726).

Owen, John. *The Spirit and the Church*, ed. R. J. K. Law (Edinburgh, 2002).

Pareus, David. *A commentary upon the divine Revelation of the apostle and evangelist, John*, trans. Elias Arnold (London, 1644: Wing P353).

Parker, Thomas. *The copy of a letter written by Mr. Thomas Parker, pastor of the church of Newbury in New-England, to his sister, Mrs Elizabeth Avery* (London, 1649).

Patrick, Simon. *Mensa mystica: A discourse concerning the sacrament of the Lords Supper* (London, 1684: Wing P825A).

Patrick, Simon. *The Virgin Mary misrepresented by the Roman Church, in the traditions of that Church* (London, 1688).

Pepys, Samuel. *The Diary of Samuel Pepys*, ed. Henry B. Wheatley (London, 1893–99).

Perkins, William. *A reformed Catholike, or, A declaration shewing how neere we may come to the present Church of Rome in sundrie points of religion* (Cambridge, 1597: RSTC 19735.8).

Perkins, William. *A golden chaine: or The description of theologie, containing the order of the causes of sauation and damnation, according to Gods word* (Cambridge, 1600: RSTC 19646).

Perkins, William. *Lectures vpon the three first chapters of the Reuelation: preached in Cambridge anno Dom. 1595* (London, 1604).

Perkins, William. *Of the calling of the ministerie two treatises, describing the duties and dignities of that calling* (London, 1605: RSTC 19733).

Perkins, William. *A godly and learned exposition or commentarie vpon the three first chapters of the Reuelation* (London, 1606: RSTC 19732).

Perkins, William. *The whole treatise of the cases of conscience, distinguished into three bookes* (Cambridge, 1606: RSTC 19669).

Phelpes, Charles. *A commentary: Or an exposition with notes on the five first chapters of the Revelation of Jesvs Christ* (London, 1678).

Phillips, Edward. *Theatrum poetarum, or A compleat collection of the poets, especially the most eminent, of all ages* (London, 1675: Wing P2075).

Playfere, Thomas. *Hearts delight. A sermon preached at Pauls crosse in London in Easter terme. 1593* (London, 1603: RSTC 20010).

Prynne, William. *Mount-Orgveil: or Divine and profitable meditations* (London, 1641: Wing P4013).

Pseudo-Dionysius, *The Complete Works*, trans. Colm Luibheid (New York, 1987).

Puccini, Vincenzio. *The life of the holy and venerable mother Suor Maria Maddalena De Patsi a Florentine lady* (St. Omer, 1619: RSTC 20483).

Puente, Luis de la. *Meditations vppon the mysteries of our holy faith*, trans. F. Rich. Gibbons (Douai, 1610: RSTC 20485).

Quarles, Francis. *Diuine poems: containing the history of Ionah. Ester. Iob. Sampson. Sions sonets. Elegies* (London, 1633: RSTC 20534).

Quarles, Francis. *Emblemes* (London, 1639: RSTC 20542).

R. B., *Delights for the ingenious, in above fifty select and choice emblems, divine and moral, ancient and modern* (London, 1684).

Reading, John. *Dauids soliloquie: Containing many comforts for the afflicted mindes* (London, 1627).

Reyner, Edward. *Considerations concerning marriage, the honour, duties, benefits, troubles of it* (London, 1657).

206 BIBLIOGRAPHY

Reynolds, Edward. *Meditations on the holy sacrament of the Lords last Supper* (London, 1638: RSTC 20929a).

Reynolds, Edward. *A treatise of the passions and faculties of the soule of man* (London, 1640: RSTC 20938).

Richards, Nathanael. *The celestiall publican. A sacred poem* (London, 1630).

Robe, James. *Narratives of the Extraordinary Work of the Spirit of God* (Glasgow, 1790).

Rogers, Richard. *Seuen treatises, containing such direction as is gathered out of the Holie Scriptures* (London, 1603: RSTC 21215).

Rogers, Richard. *A commentary vpon the whole booke of Iudges* (London, 1615).

[Rogers, Richard, William Perkins, Richard Greenham, Miles Mosse, and George Webbe]. *A garden of spirituall flowers* (London, 1609).

Rogers, Thomas. *Celestiall elegies of the goddesses and the Muses* (London, 1598).

Rolle, Richard. *The Fire of Love*, trans. Clifton Wolters (New York, 1972).

Rolle, Richard. *Richard Rolle: Prose and Verse, Edited from MS Longleat 29 and Related Manuscripts*, ed. S. J. Ogilvie-Thomson (Oxford, 1998).

Ross, Alexander. *The philosophicall touch-stone: or Observations upon Sir Kenelm Digbie's Discourses of the nature of bodies, and of the reasonable soule* (London, 1645: Wing R1979).

Rous, Francis. *The mysticall marriage. Experimentall discoveries of the heavenly marriage between a soule and her savior* (London, 1631: RSTC 21342.5).

Rous, Francis. *Treatises and meditations dedicated to the saints, and to the excellent through-out the three nations* (London, 1657: Wing R2031).

Sales, Francis de. *A treatise of the loue of God. Written in French by B. Francis de Sales...translated into English by Miles Car priest of the English College of Doway* (Douai, 1630).

Sandys, George. *A paraphrase vpon the divine poems* (London, 1638).

Scot, Reginald. *The discovery of witchcraft; proving, that the compacts and contracts of witches with devils and all infernal spirits or familiars, are but erroneous novelites and imaginary conceptions* (London, 1665: Wing S945).

Scott, John. *The Christian life, from its beginning to its consummation in glory* (London, 1683: Wing S2044).

Scrivener, Matthew. *The method and means to a true spiritual life* (London, 1688).

Scupoli, Lorenzo. *The Christian pilgrime in his spirituall conflict, and conquest* (Paris [i.e. London?], 1652: Wing S2166A).

Serre, Puget de la. *The sweete thoughts of death, and eternity*, trans. Henry Hawkins (Paris [i.e. St. Omer: Printed by the English College Press], 1632).

Shaftesbury, Anthony Ashley Cooper, Earl of. *A letter concerning enthusiasm, To My Lord****** (London, 1708).

Shakespeare, William. *Poems: vvritten by Wil. Shake-speare. Gent* (London, 1640: RSTC 22344).

Sharpe, James. *The triall of the protestant priuate spirit* (St. Omer, 1630).

Sherlock, Richard. *The Quakers wilde questions objected against the ministers of the Gospel, and many sacred acts and offices of religion* (London, 1655: Wing S3255).

Sidney, Phillip. *The defence of poesie* (London, 1595: RSTC 22535).

Simon, Richard. *A critical history of the text of the New Testament, wherein is firmly establish'd the truth of those acts on which the foundation of Christian religion is laid* (London, 1689).

Smith, John. *Select discourses treating* (London, 1660: Wing S4117).

Southwell, Robert. *Moeoniae. Or, Certaine excellent poems and spirituall hymnes* (London, 1595: RSTC 22955.5).

BIBLIOGRAPHY   207

Spencer, John. *A discourse concerning vulgar prophecies wherein the vanity of receiving them as a certain indications of any future event is discovered* (London, 1665: Wing S4949).

Spenser, Edmund. *Fovvre hymnes* (London, 1596).

Spinoza, Baruch. *The Correspondence of Spinoza*, trans. A. Wolf (London, 1966).

Spinoza, Baruch. *Theological-Political Treatise* (2nd edn., Cambridge, MA, 1998).

Sternhold, Thomas, John Hopkins, et al. *The vvhole book of Psalmes: collected into English meeter* (1638: RSTC 2678.4).

Sterry, Peter. *The commings forth of Christ in the power of his death. Open in a sermon preached before the High Court of Parliament…November 1649* (London, 1649).

Stillingfleet, Edward. *Origines sacrae, or A rational account of the grounds of Christian faith, as to the truth and divine authority of the scriptures, and the matters therein contained* (London, 1663: Wing S5617).

Stillingfleet, Edward. *A discourse concerning the idolatry practised in the Church of Rome, and the hazard of salvation in the communion of it* (London, 1671: Wing S5577).

Strong, William. *Discourse of the two covenants: wherein the nature, differences, and effects of the covenant of works and of grace are distinctly, rationally, spiritually and practically discussed* (London, 1678).

Strype, John. *Annals of the Reformation and Establishment of Religion, vol. I* (London, 1725).

Stubbes, Philip. *A cristal glasse for Christian vvomen containing, a most excellent discourse, of the godly life and Christian death of Mistresse Katherine Stubs* (London, 1592: RSTC 23382).

Stubbes, Philip. *The anatomie of abuses: containing a discouerie, or briefe summarie of such notable vices and imperfections* (London, 1595: RSTC 23379).

St. Victor, Richard of. *Richard of St. Victor: The Twelve Patriarchs, The Mystical Ark, and Book Three of The Trinity*, trans. Grover A. Zinn (New York, 1979).

Sutton, Christopher. *Godly Meditations upon the Most Holy Sacrament of the Lord's Supper* (new edition, Oxford, 1866).

Taylor, Jeremy. *XXV sermons preached at Golden-Grove being for the vvinter half-year, beginning on Advent-Sunday, untill Whit-Sunday* (London, 1653).

Taylor, Jeremy. *Antiqvitates Christianae: or, The history of the life and death of the Holy Jesus: as also the lives, acts and martyrdoms of his Apostles* (London, 1684).

Tenison, Thomas. *Of idolatry: a discourse, in which is endeavoured a declaration of, its distinction from superstition* (London, 1678: Wing T704).

Throkmorton, Job. *The defence of Iob Throkmorton, against the slaunders of Maister Sutcliffe* (London, 1594: RSTC 24055.5).

Toland, John. *Christianity not mysterious: or, A treatise shewing, that there is nothing in the Gospel contrary to reason, nor above it* (London, 1696: Wing T1763).

Torsellino, Orazio. *The admirable life of S. Francis Xavier Deuided into VI. bookes…translated into English by T.F.* (St. Omer, 1632).

Toxander, Theophilus. *Vox coeli to England, or Englands fore-warning from heaven* (London, 1646).

Traherne, Thomas. *The Poetical Works of Thomas Traherne*, ed. Gladys I. Wade (New York, 1965).

Traherne, Thomas. *Christian Ethicks*, eds Carol L. Marks and George Robert Guffey (Ithaca, NY, 1968).

Trapnel, Anna. *A legacy for saints; being several experiences of the dealings of God with Anna Trapnel* (London, 1654).

Trapp, John. *A Commentary or Exposition upon all the Epistles, and the Revelation of John* (London, 1647).

Trench, Edmund. *Some remarkable passages in the holy life and death of the late Reverend Mr. Edmund Trench* (London, 1693).

208 BIBLIOGRAPHY

Troughton, William. *Of the causes and cure of sad disconsolate thoughts in Christians* (London, 1677).

Valentine, Henry. *Private devotions, digested into six letanies* (London, 1654: Wing V23B).

Vaughan, Henry. *Silex scintillans: or sacred poems and priuate eiaculations* (London, 1650: Wing V125).

Vennard, Richard. *The right vvay to heauen, and a good presedent for lawyers and all other good Christians* (London, 1602).

Vermigli, Peter. *The common places of Peter Martyr*, trans. Anthonie Marten (London, 1583).

Vicars, John. *Gods arke overtopping the worlds waves, or the third part of the Parliamentary chronicle* (London, 1645).

Voragine, Jacobus. *Legenda aurea sanctorum, sive, Lombardica historia* (London, 1483).

Wadsworth, Thomas. *Wadsworth's remains: being a collection of some few meditations with respect ot the Lords Supper* (London, 1680).

Walker, Obadiah. *Paraphrases and Annotations upon the Epistles of St. Paul written to the Romans, Corinthians and Hebrews* (Oxford, 1684).

Walton, Izaak. *The lives of Dr. John Donne, Sir Henry Wotton, Mr. Richard Hooker, Mr. George Herbert* (London, 1670: Wing W671).

Watson, Thomas. *A body of practical divinity, consisting of above one hundred seventy six sermons on the lesser catechism* (London, 1692).

Wesley, John. *A Letter to the Author of the Enthusiasm of the Methodists and Papists Compared* (London, 1750).

Wesley, Samuel. *The life of our blessed Lord & Saviour Jesus Christ. An heroic poem* (London, 1693: Wing W1371).

Wettenhall, Edward. *Enter into thy closet: or, A method and order for private devotion* (London, 1676: Wing W1499).

Whitaker, William. *A Disputation on Holy Scripture*, trans. Rev. William Fitzgerald (Cambridge, 1849).

[Whitford, Richard]. *The pomander of prayer* (London, 1528).

Winstanley, William. *England's vvorthies. Select lives of the most eminent persons from Constantine the Great, to the death of Oliver Cromwell late Protector* (London, 1660: Wing W3058).

Winthrop, John. *Winthrop Papers, 1498–1628, vol. I* (Boston, 1929).

Wither, George. *A collection of emblems, ancient and modern quickened vvith metricall illustrations, both morall and divine* (London, 1635: RSTC 25900a).

Woodhead, Abraham. *Concerning images and idolatry* (Oxford, 1689: Wing W3441).

Woolton, John. *A treatise of the immortalitie of the soule wherein is declared the origine, nature, and powers of the same* (London, 1576).

Secondary Sources

Abraham, William J. *Divine Revelation and the Limits of Historical Criticism* (Oxford, 1982).

Abraham, William J. *Crossing the Threshold of Divine Revelation* (Grand Rapids, MI, 2006).

Adams, Gwenfair Walters. *Visions in Late Medieval England: Lay Spirituality and Sacred Glimpses of the Hidden Worlds of Faith* (Leiden, 2007).

Adlington, Hugh, David Griffith, and Tara Hamling. 'Beyond the Page: Quarles's *Emblemes*, Wall-Painting, and Godly Interiors in Seventeenth-Century York', *Huntington Library Quarterly*, 78 (2015): 521–51.

Ainsworth, David. *Milton, Music, and Literary Interpretation* (New York, 2020).

BIBLIOGRAPHY

Allen, Hope Emily. *Writings Ascribed to Richard Rolle the Hermit of Hampole and Materials for His Biography* (Oxford, 1927).

Allen, Keith. 'Cudworth on Mind, Body, and Plastic Nature', *Philosophy Compass* 8 (2013): 337–47.

Alston, William P. *Perceiving God: The Epistemology of Religious Experience* (Ithaca, NY, 1991).

Astell, Ann W. *The Song of Songs in the Middle Ages* (Ithaca, NY, 1990).

Astell, Ann W. *Eating Beauty: The Eucharist and the Spiritual Arts of the Middle Ages* (Ithaca, NY, 2006).

Aston, Margaret. 'The Bishops' Bible Illustrations', in *The Church and the Arts*, ed. Diana Wood (Oxford, 1992), 267–85.

Aston, Margaret. *The King's Bedpost: Reformation and Iconograpy in a Tudor Group Portrait* (Cambridge, 1993).

Aston, Margaret. 'Bibles to Ballads: Some Pictorial Migrations in the Reformation'. In *Christianity and Community in the West: Essays for John Bossy*, ed. Simon Ditchfied (Aldershot, 2001), 106–30.

Aston, Margaret. *Broken Idols of the English Reformation* (Cambridge, 2015).

Auger, Peter. *Du Bartas' Legacy in England and Scotland* (Oxford, 2019).

Backus, Irena. *Reformation Readings of the Apocalypse: Geneva, Zurich, and Wittenberg* (Oxford, 2000).

Baker, Denise Nowakowski. *Julian of Norwich's Showings: From Vision to Book* (Princeton, NJ, 1994).

Ball, Bryan. *A Great Expectation: Eschatological Thought in English Protestantism to 1660* (Leiden, 1975).

Balthasar, Hans Urs von. *Love Alone: The Way of Revelation* (London, 1992).

Barfield, Owen. *Saving the Appearances: A Study in Idolatry* (2nd edn., Middletown, CT, 1988).

Bauckham, Richard. *Tudor Apocalypse: Sixteenth Century Apocalypticism, Millennarianism, and the English Reformation: From John Bale to John Foxe and Thomas Brightman* (Ann Arbor, MI, 1979).

Bebbington, David. *Evangelicalism in Modern Britain* (Abingdon, 2003).

Beckwith, Carl L., ed. *Reformation Commentary on Scripture: Old Testament, vol. XII: Ezekiel and Daniel* (Downers Grove, IL, 2012).

Beiser, Frederick. *The Sovereignty of Reason: The Defense of Rationality in the Early English Enlightenment* (Princeton, NJ, 2016).

Bestul, Thomas H. 'Meditatio/Meditation', in *The Cambridge Companion to Christian Mysticism*, eds Amy Hollywood and Patricia Z. Beckman (Cambridge, 2012), 164–6.

Betteridge, Tom. *Literature and Politics in the English Reformation* (Manchester, 2004).

Blosser, Jacob M. 'John Tillotson's Latitudinarian Legacy: Orthodoxy, Heterodoxy, and the Pursuit of Happiness', *Anglican and Episcopal History* 80 (2011): 142–73.

Boersma, Hans. *Seeing God: The Beatific Vision in the Christian Tradition* (Grand Rapids, MI, 2019).

Boffey, Julia. 'From Manuscript to Print: Continuity and Change', in *A Companion to the Early Printed Book in Britain, 1476–1558*, ed. Vincent Gillespie and Susan Powell (Cambridge, 2014), 13–26.

Burgess, Glenn and Matthew Festenstein, eds. *English Radicalism, 1550–1850* (Cambridge, 2007).

Burks, Deborah. 'Polemical Potency: The Witness of the Word and the Woodcut', in *John Foxe and His World*, eds Christopher Highley and John N. King (Aldershot, 2002), 263–76.

210 BIBLIOGRAPHY

Burns, Norman T. *Christian Mortalism from Tyndale to Milton* (Cambridge, MA, 1972).

Bynum, Caroline Walker. *Fragmentation and Redemption: Essays on Gender and the Human Body in Medieval Religion* (New York, 1991).

Canlis, Julie. *Calvin's Ladder: A Spiritual Theology of Ascent and Ascension* (Grand Rapids, MI, 2010).

Carter, Benjamin. 'Ralph Cudworth', in *Early Modern Philosophy of Religion: The History of Western Philosophy of Religion, vol. III*, eds Graham Oppy and N. N. Trakakis (Abingdon, 2014), 113–26.

Cefalu, Paul. *The Johannine Renaissance in Early Modern English Literature and Theology* (Oxford, 2017).

Christianson, Paul. *Reformers and Babylon: English Apocalyptic Visions from the Reformation to the Eve of the Civil War* (London, 1978).

Clark, John P. H. and Dorwood, Rosemary. 'Introduction', in Walter Hilton, *The Scale of Perfection*, eds. John P. H. Clark and Rosemary Dorwood (Mahwah, NJ, 1991), 13–57.

Clark, Stuart. *Vanities of the Eye: Vision in Early Modern European Culture* (Oxford, 2007).

Clarke, Elizabeth. *Politics, Religion, and the Song of Songs in Seventeenth-Century England* (London, 2011).

Clifton, James. 'A Variety of Spiritual Pleasures: Anthonis Sallaert's Glorification of the Name of Jesus', in *Jesuit Image Theory*, eds Wietse de Boer, Karl A. E. Enekel, and Walter S. Melion (Leiden, 2016), 318–52.

Collinson, Patrick. *Elizabethan Essays* (London, 1994).

Collinson, Patrick. *Richard Bancroft and Elizabethan Anti-Puritanism* (Cambridge, 2013).

Como, David R. *Blown by the Spirit: Puritanism and the Emergence of an Antinomian Underground in Pre-Civil-War England* (Cambridge, 2004).

Coster, Will and Andrew Spicer, eds. *Sacred Space in Early Modern Europe* (Cambridge, 2005).

Craig, William Lane. 'Men Moved by the Holy Spirit Spoke from God' (2 Peter 1.21): A Middle Knowledge Perspective on Biblical Inspiration', in *Oxford Readings in Philosophical Theology vol. II: Providence, Scripture, and Resurrection*, ed. Michael Rea (Oxford, 2009), 157–91.

Cressy, David. 'Books as Totems in Seventeenth-Century England and New England', *Journal of Library History*, 21 (1986): 92–106.

Cummings, Brian. *The Literary Culture of the Reformation: Grammar and Grace* (Oxford, 2007).

Dailey, Barbara Ritter. 'The Visitation of Sarah Wight: Holy Carnival and the Revolution of the Saints in Civil War London', *Church History*, 55 (1986): 438–55.

Darley, Gillian. *John Evelyn: Living for Ingenuity* (New Haven, CT, 2006).

Davidson, Clare. 'Erotic Devotion: Richard Rolle's The Form of Living', *Limina: A Journal of Historical and Cultural Studies*, 20 (2015): 1–13.

Davies, Horton. *Worship and Theology in England: From Cranmer to Hooker, 1534–1603; From Andrewes to Baxter and Fox, 1603–1690*, Combined edition (Grand Rapids, MI, 1996).

Davis, David J. 'Images on the Move: The Virgin, the *Kalendar of Shepherds*, and the Transmission of Woodcuts in Tudor England', *The Journal of the Early Book Society* 12 (2009): 99–132.

Davis, David J. *Seeing Faith, Printing Pictures: Religious Identity during the English Reformation* (Leiden, 2013).

Davis, David J. *From Icons to Idols: Documents on the Image Debate in Reformation England* (Eugene, OR, 2016).

Davis, David J. 'Rapt in the Spirit: The Ritualizing of Divine Revelation in Early Modern England', *Journal of Medieval and Early Modern Studies* 48 (2018): 341–64.

Davis, David J. 'Reforming the Holy Name: The Afterlife of the IHS in Early Modern England', *Journal of Early Modern Christianity* 8 (2021): 275–98.

Davis, David J. 'The Visual Culture of Reformation Bibles', in *The Oxford Handbook of the Bible and the Reformation*, eds Jennifer McNutt and Herman Selderhuis (Oxford, forthcoming).

Duffy, Eamon. *Stripping of the Altars: Tradition Religion in England, 1400–1580* (London, 1992).

Duffy, Eamon. *Marking the Hours: English People and their Prayers, 1240–1570* (New Haven, CT, 2006).

Duffy, Eamon. 'Praying the Counter-Reformation', in *Early Modern English Catholicism: Identity, Memory, and Counter-Reformation*, eds James E. Kelly and Susan Royal (Leiden, 2016), 206–25.

Dugan, Holly. *The Ephemeral History of Perfume: Scent and Sense in Early Modern England* (Baltimore, 2011).

Edwards, David L. *John Donne: Man of Flesh and Spirit* (Cambridge, 2001).

Elliott, Dyan. 'The Physiology of Rapture and Female Spirituality', in *Medieval Theology and the Natural Body*, eds Peter Biller and A. J. Minnis (York, 1997), 141–74.

Evans, Jennifer. *Aphrodisiacs, Fertility, and Medicine in Early Modern England* (Woodbridge, 2014).

Fairfield, Leslie P. *John Bale: Mythmaker for the English Reformation* (West Lafayette, IN, 1976).

Fincham, Kenneth and Nicholas Tyacke. *Altars Restored: The Changing Face of English Religious Worship, c.1570–1700* (Oxford, 2007).

Finocchiaro, Maurice A. *The Routledge Guidebook to Galileo's Dialogue* (London, 2014).

Firth, Keith. *The Apocalyptic Tradition in Reformation Britain, 1530–1645* (Oxford, 1979).

Flinker, Noam. *The Song of Songs in English Renaissance Literature* (Cambridge, 2000).

Freeman, Thomas S. and Thomas F. Mayer, eds. *Martyrs and Martyrdom in England, 1400–1700* (Rochester, NY, 2007).

Furey, Constance. *Poetic Relations: Intimacy and Faith in the English Reformation* (Chicago, 2017).

Garber, David. 'Soul and Mind: Life and Thought in the Seventeenth Century', *Cambridge History of Seventeenth Century Philosophy*, vol. I, eds Daniel Garbert and Michael Ayers (Cambridge, 1998), 759–95.

Gaudio, Michael. *The Bible and the Printed Image in Early Modern England: Little Gidding and the Pursuit of Scriptural Harmony* (London, 2017).

Glanz, Elaine. 'Richard Rolle's Imagery in *Meditations on the Passion B*: A Reflection of Richard of St. Victor's *Benjamin Minor*', *Mystics Quarterly* 22 (1996): 58–68.

Glasscoe, Marion ed. *The Medieval Mystical Tradition in England V: Papers Read at Dartington Hall* (Cambridge, 1992).

Glasscoe, Marion. *English Medieval Mystics: Games of Faith* (Harlow, 1993).

Glasscoe, Marion ed. *The Medieval Mystical Tradition in England, Ireland, and Wales: Exeter Symposium VI: Papers Read at Chareny Manor, July 1999* (Woodbridge, 1999).

Gravdal, Kathryn. *Ravishing Maidens: Writing Rape in Medieval French Literature and Law* (Philadelphia, 1991).

Green, Ian. *Print and Protestantism in Early Modern England* (Oxford, 2000).

Gregory, Brad S. 'The "True and Zealouse Service of God": Robert Parsons, Edmund Bunny, and The First Booke of the Christian Exercise', *Journal of Ecclesiastical History*, 45 (1994): 238–68.

212 BIBLIOGRAPHY

Gregory, Brad S. *Salvation at Stake: Christian Martyrdom in Early Modern Europe* (Cambridge, MA, 1999).

Greyerz, Kaspar von. *Religion and Culture in Early Modern Europe* (Oxford, 2008).

Griffin, Jr., Martin I. J. *Latitudinarianism in the Seventeenth Century Church of England*, ed. Lila Freedman (Leiden, 1992).

Grisé, C. Annette 'Holy Women in Print' in *Medieval Mystical Tradition in England: Exeter Symposium VII* ed. E. A. Jones (Woodbridge, 2004), 83–96.

Guy, Nathan. *Finding Locke's God* (New York, 2020).

Hamling, Tara. *Decorating the 'Godly' Household: Religious Art in Post-Reformation Britain* (London, 2010).

Hamling, Tara and Richard Williams, eds. *Art Re-formed: Re-assessing the Impact of the Reformation of the Visual Arts* (Newcastle upon Tyne, 2007).

Harris, Tim. *London Crowds in the Reign of Charles II: Propaganda and Politics from the Restoration until the Exclusion Crisis* (Cambridge, 1987).

Harrison, Peter. 'Prophecy, Early Modern Apologetics, and Hume's Argument against Miracles', *Journal of the History of Ideas*, 60 (1999): 241–56.

Haynes, Clare. *Pictures and Popery: Art and Religion in England, 1660–1760* (London, 2006).

Hellinga, Lotte. *William Caxton and Early Printing in England* (London, 2010).

Helm, Paul. *John Calvin's Ideas* (Oxford, 2004).

Helm, Paul. *The Divine Revelation: The Basic Issues* (Vancouver, 2004).

Hessayon, Ariel, ed. *Jane Lead and Her Transnational Legacy* (London, 2016).

Hessayon, Ariel and David Finnegan, eds. *Varieties of Seventeenth and Early Eighteenth Century English Radicalism in Context* (Aldershot, 2011).

Heyd, Michael. *'Be Sober and Reasonable': The Critique of Enthusiasm in the Seventeenth and Eighteenth Centuries* (Leiden, 2000).

Hill, Christopher. '"Reason" and "reasonableness" in Seventeenth-Century England', *The British Journal of Sociology* 20 (1969): 235–52.

Hill, Christopher. *The World Turned Upside Down: Radical Ideas During the English Revolution* (London, 1972).

Hill, Christopher. *Change and Continuity in 17th Century England* (New Haven, CT, 1974).

Hodnett, Edward. *Francis Barlow: First Master of English Book Illustration* (Ilkley, 1978).

Hollywood, Amy and Patricia Beckman, eds. *The Cambridge Companion to Christian Mysticism* (Cambridge, 2012).

Hudson, Elizabeth. 'English Protestants and the *imitatio Christi*, 1580–1620', *Sixteenth Century Journal* 19 (1988): 541–58.

Hunter, Michael. *Science and the Shape of Orthodoxy: Intellectual Change in Late Seventeenth-Century Britain* (London, 1995).

Hunter, Michael. ed. *Robert Boyle Reconsidered* (Cambridge, 2003).

Hunter, Michael. ed. *Printed Images in Early Modern England: Essays of Interpretation* (London, 2010).

Hunter, Michael. *Boyle: Between God and Science* (New Haven, CT, 2010).

Huray, Peter Le. *Music and the Reformation in England, 1549–1660* (Cambridge, 1978).

Iliffe, Rob. *Priest of Nature: The Religious Worlds of Isaac Newton* (Oxford, 2017).

Israel, Jonathan I. *Enlightenment Contested: Philosophy, Modernity, and the Emancipation of Man 1670–1752* (Oxford, 2006).

Janacek, Bruce. *Alchemical Belief: Occultism in the Religious Culture of Early Modern England* (University Park, PA, 2011).

Johnston, Warren. *Revelation Restored: The Apocalypse in Late Seventeenth-Century England* (Woodbridge, 2011).

Jones, E. A. ed. *Medieval Mystical Tradition in England: Exeter Symposium VII* (Woodbridge, 2004).

Katz, Steven T. ed. *Mysticism and Philosophical Analysis* (Oxford, 1978).

Katz, Steven T. ed. *Mysticism and Language* (Oxford, 1992).

Kenney, John Peter. *The Mysticism of Saint Augustine: Rereading the Confessions* (Abingdon, 2003).

King, John N. *Tudor Royal Iconography* (Princeton, NJ, 1989).

King, Rolfe. *Obstacles to Divine Revelation: God and the Reorientation of Human Reason* (London, 2011).

Knell, Matthew. *The Immanent Person of the Holy Spirit from Anselm to Lombard: Divine Communion in the Spirit* (Eugene, OR, 2009).

Koerner, Joseph. *The Moment of Self-Portraiture in German Renaissance* Art (Chicago, 1993).

Krakowsky, Posey. 'The Ecclesiology of Prayerbook Illustrations', *Anglican and Episcopal History*, 83 (2014): 243–91.

Kroll, Richard, Richard Ashcraft, and Perez Zagorin, eds. *Philosophy, Science, and Religion in England, 1640–1700* (Cambridge, 1992).

Kuchar, Gary. *Divine Subjection: The Rhetoric of Sacramental Devotion in Early Modern England* (Pittsburgh, 2005).

Kuchar, Gary. *George Herbert and the Mystery of the Word: Poetry and Scripture in Seventeenth Century England* (London, 2017).

Lake, Peter and Isaac Stephens. *Scandal and Religious Identity in Early Stuart England: A Northamptonshire Maid's Tragedy* (Woodbridge, 2015).

LeBuffe, Michael. *Spinoza on Reason* (Oxford, 2018).

Leeuwen, Peter van. *Discourse and Practice: New Tools for Critical Analysis* (Oxford, 2008).

Leppin, Volker. 'Luther and John Tauler: Some Observations about the Mystical Impact on Reformation Theology', *Theology and Life*, 36 (2013): 339–45.

Lewalski, Barbara. *Protestant Poetics and the Seventeenth-Century Religious Lyric* (Princeton, NJ, 1979).

Longfellow, Erica. *Women and Religious Writing in Early Modern England* (Cambridge, 2004).

Luborsky, Ruth and Elizabeth Ingram. *A Guide to English Illustrated Books, 1536—1603*, 2 vols. (Tempe, AZ, 1998).

Mack, Phyllis. *Visionary Women: Ecstatic Prophecy in Seventeenth Century England* (Berkeley, CA, 1992).

MacNamer, Sarah. *Affective Meditation and the Invention of Medieval Compassion* (Philadelphia, 2010).

Malcolm, Noel. *Aspects of Hobbes* (Oxford, 2002).

Maltby, Judith. *The Prayerbook and the English People* (Cambridge, 1998).

Marshall, Peter. *Beliefs and the Dead in Reformation England* (Oxford, 2002).

Marshall, Peter. *Heretics and Believers: A History of the English Reformation* (New Haven, CT, 2017).

Martin, Jessica A. and Alec Ryrie, eds. *Private and Domestic Devotion in Early Modern Europe* (Abingdon, 2016).

McCarthy, Erin A. *Doubtful Readers: Print, Poetry, and the Reader in Early Modern England* (Oxford, 2020).

McColley, D. K. *Poetry and Music in Seventeenth-Century England* (Cambridge, 1997).

McDowell, Nicholas. *The English Radical Imagination: Culture, Religion, and Revolution, 1630–1660* (Oxford, 2003).

McGinn, Bernard. *The Varieties of Vernacular Mysticism, 1350–1550* (New York, 2012).

214   BIBLIOGRAPHY

McIlroy, Claire. *The English Prose Treatises of Richard Rolle* (Woodbridge, 2004).

McMahon, Robert. *Understanding the Medieval Mystical Ascent: Augustine, Anselm, Boethius and Dante* (Washington DC, 2006).

Mezei, Balázs M., Francesca Aran Murphy, and Kenneth Oakes, eds. *The Oxford Handbook of Divine Revelation* (Oxford, 2021).

Michaud, David A. *Reason Turned into Sense: John Smith on the Spiritual Senses* (Leuven, 2017).

Milbank, John. *Beyond the Secular Order: The Representation of Being and the Representation of the People* (Hoboken, NY, 2013).

Milne, G. H. *The Westminster Confession of Faith and the Cessation of Special Revelation* (Milton Keynes, 2007).

Milner, Matthew. *The Senses and the English Reformation* (Abingdon, 2011).

Milton, Anthony. *Catholic and Reformed: The Roman and Protestant Churches in English Protestant Thought, 1600–1640* (Cambridge, 1995).

Monk, James Henry. *The Life of Richard Bentley* (London, 1833).

Morgan, David. *Visual Piety: A History and Theory of Popular Religious Images* (London, 1998).

Mortimer, Sarah. *Reason and Religion in the English Revolution: The Challenge of Socinianism* (Cambridge, 2010).

Mukherji, Subha and Tim Stuart-Battle, eds. *Literature, Belief and Knowlede in Early Modern England: Knowing Faith* (Cham, 2018).

Muller, Richard. *Post-Reformation Reformed Dogmatics, Vol. 2: Holy Scripture: The Cognitive Foundation of Theology* (Grand Rapids, MI, 2003).

Muller, Richard. *Grace and Freedom: William Perkins and the Early Modern Reformed Understanding of Free Choice and Divine Grace* (Oxford, 2020).

Nadler, Steven. *A Book Forged in Hell: Spinoza's Scandalous Treatise and the Birth of the Secular Age* (Princeton, NJ, 2011).

Noll, Mark A. *The Rise of Evangelicalism: The Age of Edwards, Whitefield and the Wesleys* (Westmont, IL, 2015).

Ó hAnnracháin, Tadhg. 'Early Modern Catholic Perspectives on the Biblical Text: The Bellarmine and Whitaker Debate', in *The English Bible in the Early Modern World*, eds Robert Armstrong and Tadhg Ó hAnnracháin (Leiden, 2018), 104–30.

O'Banion, Patrick. 'The Pastoral Use of the Book of Revelation in Late Tudor England', *Journal of Ecclesiastical History*, 57 (2006): 711–37.

Oberman, Heiko. '*Simul gemitus et raptus*: Luther and Mysticism', in *The Dawn of the Reformation: Essays in Late Medieval and Early Reformation Thought*, ed. Heiko Oberman (Edinburgh, 1986), 126–54.

Osler, Margaret J. ed. *Rethinking the Scientific Revolution* (Cambridge, 2000).

Osler, Margaret J. 'Early Modern Uses of Hellenistic Philosophy: Gassendi's Epicurean Project', in *Hellenistic and Early Modern Philosophy*, eds Brad Inwood and Jon Miller (Cambridge, 2003), 30–44.

Ozment, Steven. *Homo Spiritualis: A Comparative Study of the Anthropology of Johannes Tauler, Jean Gerson, and Martin Luther in the Context of Their Theological Thought* (Leiden, 1969).

Ozment, Steven. *Mysticism and Dissent: Religious Ideology and Social Protest in the Sixteenth Century* (New Haven, CT, 1973).

Parish, Helen. *Monks, Miracles, and Magic: Reformation Representations of the Medieval Church* (Abingdon, 2005).

Park, G. Sujin. *The Reformation of Prophecy* (Oxford, 2018).

Parker, Kenneth. *The English Sabbath: A Study of Doctrine and Discipline from the Reformation to the Civil War* (Cambridge, 2002).

Parker, Kim Ian. 'Spinoza, Locke, and Biblical Interpretation', in *Locke and Biblical Hermeneutics*, ed. Luisa Simonutti (Cham, 2019), 169–70.

Parker, T. H. L. *Calvin's Old Testament Commentaries* (Edinburgh, 1986).

Parry, Graham. *Glory, Laud and Honor: The Arts of the Anglican Counter-Reformation* (Woodbridge, 2006).

Passmore, J. A. *Ralph Cudworth: An Interpretation* (Cambridge, 1951).

Plantinga, Alvin. 'Against Materialism', *Faith and Philosophy*, 23 (2006): 3–32.

Popkin, Richard H. *The History of Scepticism from Erasmus to Spinoza* (London, 1979).

Raymond, Joad. *Milton's Angels: The Early Modern Imagination* (Oxford, 2010).

Riehle, Wolfgang. *The Middle English Mystics* (London, 1981).

Riehle, Wolfgang. *The Secret Within: Hermits, Recluses, and Spiritual Outsiders in Medieval England*, trans. Charity Scott-Stokes (Ithaca, NY, 2014).

Robbie, H. J. L. 'Benlowes: A Seventeenth-Century Plagiarist', *Modern Language Review*, 23 (1928): 342–4.

Rozenski, Steven. 'The *Chastising of God's Children* from manuscript to print', *Études Anglaises* 66 (2013): 369–78.

Rubin, Miri. *The Mother of God: A History of the Virgin Mary* (New Haven, CT, 2005).

Rupp, Gordon. 'Word and Spirit in the First Years of the Reformation', *Archiv für Reformationsgeschichte* 49 (1958): 13–26.

Ryrie, Alec. *Being Protestant in Reformation Britain* (Oxford, 2013).

Ryrie, Alec. *Unbelievers: An Emotional History of Doubt* (Cambridge, MA, 2019).

Sargent, Michael. 'Contemporary Criticism of Richard Rolle', *Analecta Cartusiana* 55 (1981): 160–205.

Saunders, Corinnne J. *Rape and Ravishment in the Literature of Medieval England* (Woodbridge, 2001).

Saveson, J. E. 'Differing Reactions to Descartes among the Cambridge Platonists', *Journal of the History of Ideas*, 21 (1960): 560–67.

Schlosser, Marianne. 'Bonaventure: Life and Works', in *The Companion to Bonaventure*, eds Jay M. Hammond, Wayne Hellmann, and Jared Goff (Leiden, 2014).

Schwanda, Tom. *Soul Recreation: The Contemplative-Mystical Piety of Puritanism* (Eugene, OR, 2012).

Screech, M. A. *Erasmus: Ecstasy & The Praise of Folly* (London, 1980).

Scribner, Robert. *For the Sake of the Simple Folk: Popular Propaganda for the German Reformation* (Cambridge, 1981).

Scribner, Robert. *Religion and Culture in Germany (1400–1800)*, ed. Lyndal Roper (Leiden, 2001).

Shagan, Ethan. *The Birth of Modern Belief* (Princeton, NJ, 2019).

Sherman, William. *Used Books: Marking Readers in Renaissance England* (Philadelphia, 2008).

Simpson, James. *Permanent Revolution: The Reformation and the Illiberal Roots of Liberalism* (Cambridge, MA, 2019).

Skouen, Tina. 'The Rhetoric of Passion in Donne's Holy Sonnets', *Rhetorica*, 27 (2009): 159–89.

Smith, Michael Jaeger. 'Imagination, Authority, and Community in Spinoza's Theological-Political Treatise' (Boston College PhD thesis, 2014).

Spinks, Brian. *Sacraments, Ceremonies, and Stuart Divines: Sacramental Theology in England and Scotland, 1603–1662* (Aldershot, 2002).

Spufford, Margaret. *Contrasting Communities: English Villages in the Sixteenth and Seventeenth Centuries* (Cambridge, 1979).

216 BIBLIOGRAPHY

Stronks, Els. *Negotiating Differences: Word, Image and Religion in the Dutch Republic* (Leiden, 2011).

Swann, Elizabeth L. 'Nosce Teipsum: The Senses of Self-Knowledge in Early Modern England', in *Literature, Belief and Knowledge in Early Modern England*, eds Subha Mukherji and Tim Stuart-Battle (Cham, 2018), 195–214.

Swann, Elizabeth L. *Taste and Knowledge in Early Modern England* (Cambridge, 2020).

Swann, Joel. '"In the hands and hearts of all true Christians": Herbert's *The Temple* (1633–1709) and Its Readers', *Journal of Medieval and Early Modern Studies*, 50 (2020): 115–37.

Swinburne, Richard. *The Evolution of the Soul* (Oxford, 1986).

Swinburne, Richard. *Revelation: From Metaphor to Analogy* (Oxford, 1992).

Sytsma, David. *Richard Baxter and the Mechanical Philosophers* (Oxford, 2017).

Taliaferro, Charles. *Evidence and Faith: Philosophy and Religion since the Seventeenth Century* (Cambridge, 2005).

Tamburello, Dennis. *Union with Christ: John Calvin and the Mysticism of St. Bernard* (Louisville, KY, 1994).

Targoff, Ramie. *John Donne, Body and Soul* (Chicago, 2008).

Taylor, Charles. 'Interpretation and the Sciences of Man', *The Review of Metaphysics*, 25 (1971): 3–51.

Taylor, Charles. *A Secular Age* (Cambridge, MA, 2007).

Taylor, Mark. *After God* (Chicago, 2007).

Temple, Liam Peter. *Mysticism in Early Modern England* (Woodbridge, 2019).

Thomas, Keith. *Religion and the Decline of Magic: Studies in Popular Belief in Sixteenth- and Seventeenth-Century England* (London, 1991).

Thomson, Ann. *Bodies of Thought: Science, Religion, and the Soul in the Early Enlightenment* (Oxford, 2008).

Thornton, Tim. *Prophecy, Politics and the People in Early Modern England* (Woodbridge, 2006).

Walker, Christopher. *Reason and Religion in Late Seventeenth-Century England: The Politics and Theology of Radical Dissent* (London, 2013).

Walker, D. P. 'The Cessation of Miracles', in *Hermeticism and the Renaissance*, eds Ingrid Merkel and Allen Debus (Washington DC, 1988), 111–24.

Walsham, Alexandra. '"Frantic Hackett": Prophecy, Sorcery, Insanity, and the Elizabethan Puritan Movement', *The Historical Journal*, 41 (1998): 27–66.

Walsham, Alexandra. *Providence in Early Modern England* (Oxford, 1999).

Walsham, Alexandra. 'Jewels for Gentlewomen: Religious Books as Artefacts in Late Medieval and Early Modern England', in *The Church and the Book: Papers Read at the 2000 Summer Meeting and the 2001 Winter Meeting of The Ecclesiastical History Society*, ed. R. N. Swanson (Woodbridge, 2004), 123–42.

Walsham, Alexandra. *The Reformation of the Landscape: Religion, Identity, and Memory in Early Modern Britain and Ireland* (Oxford, 2011).

Walsham, Alexandra. *The Catholic Reformation in Protestant Britain* (Aldershot, 2014).

Walsham, Alexandra. 'Domesticating the Reformation: Material Culture, Memory, and Confessional Identity in Early Modern England', *Renaissance Quarterly*, 69 (2016): 566–616.

Wandel, Lee Palmer. *The Eucharist in the Reformation* (Cambridge, 2006).

Watt, Tessa. *Cheap Print, Popular Piety, 1550–1640* (Cambridge, 1991).

Wells-Cole, Anthony. *Art and Decoration in Elizabethan and Jacobean England* (New Haven, CT, 1997).

Westfall, Richard S. *Science and Religion in Seventeenth-Century England* (New Haven, CT, 1958).

Willis, Jonathan. *Church Music and Protestantism in Post-Reformation England: Discourses, Sites and Identities* (Aldershot, 2010).

Wojcik, Jan W. 'The theological context of Boyle's *Things above Reason*', in *Robert Boyle Reconsidered*, ed. Michael Hunter (Cambridge, 2003), 139–56.

Wolterstorff, Nicholas. *Divine Discourse: Philosophical Reflections on the Claim that God Speaks* (Cambridge, 1995).

Young, R. V. *Doctrine and Devotion in Seventeenth-Century Poetry* (Woodbridge, 2000).

Zachman, Randall. *Image and Word in the Theology of John Calvin* (South Bend, IN, 2007).

Zwollo, Laela. 'St. Augustine on the Soul's Divine Experiences: *Visio intellectualis* and *imago dei* from book 12 of *De genesi ad litteram libri XII*', *Studia Patristica* LXX (2013): 85–92.

Zwollo, Laela. *Augustine and Plotinus* (Leiden, 2019).

Index

Note: Figures are indicated by an italic "*f*" and notes are indicated by "n" following the page numbers.

For the benefit of digital users, indexed terms that span two pages (e.g., 52–53) may, on occasion, appear on only one of those pages.

A bryefe summe of the whole Byble 85–7
Abbot, George 150n.30, 151
accommodation, language of 120n.11, 133
Act of Uniformity (1662) 148
active life 21–3, 104
Adams, Thomas 47, 81–2
affections 23, 48, 50, 52–5, 102, 104–5, 108–9, 114–15, 123, 126, 133, 140, 146–7
Alexander VII (pope) 174
Ambrose, Isaac 99, 107, 114, 117, 134, 192
analytic philosophy 183n.82
Andrewes, Lancelot 51–2, 114n.86
Andries, Jodocus 85
Anglicans 10–11, 43–4, 59, 163–4, 182n.79
Annand, William 37
Apocalypse, Last Judgment 25–6, 40–3, 137, 146
Aquinas, Thomas 16–17, 22–3, 43, 160, 182n.75
Ascension of Christ 37
atomism 181–2, 184–5
Augustine of Hippo 4–6, 23, 33–4, 40–1, 47, 58, 62–3, 98, 125, 167, 183
Austin, William 87
Avery, Elizabeth 156
Avila, Theresa of 132–3
Aylett, Robert 125n.30, 135

Baker, Augustine 106, 159
Bale, John 39–40, 41n.18
Bampfield, Francis 10–11, 148
Bancroft, Richard 150n.31, 155
Barfield, Owen 2, 58
Barker, Jane 126
Barnes, Barnabe 122, 135
Baxter, Richard 6–7, 25n.40, 58, 72–4, 100, 122n.18, 152, 169n.15, 172n.29, 177n.51, 182–3
beatific vision 6, 25n.40, 36, 52–4, 100, 102, 106, 119, 125, 136–7, 160, 164, 187, 192–4
bedchamber/marital bed 108, 137
Benlowes, Edward 9–10, 139–40
Bentley, Richard 176, 179–80
Bentley, Thomas 63–4, 98

Bethell, Alathea 54, 115n.89, 136–7
Beza, Theodore 39–40, 43n.22, 108, 124, 133
Bible (texts)
 Genesis 124
 Exodus 131
 2 Chronicles 131
 Psalms 62n.18, 66, 79–81, 124, 125n.31, 129–32
 Proverbs 153–4
 Song of Songs (Canticles) 32, 64, 102–3, 108, 114, 128, 133
 Daniel 81–2, 170–1
 Matthew 26
 Luke 26
 John 28–9, 83, 172
 Acts 25–6, 34–5, 37, 72, 79, 104
 Romans 134
 1 Corinthians 23–4
 2 Corinthians 6–7, 43
 Ephesians (Eph.) 70
 1 John 70, 136–7
 Revelation 39–44, 46, 52, 113–14, 146
Blondel, David 162–3
Bonaventure (saint) 8–9, 16–17, 62–3, 85n.76, 107–8, 115
Book of Common Prayer 56, 67, 91n.92, 113–14
Bouche, Peter Paul 56
Boyle, Robert 10–11, 177, 179–80
Brightman, Thomas 45–6
Brough, William 74n.48, 115–16
Browne, Thomas 149nn.24,26, 165, 175
Bullinger, Heinrich (Henry) 9–10, 39–40, 43n.23, 44, 82n.65
Bunny, Edmund 100
Burgess, Anthony 53–4
Burton, Robert 126, 157–8

Calvin, John 5–6, 37–9, 39n.9, 45n.29, 58, 66, 155n.50, 160, 193
Cambridge Platonists 185–6, 187n.104
Capua, Raymond of 29–30, 30nn.73–5
Cary, Grace 146–7

220 INDEX

Cartwright, Thomas 45–6, 62–3
Casaubon, Meric 162–3
Castiglione, Baldassare 128
Cave, William 87
Cavendish, Margaret 124, 139–40
cessationism, of prophecy 149–54, 164
Charleton, Walter (William) 184–5
chastysing of goddess children, The 33–4, 48, 101
Clairvaux, Bernard of 15, 40, 97–8, 107–8, 174
Clarke, Samuel 104n.37, 114n.85, 134n.74, 161
Clerc, Jean le 72–4, 172
Climacus, John (saint) 105
Cloud of Unknowing, The 18–19, 25–6, 48, 101
Cockin (Cockayne), Francis 126n.38, 128–9
collective representation 2–3, 7–8, 10, 16, 62,
    189–90, 194
Comber, Thomas 157–9, 163
commentaries 3, 7, 10, 20, 37–41, 43–6, 48, 50,
    55, 57, 96, 121–2
communion, Eucharist, Lord's Supper 1–2, 7, 10,
    24–5, 30, 32–3, 83, 102–3, 111–17, 129, 173
consolation, images of 66, 78–9, 82, 99
contemplation 4–5, 17–20, 22–6, 28–9, 32–3,
    35–6, 44, 46–7, 50–4, 97–8, 104–6, 108, 118,
    130–1, 135–7, 161–3, 179–80, 187
contemplative life 21–3, 48, 51, 97–8
Cosin, John 109–10
Cowper (Couper), William 46n.36, 47,
    50, 109–10
Crashaw, Richard 122–3, 125
Cressy, Serenus 106–7, 107n.53
Crucifixion 59–60, 61f, 62n.18, 64–6, 85–9,
    99n.19, 132–3
Cudworth, Ralph 170–1, 185

Davies (of Hereford), John 124, 126
death, deathbed visions 5n.14, 7, 15–16, 18,
    21–2, 24–31, 33–6, 54, 64–6, 88–9, 95,
    98–9, 111, 118–19, 134, 136–7, 180–1,
    186–7, 191
décor, domestic 9–10, 57–8, 62, 69n.36
demonic possession 157–9
Dent, Arthur 45–6, 101–2, 108
Descartes, Rene 170–1, 177–8, 183–4
devotionals 16, 32n.78, 85–7, 96, 99–102, 121–2
Digby, Kenelm 183–5
discourse
    recontextualization 10, 17n.11, 145
Donne, John 89, 118–20, 118n.2, 164, 192
dreams 45–6, 150, 173–4, 191
drunkenness 109n.64, 116–17
Du Bartas, Guillaume de Salluste 1n.1, 9–10,
    124–5, 127, 133
Durer, Albrecht 40–1, 42f
Durham, James 50–1

Earbery, Matthias 169–70
Easter 15–16, 51–2, 104
Ecstasy 19, 134, 155n.50, 174, 190–1
Edwards, Jonathan 188, 190, 191n.3
Edwards, Thomas 144, 155
Eliza's babes 136–7
Elizabeth of Hungary (saint) 26–7, 105
English Civil War 60–2, 104–5, 130, 154–5, 160
enthusiasm 10–11, 145, 154–64, 166, 172,
    178, 190–3
epistemology 3n.6, 7, 11–12, 187
erotic/sensual imagery 32, 106, 108–9, 124, 186
Evans, Arise 147, 148n.21
Evelyn, John 181–2, 182nn.75,78
Eynsham, Edmund of 17–18

Fairclough, Samuel 114
Faithorne, William 56, 67, 87, 89–90
Falconer, John 111
fasting 18, 157n.59
feast (banquet), imagery of 115, 129–31, 133,
    137, 140, 174
Fifth Lateran Council 180
Fisher, Samuel 152–3, 173
Fox, George 153, 158–9
Foxe, John 49, 87, 103
Fulke, William 44–5

Galilei, Galileo 184
garden, imagery of 10, 75–6, 133, 137, 140
garden of spirituall flowers, A 101–2
Gassendi, Pierre 181–4
Gauden, John 154–5
gender 7–8, 32, 156
Gilpin, Richard 158–9
Gifford, George 45n.28, 49, 113–14
Glanvill, Joseph 171–2, 177, 188
Granada, Luis de 66, 99–100, 102n.31, 108
Great Awakening 190
Gunpowder Plot 74, 155

Hakewill, George 76–8, 77f
Hall, Elizeus 145–7
Hall, Joseph 64n.26, 97, 102, 104, 133
Hammond, Henry 54, 55n.64, 60–2
Harrington, James 9–10, 104–5
Hayter, Richard 38n.6
Herbert, George 119n.4, 122–3, 126n.36, 129,
    130n.54, 131n.61, 135, 164
hermit 7–9, 16, 20, 102, 171–2
Heylyn, Peter 75–6, 155–8, 162n.80
Hicks, William 43n.22
Hilton, Walter 3, 8–9, 23, 24n.37, 40, 106–7
Hobbes, Thomas 169–70, 173–4, 188
Holy Name, image of (I.H.S.) 58, 62–3, 67–70

INDEX 221

Holbein, Hans 40–1, 62, 79–82, 81*f*
Hove, Frederick Hendrick van 56, 79
Hugo, Hermann 64
Hume, David 149

idolatry 57, 59–60, 81–2, 153–4
illustrations (engravings, woodcuts) 40–1, 56, 59, 63–4, 79–82, 85–7, 89–91, 97–100, 111–13, 121–2, 139–40
imagination 4–7, 34–5, 58–9, 63–4, 82, 87, 121–2, 135–6, 167–74, 183
imitatio Christi 100n.24
immanence, images of 72
innatism 185
Interregnum 89, 128–9
invocation 119–20, 131–2

James, John 159–60
Jessey, Henry 146–7
Johnson, Samuel 149
judgment, divine 41, 66, 72, 76–8, 99, 165
Junius, Franciscus 44–5, 49n.43

Keith, George 146–7, 153–4
Kempe, Margery 28, 28n.63, 29nn.65–7, 110
Kempis, Thomas 8–10, 23, 33, 35–6, 82, 100–1

latitudinarian/latitudinarianism 182–3
Laud, William (Laudianism) 115–16, 155–6
Lead, Jane 146–7
Leo X (pope) 180
Loarte, Gaspar 9–10, 99–100, 102n.31, 105, 108
Locke, John 10–11, 164, 176–9
Lucretius 181–4
Luther, Martin 38–40, 149–50

Malone, William 74–5, 75*f*, 159nn.69–70
Manningham, Thomas 177–9
manual of prayers, A 81–2, 81n.60
Marlorat, Augustine 39–40, 43n.23, 49n.43
Marprelate Tracts 143–4
marriage (human) 108, 110
materialism 182, 184–6
Mayer, John 45–6
meditation 17–18, 20–1, 23–6, 33, 51–4, 62–4, 87, 95–101, 104, 113, 115–16, 129–31, 134, 136–7, 139–40, 160, 165–6
memorial, images of 60–2, 64–6, 69–70, 74, 82–5, 87, 89–91, 101, 130, 132–3
memory 53, 57–60, 62–4, 70, 135–6, 161, 172, 179–80, 183
Milton, John 1n.1, 9n.26, 120n.11, 122n.17, 125, 180n.67
miracles 33–4, 130–1, 149–50, 167–8
Montaigne, Michel de 175–7

More, Henry 60, 157–8, 165, 170–1, 185–6, 185n.90
mortalism 179n.62, 180–1, 184–6
Muggleton, Lodowick 146–7, 158–9
music 22–3, 89n.86, 100, 104–5, 125–6, 135n.79, 136–7, 157–8
mystical marriage (Bride and Bridegroom) 32, 108–13, 117, 128–9, 133
mysticism 3n.6, 4n.9, 5nn.13–14, 32, 40n.12, 101, 106n.50, 107n.52, 158n.62, 159n.67, 71, 167n.8

Napier, John 45–6, 50
Newton, Isaac 165–6, 180n.64, 187–8
nonconformists 6n.16, 158
Norwich, Julian of 3, 18, 23n.36, 27–8, 36, 97, 106–7, 117, 146–7, 183, 192

Oldenburg, Henry 167–70
Oringa (saint) 174
Overton, Richard 180–2
Owen, John 10–11, 83, 115n.92, 152–3, 161n.75, 163, 170, 172n.29

painting 1–4, 30, 57–9, 85n.78
Pater Noster 30
Pareus, David 39–40, 43n.23, 45–6
Parker, Thomas 156
Parsons, Robert 100
Passion (wounds, suffering) of Christ 24–5, 85–9, 100, 105, 113, 119–20, 133, 139–40
Patrick, Simon (bishop) 9–11, 116–17, 174–5, 188, 192–3
Pepys, Samuel 125–6
Perkins, William 46–9, 60–2, 66n.30, 83n.73, 150–1, 150n.31, 153
Perpetval Crosse, The 85
Pius II (pope) 29–30
plastick principle 185–6
Poor Caitiff 21–2, 33, 36
preaching 69–70, 155–6
prophecy 3–4, 10–11, 47–8, 149–55, 158–9, 164–9, 171–3, 177, 187–8
providence, images of 66, 72–8, 91
Prynne, William 119n.4, 130, 133
Psalms 124, 130n.54
purgation 21–2, 24–5, 28–9, 51, 109–10

Quarles, Francis 64–6, 65*f*, 79, 89, 119n.4, 121–3, 125n.31, 128, 129nn.50, 51, 137, 138*f*

rape, sexual violence 16–17, 127–8
raptus/ravishment 4–7, 10, 16–17, 19–30, 33–48, 51–3, 55, 96–105, 109, 111–18, 120–3, 128, 134, 136–7, 139–40, 144–6, 148–53, 161–4, 166, 170, 179

222 INDEX

Radegund (saint) 26–7
Reading, John 52, 52n.55
Reeve, John 146
reflection, images of (mirrors) 64–6, 85,
134n.74, 157–8
Restoration of the monarchy 1, 56, 104–5, 154–5
Reynolds, Edward 6–7, 114–15, 121–2, 170
Rogers, Thomas 82, 100–1
Rolle, Richard 8–9, 20, 21n.24, 23n.33, 33n.81,
39n.10, 58, 109, 157n.61, 192
Rous, Francis 109–10, 128, 192–3
Royal Society 167, 171–2, 177–8, 181–4

Sabbath 7, 10, 39–40, 44, 48–51, 101–2, 104,
130–1, 147
Salvator Mundi, images of 89–90
Sandys, George 119n.4, 123, 123n.23,
125n.31, 129–30
Scrivener, Matthew 66n.28, 157, 163
Scupoli, Lorenzo 102, 131
Scutum Fidei 59–60, 69–70
sectarianism
Fifth Monarchists 144
Levellers 180–1
Philadelphian Society 146–7
Ranters 144, 146, 154–5
Quakers 3n.5, 144, 146–7, 153–9, 161–2,
162n.78, 173
sermons 3, 10, 38–9, 38n.3, 43n.23, 44n.25, 27–8,
47n.39, 49nn.42–3, 52n.52, 54–5, 54nn.59–60,
57, 82, 83n.68, 89n.88, 96, 101, 103, 108,
111, 114n.82, 119, 121–2, 126, 133, 135,
153–4, 159–60
Shaftesbury, Anthony Ashley Cooper
(Lord) 164, 166, 172, 190
Shakespeare, William 9n.26, 125
Sharpe, James 159
Sheldonian Theatre 1, 194
Sherlock, Richard 156, 161–3
sickness 18, 161
Siena, Catherine of 8–10, 29–30, 30n.72, 31f, 36,
40n.11, 105, 147n.17
sight, sense of 98–9, 134–9, 146–7, 160
Simon, Richard 172
smell, imagery of 129–30
Smith, John 179n.62, 185n.90, 186, 192–3
sola scriptura 150
soul
ascent (Platonic) 16–20, 23, 48, 62–3, 87,
97–8, 113, 115, 134–5, 137–9, 163–4, 186
dissociation from the body 5n.14, 6–7, 45–7,
145–6, 162–3
immortality of 126n.36, 179–81, 184–6,
185n.90

Southwell, Robert 130, 133
Spenser, Edmund 134–5, 137–9
Spinoza, Benedict 149, 152, 167–75, 177–8, 188
Stillingfleet, Edward 150n.31, 158–9, 172n.29,
174–5
Streater, Robert 1–4
Strong, William 37, 160–1, 164
Stubbes, Katherine 192
Stubbes, Philip 49–50, 49n.44, 98–9
St. Victor, Richard of 17–20, 19nn.17, 19–20,
22–3, 25–6, 62–3
Sutton, Christopher 115–16
Sylvestre, Joshua 124

Taylor, Jeremy 83, 83n.68, 87, 131–2, 163–4,
163n.83, 182–3
Tenison, Thomas 60, 67–70, 174–5
Tetragrammaton 57–60, 62, 69–70, 75–8,
82–3, 98
Throkmorton, Job 143–4, 155
Toland, John 178–9
Tomkins, Thomas 103, 135n.79, 146
Traherne, Thomas 6n.18, 137–40, 140n.98, 189
Trapnel, Anna 146–7, 158–9
Trinity, images of 58–9, 69–70, 71f, 74–5, 79–83,
106, 148

understanding 1–11, 16–19, 22–8, 36–8, 40,
45–8, 52–3, 55, 57–8, 62–3, 70, 78, 83, 91, 95,
99–100, 102, 104–5, 108, 115–17, 120–1,
127–9, 133–6, 148–51, 153–4, 157–73,
164n.86, 173n.36, 175–82, 183n.83,
187–90, 193–4
unio mystica 40, 113–17
Ussher, James (bishop) 74–5

Vaughan, Henry 119n.4, 129n.50, 130–2,
135–9, 136n.81
Vermigli, Peter 83n.73, 149–50
Venner's Rising 159–60
visio intellectualis 4–5, 47–8, 167
visio spiritualis 4–5, 58–9, 170
visions, divine
Paul's vision of the third heaven 6–7, 22–3, 43,
95, 108, 121–2, 146–7, 162–3
Saul's vision on the Damascus road 72, 74,
146–7, 191–2
Stephen's vision 139–40

Walker, Obadiah 162–3
Wesley, Charles 89–90
Wesley, John 89–90, 188, 191
Westminster Assembly/Confession 121–2,
151–2, 160

Whichcote, Benjamin 185
Whitaker, William 150–1
Whitford, Richard 35–6
William of Perth (saint) 26–7
Winefride (saint) 111

Winthrop, John 95–7, 109–10, 117
Wight, Sarah 146–7

Yepes y Alvarez, Juan de (John of the Cross)
135–6, 193